THE
PERSISTENT VOICE

ESSAYS ON HELLENISM
IN FRENCH LITERATURE
SINCE THE 18TH CENTURY
IN HONOR OF PROFESSOR
HENRI M. PEYRE

Edited by
Walter G. LANGLOIS

New York University Press
New York 1971

Copyright © 1971 New York University and Librairie Droz Geneva
Library of Congress Catalogue Card Number: 71-150982
SBN: 8147-4952-6
Manufactured in Switzerland

« Une Grèce secrète repose au cœur de tous les hommes d'Occident. »

André MALRAUX, Athens, 1959

Henri Peyre cannot help but be touched by this volume, a symbol of the affection and esteem in which he is held by his former students. Yet since he is fundamentally a deeply modest man, he will also be uneasy at being the object of a Festschrift. *His pride never lay in the shaping of " disciples"; nor does it feed on gratitude. What has always mattered to him is the worthier satisfaction, and the more constant challenge, of continuing to stimulate, to provoke and to help—not only his own students, but those of others, and colleagues as well, and friends everywhere. To help with generosity of mind and deed.*

There exists a Peyre myth: the image of the remarkable, ebullient man capable of carrying on a telephone conversation, of writing a letter, and of advising a Ph. D. candidate, all at the same time; a man endowed with gifts of ubiquity: chairing a department, advising Foundations, sitting on committees, giving scintillating lectures— all the while never neglecting his students, and still finding time and strength to write book after book!

The reality that stands behind the myth is, however, far more impressive. It is a unique blend of scholarship, youthful fervor... and goodness. I am not ashamed to use that banal word—for of that goodness many of us have had numerous personal experiences. One could go on and speak of his wide-ranging intelligence, his tolerance for others, his amusing prejudices, his sense of excellence, his touching capacity for enthusiasm.

But Henri Peyre is so much with us that such clichés of praise seem superfluous. In any case, they are truths that hardly need to be proclaimed. French Studies in the United States would not be what they are without him.

VICTOR H. BROMBERT

Yale University

CONTENTS

PREFACE

In most lands of the Near and Far East, a master who wakes his students to an intellectual or spiritual life is considered to be their father in no less real a sense than the man who actually sires them from his flesh. Although no comparable tradition as such exists in our Western culture, we have always recognized that a great professor indelibly marks the minds and characters of the young people who pass through his hands, and that they in turn (particularly if they become teachers) mark others, so that the echoes of the master's voice literally never die.

A rare combination of intelligence, learning, skill, wit, and human warmth is required to produce a truly great teacher, and these are precisely the qualities of Professor Henri M. Peyre. For more than three decades, Yale undergraduates have found him to be "brilliant, irreverent, and personable," as a recent course critique put it.[1] Whether the class is relatively small (when it is taught in French) or very large (in English), each student is touched by his "sparkling wit and deep humanity." His courses are not easy, for he makes "rigorous demands upon the students to read and produce," but so remarkable an educational and human experience has attracted undergraduates from every conceivable discipline, and the memory of his classes is now part of the treasured past of Yale men in every walk of private and professional life.

Those of us who knew Professor Peyre both as undergraduates and as graduate students were even more fortunate, not only because we experienced the full range of his intellectual and human qualities, but because he offered so outstanding an example to us as future professionals. An incredible memory, great sensitivity, an enormous breadth of intellectual interests and competence, a teaching technique which sparked the mind to undertake voyages of discovery rather than to undergo an indoctrination—coupled with wit, great kindness, patience, and modesty, these were the qualities that we admired (and hoped to emulate), both in him and in the remarkable group of men he gathered about him in the Yale French department during the years following World War II. The quietly brilliant Georges May, the saintly Andrew Morehouse, the incisively perceptive Jean Boorsch, and the gentle, superbly learned Erich Auerbach were part of a faculty that gave a generation of young American teachers a truly remarkable professional and human formation in the

1950's, a formation which now—hopefully—is bearing fruit at other institutions of higher learning, all over the United States.

Professor Peyre once made a very revealing comment about his view of his profession when he said: "When we teach, we teach what we *are*, not really what we know and not always what we think. We teach what we feel deep down, and we teach with a certain personality."[2] Peyre's students would agree unanimously, I think, that his influence—and that of his colleagues—has been first and foremost a human one. We are better men—and, hopefully, better teachers—because we all responded to his humanity. This intangible form of influence is most difficult to measure because it manifests itself in the dialogue of heart to heart, whether it be between teacher and students in the classroom, or between men in their daily lives.

But for those of us who are primarily university teachers and researchers, there exists a time-honored means of paying tribute to the role that a man like Henri Peyre has played in our professional lives. The *Festschrift*, a collection of scholarly essays in honor of a revered professor, is most appropriate for someone like Peyre, who is as distinguished for his learning as for his teaching and his humanity. In any case, it is a tangible way for grateful students to acknowledge the fatherhood of such a master. Nearly four years ago, a group of us began to plan the present volume, with the clear intention that the book would not be primarily our *personal* tribute to him, but rather that it would represent in a very real way the homage of all those who have been touched by his hand.

Most *Festschriften* are basically miscellanies; their only unity comes from the fact that the contributors have all been students or associates of the man in whose name it has been compiled. We decided that our collection would be distinctive in that all the essays would be written around a single theme, one closely linked to the scholarly work of Peyre himself. At first glance, it seemed that we had a very wide range of choices, because Peyre's writings cover a great variety of subject matter in nearly every major period of French literature. However it is clear that several broad themes have never ceased to preoccupy him as a scholar. Certainly one of the most persistent of these is Greece—its importance in French culture and literature, and more generally its role in the formation of the view that Western man has of himself and of the world. Indeed, Peyre's very first publication, a 1926 translation of Sir James Frazer's *Atys et Osiris* (a study of some of the ancient religious beliefs of the Mediterranean basin),[3] suggests this interest, which became clearly evident several years later with the publication of the second of his nearly 30 scholarly books, the *Bibliographie critique de l'hellénisme en France, 1843-1870.* [4]

In the opening pages of this 1932 study, Peyre notes that Renan—among others—had been particularly aware of the enormous debt which the modern Western world owed to its Greek heritage, and he quotes the following eloquent passage:

> Notre science, notre art, notre littérature, notre philosophie, notre morale, notre politique, notre stratégie, notre diplomatie, notre droit international, sont grecs d'origine. Le cadre de la culture humaine créé par la Grèce est susceptible d'être indéfiniment élargi, mais il est

complet dans ses parties. Le progrès consistera éternellement à développer ce que la Grèce a conçu, à remplir les desseins qu'elle a, si l'on peut s'exprimer ainsi, excellement échantillonnés... C'est en ce sens que tout penseur, tout savant, tout homme cultivé, est encore de nos jours, sinon un 'helléniste' conscient, du moins un disciple et un continuateur de la Grèce.[5]

Yet, Peyre himself carefully points out that in literature, "il y a évidemment autant d'hellénismes divers que d'auteurs s'inspirant de la Grèce," because each writer sought in that ancient tradition those particular elements he needed for his own expression. But on a broader plane, he concedes that it is true that in the West "on réserve, dans l'espace et dans le temps, une place privilégiée à ce petit pays et, sur le peu que l'on sait de son histoire, de son art, on bâtit un rêve lumineux, une véritable religion rétrospective: le culte de la Grèce."[6]

Nearly a decade later (in 1941), to delineate the elements that various authors had taken from Greece at different periods in French literary history and to encourage specific research in this area, Peyre published his study of *L'Influence des littératures antiques sur la littérature française moderne. Etat des travaux.*[7] This title is somewhat misleading because the book surveys in depth all the major periods from the Middle Ages to contemporary times, and the inquiry ranges over the whole spectrum of our Greek inheritance. Many of the studies Peyre has written since 1941 have treated various aspects of this broad topic in passing, but he returned to it specifically in his provocative 1950 essay, "What Greece Means to Modern France," (recently reissued in a 1968 collection),[8] and indirectly in his article, "What is Wrong With the Humanities," published in the Fall, 1969 issue of *Ventures*.[9]

Since the role of Hellenism in French literature has never ceased to interest Professor Peyre, we felt that it would be a particularly appropriate theme to guide and unify our *Festschrift* collection. It was obviously impossible to deal with all the periods of French literary history, so we decided to limit our inquiry. In one of his essays, Peyre alludes to Malraux's view that the death of Absolutes at the end of the 17th and in the 18th centuries—coupled with a growing historical awareness and an explosion of knowledge in widely separated areas—made the Age of Enlightenment a kind of watershed that marked the beginning of what is truly the "modern" Western world.[10] Moreover, since Peyre himself has achieved renown as a scholar primarily in the more recent centuries of French literary history, particularly the 20th, it did not seem unreasonable to limit our efforts to an exploration of some of the paths he had pointed out in the periods since 1700.

But an even more fundamental reason led us to believe that a book centering on Hellenism would be particularly appropriate as an homage to Professor Peyre. To most Westerners, the Greek ideals are intelligence, honesty, courage, magnanimity—the perfection of all the human virtues, the joy of living and of giving to one another in this world of men—and these are the virtues that have distinguished this great teacher. For those of us who were his students, Greece has remained alive not primarily because we found it in literature, or because we drew meaning from its myths or its philosophy, but because we have seen the kind of man it molded, the kind of life it nourished.

In short, for us the persistent voice of Greece in Western culture, particularly in French literature, is echoed in the voice of our master, Professor Henri Peyre, and it is to him—in the name of the hundreds of students whom he has touched with the greatness of his humanity—that we dedicate, with greatest affection, this volume of tribute.[11]

Oscar Haac, State University of New York, Stony Brook

Mark J. Temmer, University of California, Santa Barbara

Frank P. Bowman, University of Pennsylvania

Philip Walker, University of California, Santa Barbara

Robert Greer Cohn, Stanford University

Basil Guy, University of California, Berkeley

Wolfgang Holdheim, Cornell University

Rosette C. Lamont, Queens College, City University of New York

Konrad Bieber, State University of New York, Stony Brook

Alex Szogyi, Hunter College, City University of New York

Eric C. Hicks, University of Maryland

Walter G. Langlois, University of Kentucky.

Notes

[1] Quoted in an article in the *New Haven Register*, 21 April, 1969, p. 30.

[2] *New Haven Register, loc. cit.*

[3] *Atys et Osiris. Etude de religions orientales comparées.* Traduction... par Henri Peyre (Paris, 1926, Annales du Musée Guimet, Bibliothèque d'études, tome 35). Sir James Frazer's work was originally published in London in 1906.

[4] This was published as the sixth volume in the Yale Romanic studies, immediately following Peyre's first major scholarly work, *Louis Ménard (1822-1901)* (New Haven-Oxford, 1932).

[5] Cited by Peyre (p. 5), from Renan's *Histoire du peuple d'Israël*, vol. I (Paris, 1893), p. ii.

[6] *Bibliographie*, pp. 5-6.

[7] This book appeared as the XIXth volume in the Yale Romanic studies series (New Haven-Oxford, 1941).

[8] The article originally appeared in Yale French Studies, No. 6 (December, 1950), pp. 53-62, and was reprinted in Peyre's recent *Historical and Critical Essays* (University of Nebraska Press, 1968), pp. 100-112.

[9] Pp. 26-39.

[10] "The Crisis of Modern Man as Seen by André Malraux and Albert Camus," in *Historical and Critical Essays*, pp. 272-273.

[11] In the following essays, the preferences of each author regarding capitalization of titles, punctuation, etc. have generally been followed.

I

THE EIGHTEENTH CENTURY

A major characteristic of the 18th century intellectual was an attitude that may perhaps best be described as an explosive inquisitiveness or a devouring curiosity. Most educated people of the period were very much interested in a wide variety of things: the types of plants to be found in South American jungles, the kind of fossils in English coal-beds, the skeletal formation of the sea elephant. Discoveries in these domains were eagerly discussed not only by scholars but by members of society as well, in fashionable salons and in exchanges of personal letters. This avid curiosity also entended into the more abstract areas of philosophy, epistomology, religion and history, and it is not surprising to note the growth of a renewed interest in the classical world.

To be sure, antiquity had long been an important element in French intellectual formation because it figured prominently in the traditional educational system. However the growing new spirit of inquiry brought about a re-examination, re-evaluation, and re-use of classical materials in the second half of the century that eventually produced what Professor Peyre has called "une véritable renaissance de l'antiquité."[1] The role that Rome and Greece played in the intellectual and literary life of the times is perhaps most immediately obvious in the case of certain minor figures because they lacked the ability—or the desire—to truly assimilate these materials and make them their own. Broadly speaking, these secondary authors may be classed according to a scale that runs from "galants" to "pédants". Among the former would be a number of writers who—as Peyre put it—"ont mis à la mode la Grèce des boudoirs."[2] They were interested in the classical world primarily as a mise en scène that would embellish their amatory tales, and they used the sentimental escapades of ancient gods and goddesses simply as an excuse to present certain piquant situations that have attracted some types of readers since time immemorial. The paintings of a contemporary like Boucher are clear testimony that this current was not confined to literature.

At the other end of this scale were the various "scholarly" students of antiquity. These included the translators and/or linguists of varying abilities who prepared the texts of classical authors that were used in the schools and were read (perhaps even more widely) by the cultivated public of the day. Many of these early texts are very inadequate, but as the century advanced an ever-increasing intellectual curiosity brought about a renewed interest in Latin and Greek as languages. This in turn eventually resulted in much more satisfactory editions and translations. The large number of what might be called "adaptations" of classical materials in the 18th century ranged all the way from a Greek or Roman original that had been expurgated of unsuitable elements or restructured to make it more immediately comprehensible, to the complete reworking of an ancient theme to produce a new work, modeled more or less closely on a classical source.[3] Rare indeed was the youth of any literary pretensions who had not tried his hand at recasting one of the Greek myths into a tragedy or an epic poem.

The more gifted and mature minds of the period generally turned their attention toward the classical world in a much more serious or scholarly way. They wanted to learn about it in greater depth, to know it more fully so that they could see what judgments could be made about it and what meaning it held for a modern reader. This effort to try and view antiquity somewhat objectively—and thus to give it a new, contemporary meaning—figures in the famous "querelle des anciens et des modernes." Indeed the century began with a dispute over a related matter, the merits of Homer.[4] Discussions of the "foolish" or the "sublime" elements in the epics of the great Greek poet were heated—and often ridiculous, but they were symptomatic of the new inquiring spirit with which intellectuals were approaching the culture, the literature, the ideas, and even the personalities of the ancient world.

Thus, broadly speaking—and irrespective of whether conclusions on a specific point were favorable or not—antiquity was a major preoccupation of the *philosophes* of the 18th century. The classical past nourished their minds, stimulated their imaginations, and inspired their energies, and the further they explored their cultural heritage from Greece and Rome, the more treasures they discovered in it. Perhaps no one better typifies this aspect of the period than does Voltaire, and Professor Haac's revealing account of his changing interest in Plato, the giant of Greek philosophy, focuses the problem sharply.

Notes

[1] Henri M. Peyre, *L'Influence des littératures antiques sur la littérature française* (New Haven-Oxford, 1941), p. 53.

[2] *Op. cit.*, p. 48.

[3] Peyre discusses the most important of these works in his *L'Influence...*, pp. 49-50, and 53-54.

[4] Peyre calls attention to this quarrel (p. 47) and signals the need for a study on Voltaire's views on certain aspects of antiquity in his *L'Influence...*, pp. 50-51.

A 'PHILOSOPHE' AND ANTIQUITY:
VOLTAIRE'S CHANGING VIEWS OF PLATO

By Oscar Haac

Voltaire's preoccupation with the various works of Plato extends from his earliest (1716) to his latest writings and owes much to the extensive classical background he acquired at the Collège de Clermont, later Collège Louis-le-Grand. It is no coincidence that his earliest reference to the Greek philosopher is found in a letter to his much-admired teacher, Charles Porée. Having composed choruses for *Oedipe*, Voltaire feels that he is wearing "la robe de Platon"[1] and thus is reminded of his days at the Collège. The catalogue of the library of the institution indeed reflects the importance of Greek authors in the curriculum at this time.[2] To be sure, Latin writers were predominant, but both the Latin and Greek languages had long been taught in Jesuit schools,[3] and the parallel curriculum of the Faculté des Arts specifically lists a number of Greek works to be studied, including the dialogues of Plato, along with the Iliad and the Odyssey, Theocritus, Demosthenes, Isocrates, and Pindar.[4]

Voltaire's life-long interest in Greek philosophical literature reflects not only his early academic training but also his involvement in certain wider issues of his time.Ever since Guez de Balzac had spoken of a "Socrate chrétien," Socrates' martyrdom had become a rationalist's equivalent to the passion of Christ. Like his contemporaries (Diderot and Rousseau in particular), and not withstanding his later objections to Dacier's Christian image of Plato, Voltaire was greatly influenced by this idea.[5] Moreover, as we shall see, when Homer and Plato come under attack during the "querelle des anciens et des modernes," Voltaire's classical formation prevented him from siding entirely with the "modernes".

Il should be remembered that there was another objection to Plato current at certain times during the eighteenth century. To many *philosophes*, the transcendental idealism of the Greek thinker seemed so distant from practical reality as to be virtually meaningless; even Cicero— whose discourses and interpretations were studied even more extensively than the original Platonic dialogues themselves—seemed more in touch with everyday human existence. In one of his articles, Bayle defined this issue as it appeared to Voltaire and the other *philosophes*:

Qu'on fasse ce qu'on voudra, qu'on bâtisse des systèmes meilleurs que la République de Platon, que l'*Utopie* de Morus, que la *République du Soleil* de Campanella, etc.: toutes ces belles idées se trouveraient courtes et défectueuses dès qu'on les voudrait réduire en pratique. Les passions des hommes, qui naissent les unes des autres dans une variété prodigieuse, ruineraient bientôt les espérances qu'on aurait conçues de ces beaux systèmes.[6]

When Voltaire studied the Dacier translation of Homer, he constantly referred to the more practical Cicero, and in passing often criticized Plato's fantasies. Yet it is clear that he remains committed to the authors he had first come to know in his days at the Collège, and that he continues to admire figures like Plato and Homer, even as he speaks of the barbarous times in which they lived. But while he recognizes and admires Plato as a supreme manifestation of the Greek spirit, he also is delighted when he can find an ally in him for certain contemporary causes. Thus, to a certain extent one may say that Voltaire's devotion to the classics was pragmatic, and in his various writings individual references to Greek authors—including Plato—may sometimes appear to be contradictory. However, his sustained interest in the Greek masters of his youth is clear evidence of his fundamental affection for them.

Voltaire's interest in Plato is greatest during three different periods of his life: at Cirey, in 1736-37, when he shared the philosophical pursuits of Mme du Châtelet; around 1749-50 when, under the pressure of events, he felt a particular kinship with Plato's homeless and persecuted Socrates; and finally between 1765 and 1772 at Ferney, when his studies made him aware of the Platonic tradition in early Christian thought. Through his lifetime, he was attracted to the human portrait of Socrates that Plato presents in the *Crito*, the *Apology*, and the *Phaedo*, but Plato became increasingly important to Voltaire as a thinker, an ally in his defense of theism and in his campaign for tolerance. To a large extent, Voltaire turned to Plato because the latter's writings lent universality to certain religious concepts that the Sage of Ferney was anxious to discover outside the Christian tradition. With these points of reference in mind, we shall survey chronologically the major references to Plato and Socrates in Voltaire's works and correspondence, to define his attitude and better understand his progressive encounters with Greek philosophy.[7]

As we have seen, when young Voltaire wrote Porée that he was wearing "la robe de Platon," he was expressing his general enthusiasm for the classical tradition because it had furnished him with the material for his play, *Oedipe*. A few years later, however, we find that he makes a very personal identification with a classical event; when he sends his drama to M. Genonville, he takes care to point out that Socrates had been maligned by Aristophanes just as he himself was being mistreated by his critics (1719).[8] But, characteristically, Voltaire cannot confine himself for long to bland expressions of kinship and admiration. His critical temperament and verve make him rebel, and he can become bitingly ironic, as—for example—several years later when he discovers the androgynes in note F to Bayle's article, *Adam*.

According to Plato's *Symposium*, Aristophanes had set forth the legend of the androgynes in order to explain the three modes of sexuality, i.e. the normal, the homosexual, and the lesbian. Originally, says Plato's speaker, human beings lived as winged couples; when these couples were cut apart, each of the halves set out in search of a partner. When the reunited halves were both men or both women, homosexuals or lesbians resulted. Although Voltaire shrinks from spelling out the details of this unorthodox morality, Plato's androgynes remain for him a source of constant amusement,[9] and he uses them in his burlesque scene in the castle of Hermaphrodix.[10]

During his stay in England, Voltaire became convinced of the validity of the intellectual discoveries of contemporary thinkers like Locke and Newton. From this moment on, he measures such Platonic "galimatias" as the myth of the androgynes and the metaphysical naïveté criticized by Bayle[11] against the superior understanding of man and the universe achieved by the modern philosophers. Many of Plato's speculations appear as pure fantasy, as do the Christian concepts of evil and original sin: "Le grand point [est de] savoir si la raison humaine suffit pour prouver deux natures dans l'homme ... idée ingénieuse mais il s'en faut bien qu'elle soit philosophique. Je crois le péché originel quand la religion l'a révélé, mais je ne crois pas les androgynes quand Platon a parlé." Actually, Voltaire does not believe in original sin either, for he says: "Les misères de la vie ne prouvent pas plus, philosophiquement parlant, la chute de l'homme, que les misères d'un cheval de fiacre."[12]

It is important to note that, compared to the defenders of religious orthodoxy, Plato appears to Voltaire as an enlightened ally. As he saw it, the Greek philosopher—like Shaftesbury, Bolingbroke, and Pope—had set out to discover order in the diversity of creation.[13] Moreover, Plato is not haunted by original sin, and he does not claim to be the spokesman for God. He believes neither in individual creation nor in some special individual providence. In short, he is not an inspired fanatic like the prophets, but a rationalist in awe before the "éternel géomètre" and "machiniste". Even so, in Voltaire's view Plato seems separated from modern thinkers by a long period of darkness and fruitless speculation. As he points out, those who are familiar with the philosophy of Locke can only mock the adjective "divin"as attached to Plato, for contemporary men have become acutely aware that ancient Greece was both "le berceau des arts et des erreurs."[14]

As we have suggested, Voltaire's ambivalent attitude is the result of a fundamental admiration for the classics that was often tempered by the perceptive irreverence of a "moderne". He will not blindly accept the attitude of pious adulation that he finds in certain works, like the commentary of Dacier's Oeuvres de Platon (1700), and his reserve sometimes becomes explicit, as in 1736 when he studies Cicero's Tusculanes with Mme du Châtelet.[15] In the Tusculanes, Cicero expresses his admiration for Plato, particularly for his idea of the immortal soul and for Socrates' call to a moral life. This text arouses the interest of both Mme du Châtelet and Voltaire, who set out to reread Dacier's translation of Plato along with Ficino's Latin text and commentary, as well as the comments of Plutarch and Diogenes Laertius. As they pursue their studies, they both write revealing marginal comments into their edition of Dacier's Oeuvres de Platon.[16]

Not unexpectedly, some of these notes indicate a critical attitude on Voltaire's part. Even in the matter of the immortality of the soul, where he sympathizes with Plato's views (later he will consider him an important ally in opposing atheism), he complains: "Chose pitoyable que ces prétendues preuves de l'immortalité de l'âme alléguées par Platon... Qui a lu Locke, ou plutôt a son Locke à soi-même, doit trouver les Platons des discoureurs et rien de plus." In a letter to the abbé d'Olivet, the translator of the *Tusculanes*, Voltaire pointedly includes Cicero and all ancient philosophy in this judgment (Best 978 of 1736). Plato and Cicero appear as "des hommes qui avaient recours à des mots pour cacher leur ignorance" (Best 1266 of 1737).

However there are other marginal comments in the Dacier edition that clearly express Voltaire's very considerable admiration for Plato, and the extent of his effort—his use of Ficino's Latin text, his checking Dacier against Plutarch and Diogenes Laertius—certainly indicates a deep respect and interest. Furthermore, he often seems to be objecting more strenuously to the commentary by Dacier than to the text of Plato itself. In the long tradition of interpreters from St. Augustine to the abbé Fleury,[17] Dacier saw Plato primarily as a forerunner of Christianity. Voltaire objects that these pious associations are gratuitous and hardly helpful. As he sees it, Dacier's comments on the obscurities of the Greek text serve mainly to prove his linguistic shortcomings, and his attempted Christian interpretations of *Phaedo* are little more than "des capucinades."[18] For Voltaire, *Crito*, the *Apology*, and *Phaedo* are remarkable accounts of the life and death of an admirable human being named Socrates, and no Christian apologia is needed to make them moving.

Frederick the Great shares Voltaire's respect for Socrates and, in November 1736, he honors him by sending first a bust, and then a walking cane with a carved head representing the Greek philosopher.[19] Voltaire gratefully acknowledges this generosity and replies that Frederick's gesture has inspired him to reread everything Plato said about Socrates. It is characteristic that this scholarly effort leaves Voltaire dissatisfied. After close examination, he notes that even the most passionate texts of Plato often appear to be primarily exercises in abstract analysis, rather than truly living presentations: "Nous ne sommes point nés uniquement pour lire Platon et Leibniz, pour mesurer des courbes et pour arranger des faits dans notre tête. Nous sommes nés avec un cœur qu'il faut remplir avec des passions sans en être maîtrisé."[20]

But Voltaire has another, more fundamental objection to Plato: he dislikes the basic method of speculation that the Greek philosopher employs. Plato's arguments seem like those of a man who sees the Sultan's eunuch pass by and calculates on this basis the number of caresses the Sultan has bestowed on his Odalisque, unaware that the Sultan spent the whole night in sleep (Best 1591 of 1738). Voltaire prefers to admit the limits of rational intelligence. For him the metaphysical speculations of all pre-Locke philosophers—be they Plato, Descartes, Malebranche, Leibniz, or Wolff—merely show "combien la nature de mon âme m'était incompréhensible" before Locke and "combien nous devons admirer

l'Etre suprême" (Best 1649 of 1738). Thus, even while he admires
Plato as a rational philospher who had resisted popular superstition
(Best 2044 of 1740), Voltaire attacks him for his metaphysical wan-
derings.[21]

Voltaire's few references in the decade 1740-1750 usually underline one
single theme: Socrates was maligned like myself, but he drank hemlock
while I prefer to stay alive. In deference to the Athenians, Voltaire admits
that they usually treated their citizens better, but the fate of Socrates serves
as a constant reminder that an iconoclast must be cautious.[22] Voltaire is
willing to believe that the philosopher king of Plato's *Republic* can provide
safeguards that will assure the happiness of the people and the freedom of
philosophers, but certain events in his own life—his stay with Frederick,
the subsequent difficulties and acrimony, and the exile at Ferney—hardly
permit him to be very optimistic about the contemporary situation. In a
moment of disillusionment, he notes that he considers Fenelon's hope of
being able to direct the life of a prince by writing *Télémaque* as being closer
to Plato's utopian ideas than to the real ways in which men are governed.[23]
Yet, during the 1740's Voltaire remains generally sympathetic toward
Plato and makes him an ally in his battles. In this spirit he refers to certain
of his *philosophe* friends as Socrates or Plato, and—in an excess of
flattery—on one occasion he compares the visit of Maupertuis at the court
of Frederick to that of Plato at the court of Dionysius.[24]

The *Sermon des cinquante*, composed about 1749, marks the beginning
of Voltaire's study of Platonic elements in early Christianity. It is
somewhat ironic that his campaign to "écraser l'infâme" steeps him in
theological arguments more deeply than ever before. By the time the battle
is fully engaged, Voltaire will have studied the edition of Timaeus Locrus
by the Marquis d'Argens and commented on it extensively. In a note of
1767, appended to the *Examen important de Milord Bolingbroke*, he
concludes that all Christian ideas, especially the doctrine of the
immortality of the soul, stem from Plato.[25] One passage of the *Sermon des
cinquante* states: "Je ne sais quelle métaphysique de Platon s'amalgame
avec la secte des Nazaréens," and points to the obvious link, the doctrine
of the logos (*Mél* 267). This view represents a radical shift from his earlier
objections to the Dacier interpretation, for he now accepts Platonism and
gnosticism as essential elements in early Christianity. This in turn leads
him to search all the works of Plato for parallels to the doctrine of the
Trinity, and he continues to discuss his findings in various essays, one of
which is significantly entitled, *Histoire de l'établissement du Christianisme*
(1777).

In this connection, it is interesting to examine certain of the examples
cited by Voltaire. In an initial reference to a kind of Trinity in Plato,
Voltaire calls it his "ternaire". He comments: "On a cru longtemps que la
belle morale ne pouvait être accompagnée d'une mauvaise métaphysique.
On en [of Plato] fit presque un Père de l'Eglise à cause de son ternaire que
personne n'a jamais compris." Voltaire considers the "ternaire" a futile,
metaphysical speculation but concedes to Plato a relative greatness:
"Depuis Platon jusqu'à [Locke] il n'y a rien." He is convinced that the

Apology "a rendu service aux sages," but that Locke alone meets the needs of modern philosophy.[26]

A number of subsequent passages in Voltaire specify the nature of the threefold divisions in Plato as he saw them. The *Essai sur les mœurs* refers to the *Timaeus* where Voltaire, like Dacier, finds matter classified as 1) indivisible, 2) divisible, 3) that which partakes of both properties.[27] The article *Platon* of 1765[28] repeats this presentation and adds another: 1) the force that creates, 2) creation, 3) whatever partakes of both the creator and his creation. In *Dieu et les hommes* of 1769, the following threefold divisions in Plato are noted:

1) *puissance*, 2) *sagesse*, 3) *bonté;*
1) *Dieu*, 2) *logos, le Verbe*, 3) *le monde;*
1) Isis, 2) Osiris, 3) Horus;
1) Jupiter, 2) Neptune, 3) Pluto.

In addition to the Egyptian and Roman parallels, there is an equivalent in Indian mythology (XVIII, 221-22). Finally, the article *Trinité* of 1772 adds from Timaeus Locrus: 1) the idea of logos, 2) matter created, 3) the sensible world, and from Plato's *Timaeus:* 1) God the father and creator, 2) the daimon, logos, understanding, 3) the actual world (XX, 536-38).

As his studies progress, Voltaire links Plato and Christianity ever more closely. In *Platon*, in 1765, he says that the idea of the Trinity is contained in Plato's writings *totidem litteris* if not *totidem verbis* (XX, 227). Two years later he writes: "Je pourrais dire que toutes les opinions des premiers Chrétiens ont été prises de Platon, jusqu'au dogme même de l'immortalité de l'âme," but adds that Plato never was "assez fou pour dire que cela composait trois personnes en Dieu."[29]

A thinker unconcerned with religious doctrine would hardly have provided so much detail, and it is interesting to note a few of the sources from which Voltaire draws his material. First he returns to Dacier's *Œuvres de Platon*.[30] In 1765, he again uses Plato's *Timaeus* (Best 11930, 12047) and, in the article *Platon*, shows that he has read the d'Argens edition (1763) of the *Traité de l'âme du monde* of Timaeus Locrus which includes 350 pages of commentary to accompany the 70 pages of Greek text and French translation. D'Argens explains that Plato's *Timaeus* is nothing more than a commentary on Timaeus Locrus (p. v) and a study of the tradition which links both texts to Christian thought through the important intermediary, Clement of Alexandria. D'Argens quotes Clement's *Stromata* as will Voltaire in discussing Platonism and gnosticism, and their contribution to Christianity.[31] Plato's *Timaeus* attracts Voltaire so much that he reads it in Ficino's Latin version—Dacier had not translated it— and he is proud indeed of this accomplishment (art. *Platon* of 1765; II, 224). As we have seen, it was this text that lead him to discuss concepts of the Trinity. But Voltaire found other elements as well in the *Timaeus* which fascinated him, notably Plato's ideas about the origin of matter and the world, the story of Atlantis, and his comments on the origin of Greece.[32] Moreover, Timaeus Locrus and Plato's *Timaeus* lead him to search for further parallels between Plato and the Bible. In the article *Prophéties* (of

1766; XX, 285), for example, he cites the following analogy: "Défaisons-nous du juste" from *Wisdom of Solomon* II;12, and "Le juste sera battu de verges" from the *Republic*, book II. (Not unexpectedly, the persecution of the just, i.e., the *philosophes*, is a subject close to his heart.)

From other comments and references to Plato between 1750 and 1765 it becomes clear that Voltaire does not come to really appreciate Plato's general philosophy until he discovers its importance in the development of Christianity. Thus, in a passage from the *Siècle de Louis XIV* (before 1750), quoted earlier, Voltaire still stresses Plato's "mauvaise métaphysique." The speculations of the Greek philosopher appear improbable, unprovable, and more like fantastic dreams than like rational arguments. In the *Songe de Platon* of 1756 he takes up this idea again. Plato, he tells us, was "dreaming" because in his day this was the fashionable substitute for objective observation. [33] He then lets Plato dream in the manner of a Greek Candide. Demogoron, the caretaker of the earth, believes that it is perfect, only to be told that it will take hundreds of millions of years to make it so. Thus only Demiourgos, who created the world, may boast: "Il n'appartient qu'à moi de faire des choses parfaites et immortelles."

This view of Plato as a representative of a school of dreamers is also expressed in a note of the same period (1756) added to the *Lettres philosophiques:* "Platon parlait en poète dans sa prose peu intelligible et Pope parle en philosophe dans ses admirables vers" (*Mél* 1343). Plato's concept of the chain of being seems vague indeed to Voltaire—although he will say the contrary in 1764,[34] and he merely concedes that "ce galimatias n'empêche pas qu'il y ait de temps en temps de très belles idées."[35] In 1756 Voltaire admires the ethics of Socrates but only one aspect of Plato's metaphysics is acceptable to him, namely the idea that the human soul is immortal.[36]

In 1759 Voltaire writes his play, *Socrate*. He has for some time abandoned Shakespearean models and, with his *Merope* (1743), he has returned to the classical stage. *Oreste* (1750) and *Rome sauvée* (1752) are written in the same tradition. He intends to follow Addison and show that "l'homme vertueux peut plaire sur la scène." As he says in the preface, his *Socrate* is to inspire the audience by presenting the hero as a "martyr de la sagesse."

Unfortunately, this drama strikes the modern reader as more grotesque than inspiring. Aglae and Sophronime, two young wards of Socrates, must be protected from the desires of the elderly priest, Anitus, and his equally repulsive ex-mistress, Drixa, each of whom seeks to recapture his youth by marrying one of the young people. Socrates foils their despicable schemes and resists the misguided pleadings of Xantippe but, having incurred the wrath of Anitus and the religious establishment, he must drink the hemlock. The young couple is only sorry not to be able to die for him. The play emphasizes the essential elements of Voltaire's philosophic campaign against institutionalized religion, notably the idea that priests are "des fripons" and that the idealism of the young must aim to overcome their power and empty theology. Socrates warns: "Gardez-vous de tourner jamais la religion en métaphysique. La morale est son essence" (Act III, Sc. 1). Voltaire discusses the play most seriously with Frederick (Best 7675 of 1759, etc.), and repeats most of its ideas in his later article, *Socrate*.[37]

For Voltaire, Socrates had clearly become a *philosophe*, a spokesman of enlightenment. In this spirit, around 1760 he begins to associate the names of Socrates and Plato with the sages of humanity from Confucius to Locke. His letters to close friends frequently end with a formula of greeting which means the same thing as "écrasez l'infâme": "Je m'unis à vous en Socrate, Confucius, Lucrèce, Cicéron."[38] Socrates and Plato, as much as Locke and Newton, come to represent a tradition Voltaire is proud to continue, a tradition which is occasionally said to include Jesus, the man, although Voltaire tends to prefer Plato because the latter inspires tolerance—not fanaticism—in his disciples.[39] It is no surprise to find the two Greek sages invoked in letters referring to Calas, Sirven, and the chevalier de la Barre.[40] De la Barre's sacrilege may not be comparable to Socrates' crime, but for the sake of freedom and of the *philosophes* Voltaire deliberately stresses the parallel.

This tradition of enlightenment which includes Plato becomes firmly established in Voltaire's mind during the years from 1760 to 1763. It explains in large part the enthusiastic statements he made about the Greek thinkers between 1764 and 1770. The Platonic idea of the great chain of being, for example—once called a fantasy—is accepted and defended in the article, *Chaîne des êtres* (1764): "La gradation des êtres du plus léger à l'Etre suprême me frappa d'admiration quand je lus Platon" (XVIII, 123). In the article *Platon* (1765), he commends Plato for having found order in nature and for having deduced the rule of a supreme intelligence over the universe (XX, 225). Voltaire's new-found sympathy makes him add: "Il faut toujours interpréter un auteur dans le sens le plus favorable." Thus those who accuse Socrates of heresy display malice, and "Ce n'est pas ainsi que j'en userai avec Platon" (XX, 225).

This enthusiasm explains why the Platonic conception of the universe, which seemed steeped in "galimatias philosophique" in the 1730's, now arouses Voltaire's admiration. The parallels to the idea of the Trinity which, as we have seen, were discovered by Voltaire around 1764-65, contribute to his desire to present the Greek philosopher as part of a great tradition. Indeed, the Trinity is itself "une idée archétype" that has deep roots in the Greek past, says Voltaire in the *Examen philosophique de Milord Bolingbroke* of 1767 (XXVI, 261). Then, in the *Discours de l'empereur Julien* of 1768, there is further evidence of Voltaire's enthusiasm for the Greek philosopher. Plato said, he notes, "Dieu, moi qui suis votre créateur... annonce que les choses que j'ai créées sont éternelles!" adding: "Avouons avec Cicéron que ce morceau de Platon est sublime" (XXVIII, 14-15). In contrast to his earlier critical view, Plato's idea of the logos now appears significant: "Les platoniciens d'Alexandrie nous ont appris ce que c'était que le Verbe dont nous n'avions jamais entendu parler, et que Dieu faisait tout par son Verbe, par son logos; alors Jésus est devenu le logos de Dieu."[41] Voltaire has come to feel that Platonic ideas have transformed

Christianity: "Je pourrais dire que toutes les opinions des premiers Chrétiens ont été prises dans Platon, jusqu'au dogme même de l'immortalité de l'âme que les anciens Juifs ne connurent jamais." He adds later: "Platon ne savait pas qu'un jour, par ses idées, il diviserait une église pas encore née."[42]

Plato's doctrine of the immortality of the human soul becomes an argument useful to Voltaire in his campaign against the acknowledged atheism and materialism of contemporaries like d'Holbach. He cites *Phaedo* to demonstrate the Greek belief that life rises from death, and that death is a form of life. Belligerently he agrees with Cicero that it is preferable to "se tromper avec Platon que d'avoir raison avec Epicure."[43] Although Plato's thought may be obscure at times, Voltaire finds many passages eloquent, poetic, and sublime. Plato may utter "des sophismes éblouissants" but he provides insight when he speaks of "Dieu qui forme le monde par son Verbe."[44]

1770 marks a turning point, as Voltaire's comments increasingly echo earlier conclusions and again become more critical. He will accept the idea of the immortal soul, but not most of Plato's other doctrines.[45] He stresses the superiority and greater relevance of Locke and Newton, who had always been important to him. In 1770 he rereads Plato in the translation by Grou which has just appeared, only to become more and more critical. He comments: "Le bonheur est une idée abstraite composée de quelques sensations de plaisir. Platon qui écrivait mieux qu'il ne raisonnait, imaginait son monde archétype, c'est-à-dire son monde original, ses idées du beau, du bien, de l'ordre, du juste, comme s'il y avait des êtres éternels appelés ordre, bien, beau, juste."[46] The enthusiasm he expressed earlier, in his 1764 article *Chaîne des êtres créés*, now seems excessive to Voltaire; he admonishes Plato in these words: "J'ai peur que vous n'ayez conté que des fables... Vous avez fait plus de mal que vous ne croyez."[47] The negative tone dominates increasingly: "Platon et Aristote m'ont appris de me défier de tout ce qu'ils ont écrit." In contradiction to earlier statements, Aristotle now seems the better logician of the two. The androgynes again provide cause for irony. Plato's logos, the "Verbe vivant," and even his faith in immortality often seem to be little more than "des sophismes" even though they provide "de magnifiques images toutes poétiques."[48]

As the last phrase indicates, Voltaire continues to show sympathy and some appreciation for the Greek author. In this spirit he explains: "J'ai toujours, avec Platon et Cicéron, reconnu la nature du pouvoir suprême aussi intelligent que puissant, qui a disposé l'univers tel que nous le voyons."[49] Ultimately Plato remains an important precursor of enlightenment, an ally, a spokesman for the cause of the *philosophes*, and his greatest creation—the "heretic" Socrates—is a figure with whom Voltaire likes to identify himself.

To sum it up, one may say that since Voltaire tends to seek out in the past those authors whom he can cite in support for the cause he is advancing at a given moment, his greatest moment of enthusiasm for Plato (1764-70) coincides with his realization of how much Platonism contributed to the growth of religion and philosophy, and of the tradition of the *philosophes* which he wants to safeguard and protect. As Voltaire's interests and commitments change, so do his interpretations, and his comments are favorable or unfavorable depending on what he happens to be emphasizing. Although we have found him to be generally critical before 1736 and after 1770, he never really has a totally committed view, either negatively or positively.

Above all, it is clear that Voltaire's love for classical antiquity never died, and that the Platonic Socrates remained a kind of ideal for him, a "sage au nez épaté," as R. Trousson has put it. To be sure, as this scholar points out, during much of the 18th century a certain veneration for the Greek philosopher was in the air: "Jamais les philosophes n'avaient trouvé un tel allié, un tel martyr, une telle égide."[50] However, had Voltaire not been sincerely moved by Plato, he would have studied him less thoroughly and commented on him less frequently. The death-scene of Socrates as described in one of the Platonic dialogues may seem to affect him less deeply than it did Diderot or Rousseau—this is a matter of disposition, temperament, and style—but it is certain that a lasting respect and sympathy underlie even Voltaire's most bemused and satirical comments. In the end, Plato's "galimatias" proved so fascinating that he could not help returning to it constantly, during his whole lifetime.

State University of New York
Stony Brook

Notes

[1] Best 35 of 1716. References such as these are to the Voltaire *Correspondence*, ed. Besterman. References by volume and page only are to the *Œuvres*, Moland ed. *Mél* indicates the *Mélanges* in the Pléiade edition.

[2] *Catalogue des livres de la bibliothèque des ci-devant soi-disant Jésuites du Collège de Clermont dont la vente commencera le 19 mars* . . .. Paris, 1734.

[3] According to: *Ratio atque institutio studiorum* . . .. Rome, 1586, also 1606, 1616, 1635; cf. Charles Fourrier, *L'Enseignement en France de l'antiquité à la Révolution*. Paris: Institut Pédagogique National, 1964, p. 127.

[4] *Ibid.*, p. 199. Fourrier indicates that students usually began their studies at 13 at the Faculté des Arts, p. 95, but the statute of Henri IV accorded the University the right to teach pupils 9 years old, p. 123.

[5] In his recent book *Socrate devant Voltaire, Diderot et Rousseau.—La Conscience en face du mythe* (Paris: Les Lettres Modernes, 1967), Raymond Trousson includes a chapter entitled: "Voltaire et le sage au nez épaté." This discussion of Socrates is a significant complement which I recommend to the reader's attention. R. Trousson feels that "à aucun moment Voltaire n'a réellement admiré Socrate," that he saw him as a simpleton and a blabbermouth ("un niais, un bavard") and considered himself more successful than Socrates for having been able to combat superstition while remaining alive! Voltaire rarely expresses this view in public, though the *Lettres Philosophiques* (Chapter xiii) state that a man like Socrates, boasting to own a "génie familier," must be "un peu fou ou un peu fripon." To intimate friends like Frederick II or d'Alembert, however, Voltaire admitted his strictures freely. His image of Socrates the martyr and spokesman for an ideal ethics was for public consumption. R. Trousson also shows that the formula of greetings calling for the unity of *philosophes* in the name of Confucius, Socrates, Cicero, and others does occur in the letters to intimate friends

like d'Alembert. Even so, it is clear that if Socrates incarnates the great tradition of *philosophes*, there must also have been admiration. The comments by R. Trousson mean this: Voltaire may have admired Socrates but Socrates' death was much less of a personal experience for Voltaire than for Diderot and Rousseau; Voltaire's references to the Socrates' martyrdom are a weapon of his campaigns for the *philosophes*, they express little genuine enthusiasm and even less idealism. They were useful rather than heart-felt tributes to a great man. In other chapters R. Trousson studies the parallel reactions of Diderot and Rousseau. Cf. note 50.

[6] Hobbes, "remarque E," cf. Elisabeth Labrousse, *Pierre Bayle, Hétérodoxie et rigorisme.* La Haye, 1964, p. 474; cf. Peter Gay, *The Enlightenment*, (New York, 1967), pp. 135, 195.

[7] A word of caution: Voltaire often composed the texts earlier than we indicate; except for the dates in the *Correspondence*, our dates are indicative only. It is, however, clear that the citations from the *Examen important de Milord Bolingbroke* are from the portion written around 1767, and not from 30 years earlier.

[8] Voltaire repeats this thought frequently, e.g., when he feels attacked by Palissot's play, *Les Philosophes.* Best 8134, 8136, 8237, all of 1760. The last reference is amusing: Voltaire points out that Socrates is admirable because he did not try to get even—as if he himself had ever been able to accept criticism.

[9] Best 737 of 1734, Best 2359 of 1741: Voltaire questions how Pascal could know men once were more beautiful, or winged, and had fallen; Best 3464 of 1749; *Poème sur le désastre de Lisbonne* in IX, 476; *Le Philosophe ignorant* in *Mél* 896; Best 15655 of 1770; *Dialogue d'Evhémère* in XXX, 493.

[10] *La Pucelle*, book IV, in IX, 83.

[11] Cf. note 14.

[12] Best 737 of 1734; cf. notes 9 and 26 on Locke.

[13] Prophets: *Lettres philosophiques* in *Mél* 52, 1345. "Géomètre": *Traité de Métaphysique* in *Mél* 195; Best 1268 of 1737, etc. Order: *Discours en vers sur l'homme* in *Mél* 231, cf. 226, 1369; cf. references in the text below concerning the article, *Chaîne des êtres créés*, of 1764.

[14] *Lettres philosophiques* in *Mél* 37, 43, 52, a theme often repeated.

[15] The manuscript translation of Cicero by the abbé d'Olivet seems to have reached them early in 1736 even though it was not published until the following year; Best 978 of Feb. 1736.

[16] These have been transcribed and analyzed by Edith Philips, "Mme du Châtelet, Voltaire, and Plato," *Romanic Review* 33: 250-63, 1942. She speaks of the Dacier translation of 1699 but it is usually given as 1700.

[17] Dacier bases his interpretation of Plato on Fleury's *Histoire ecclésiastique*, 1692-93.

[18] Philips, p. 260. Edith Philips defines only Voltaire's view in these earlier years for, after 1756, the Platonic tradition in Christianity comes to fascinate him. Two other limitations of her article: she tends to interpret Voltaire's objections as directed solely against Dacier, not against Plato, and she may be lending him excessive perspicacity when she credits him with sensing that *Alcibiades* I and II, Platonic dialogues according to Dacier, were not Plato's work; they are generally attributed to Plato today. With these words of caution we can only commend her discussion and extensive effort to document Voltaire's concern for Plato.

[19] Best 1144, 1203, 1247 of 1736-37.

[20] Best 1260 of 1737. This striking comment reminds us of texts cited in Delattre, *Voltaire l'impétueux.* Paris, 1957.

[21] Letter to Vauvenargues, May 1744, in *Correspondance*, ed. de la Pléiade, II, 770.

[22] Best 1290 of 1737, Best 2139, 2475 of 1742, Best 4304 of 1752, Best 7792 of 1759, Best 8153, 8164 of 1760, Best 9924 of 1761; but even Socrates accepts public sacrifices: Best 12608 of 1766, Best 13074 of 1767; his death is not typical in Athens: Best 13855 of 1768; he despises superstition: Best 18133 of 1774.

[23] On philosopher kings: *Siècle de Louis XIV*, éd. de la Pléiade of *Œuvres historiques*, p. 1001; cf. Best 13546 of 1767 favoring philosopher kings with a citation from *Républic* V, Par. 473d. On *Télémaque: Siècle de Louis XIV*, p. 1095.

[24] Best 2155 of 1740. The name is used for d'Alembert, Best 10609 of 1763, and Diderot, Best 12559 of 1765 (typical references; there are many more).

[25] Cf. note 29.

[26] *Siècle de Louis XIV*, pp. 1025-26 (for ed. see note 23).

[27] *Essai*, ed. Pomeau, Classiques Garnier, I, 92-94, discusses the parallel and reproduces page 183 of Dacier, *Œuvres de Platon*, where Dacier lists the three divisions of matter; there is an extensive marginal note by Voltaire. Dacier's *Œuvres de Platon*, pp. 143-144, discuss the *Timaeus* and, p. 192, the logos. However Dacier did not translate the *Timaeus* and Voltaire

used Ficino's Latin text. The *Essai sur les mœurs* takes the image of the world as an immense living creature from the *Timaeus:* "un grand animal," ed. Pomeau, I, 202.

²⁸ XX, 244-30. According to Beuchot's note and to Bengesco's bibliography IV, 230, item 2212, *Platon* first appeared in *Nouveaux Mélanges historiques, critiques.* Genève: Cramer, 1765, vol. III, articles 19-20.

²⁹ *Examen important* in XXVI, 261 of 1767, also a note added to this work the same year, in Voltaire, *Œuvres*, ed. Renouard, XXX, 342. The idea is repeated in 1769 in *Dieu et les hommes* in (ed. Moland) XXVIII, 245.

³⁰ Cf. the marginal notes to Dacier's *Œuvres de Platon*, see note 27.

³¹ D'Argens refers on pp. 19-20 to Clement, *Stromata* I, to his discussion of God, the nature of good and evil. Voltaire, in *Examen important de Milord Bolingbroke* of 1767 (in XXVI, 256) cites *Stromata* V, ch. 14, dealing with the difficulty of defining God, the concept of the Trinity, Son, Holy Spirit, and Resurrection. Voltaire considers Clement inferior to Plato and commends the Romans for tolerating members of gnostic sects like Clement. Cf. also his article *Prophéties* of 1766 (in XX, 285) where Voltaire speaks of gnostics attempting to reconcile Greek philosophy with Christian faith. In the *4e Homilie* of 1767 (in XXVI, 353) Voltaire speaks of Jesus as "le Socrate de Galilée." Cf. R. Pomeau, *La Religion de Voltaire.* Paris, 1956, pp. 373, also 140.

³² Atlantis, in article *Changements arrivés* of 1770 (in XVIII, 129). Athens 9000 years old: article *Platon* of 1765 (in XX, 225); cf. *Le Philosophe ignorant* of 1766-67 in *Mél* 919.

³³ XXI, 133-36 of 1756; also *Examen important* of 1767 in XXVI, 259.

³⁴ See below, on the article *Chaîne des êtres créés.*

³⁵ *Essai sur les mœurs*, ed. Pomeau, I, 94. D'Argens, in his edition of Timée de Locres, p. 124, also speaks of metaphysical "galimatias".

³⁶ Note of 1751 to the *Lettres philosophiques* in *Mél* 1333; also *Poème sur la loi naturelle* of the same period in *Œuvres*, ed. Renouard, X, 91-92.

³⁷ Of 1770, cf. Best 15722 of 1770: "mon Socrate est un philosophe intrépide." Parts of the article *Socrate* stem, however, from the *Lettres philosophiques* of 1733.

³⁸ Best 8134, 8223 of 1760; Best 9499, 9519, 9604, 9834 of 1762; Best 11035, 11249 of 1764; Best 13531 of 1767; Best 14810 of 1769, etc.

³⁹ Jesus: *Le Douteur et l'adorateur* of 1763 in *Mel* 677; *Examen des sentiments de Jean Meslier* of 1762 in *Mel* 469; *4e Homilie* of 1767 see note 31 with Pomeau references. Tolerance: *Traité sur la tolérance* of 1763 in *Mel* 585, 1429.

⁴⁰ Calas: Best 9604 of 1762. Sirven; la Barre: Best 12558 of 1766. La Barre: Best 12615, 12626, 12630, 12632 of 1766.

⁴¹ *De la Paix perpétuelle* of 1769 in XXVIII, 113 with reference to Clement of Alexandria, cf. note 31.

⁴² "Je pourrais": *Dieu et les hommes* of 1769 in XXVIII, 245, cf. note 29. "Platon ne savait": article *Sophiste* of 1771 in XX, 431, 435-36.

⁴³ *Dieu et les hommes* in XXVIII, 246; cf. article *Aristote* of 1770 in XVII, 368.

⁴⁴ *Dieu et les hommes* in XXVIII, 221.

⁴⁵ "Sans adopter ses principes." *Lettre de Memmius à Cicéron* of 1771 in XXVIII, 490.

⁴⁶ Article *Souverain bien* of 1770 in XVII, 572; cf. article *Beau* in XVII, 556. Carl Becker's *Heavenly City* notwithstanding, Voltaire is essentially a relativist.

⁴⁷ Comment of 1770 in *Dictionnaire philosophique*, ed. Naves, Classiques Garnier, note 144, p. 360.

⁴⁸ *Dialogues d'Evhémère* in XXX, 492-93 and *Histoire de l'établissement du christianisme* in XXXI, 50, both of 1777. Voltaire has reread and mentions Timaeus Locrus, the *Symposium, Phaedo, Timaeus,* also *Laws;* cf. Best 17249 of 1773 where Voltaire cites, among others, a passage from *Laws*, book II, par 656e, on ancient Egypt; also *Lois de Minos* of 1771-72 in VII, 222, and Best 15314 of 1770 where we read: "Platon raisonnait et déraisonnait."

⁴⁹ *Sophronime et Adélos* of 1776 in *Mél* 1316. Voltaire approves of the concept of God as "éternel géomètre," Best 18133 of 1774, and of Socrates "qui sait douter,"—Helvetius shares his noble soul: Best 16401, 16484 of 1771.

⁵⁰ Trousson, op. cit., note 5, pp. 21, 24-25, 44; on Socrates and Christ, p. 33 and note 39 above. Trousson sees opportunism, the enthusiasm of the *philosophe* campaign but no admiration of the Greek sage when Voltaire writes his play, *Socrate:* "il tentait soudain Voltaire," (p. 24), and concludes: "A aucun moment Voltaire n'a réellement admiré Socrate," (p. 43). Perhaps Voltaire was not capable of admiration in the sense Trousson gives this term. His study is concise, well documented, a valuable contribution to the history of ideas.

Of all the periods of French literary history, the 18th century is probably the most contradictory. While Voltaire admirably represents what was undoubtedly the dominant current of the period, one must look to another figure—a precursor of the new movements that would soon galvanize the 19th century—to see the reverse side of the coin. In a number of ways, Jean-Jacques Rousseau shared many of the preoccupations of the *philosophes*, particularly their concern with antiquity. To be sure, his interest was less scholarly than that of most of his contemporaries, because he had received little formal education and knew classical literature only somewhat haphazardly and at second hand. But Rousseau read and greatly admired translations of certain classical philosophers and mora-lists, particularly the stoics, and their influence is clearly visible in a number of his writings.

However, while Rousseau's response to antiquity was comparable in certain respects to that of his contemporaries, basically it remained distinctive because of the kind of individual he was. Highly emotional—almost unstable—Jean-Jacques tended to view everything through a richly colored personal lens, rather than through the cold eye of reason. Unlike the majority of the *philosophes*, he sought less to know, understand, and judge the past and its forms than to completely possess and rework them for his own very personal needs. In other words, one could say that he turned to the classical world and its traditions not primarily to be edified by inspiring examples or stimulated by ideas. Rather, in a much more direct way, he sought and found in antiquity an answer to new needs—the elements to create a new literature that would express more completely his particular values and his special view of the world. As Professor Peyre puts it, Rousseau admired in the classical writers "non des auteurs cultivés et polis, appliquant avec noblesse toutes les règles de l'art, mais des enfants, des primitifs, des êtres proches de la nature,"[1] precisely because these were the values he prized himself.

The fire of Rousseau's convictions usually enabled him to make original and highly personal (albeit not always successful) transformations of whatever elements he took from the classical world and its traditions. For purposes of the discussion here, Professor Temmer has centered his examination on the way in which Rousseau reworked the idyll, a classical literary form to which he was particularly attracted and which he found to be an appropriate vehicle for some of his own ideas. To be sure, he knew the idyll primarily as it had come down through Roman and/or later Italian pastoral traditions, but it seems clear that in his *Idylle des Cerises* he was consciously striving to recapture some of what he felt was the true spirit of the Golden Age of Greece, as well as to formulate a highly personal and original expression of his *Moi*.[2] In this effort—as in so many others—Rousseau was distinctively modern, and as Professor Temmer suggests his attempt to use this classical form as the vehicle for a personal artistic statement was undertaken anew by a number of other writers in the centuries that followed.

Notes

[1] Henri M. Peyre, *L'Influence des littératures antiques sur la littérature française moderne* (New Haven-Oxford, 1941), pp. 51-52.

[2] Peyre suggests other interesting aspects of Rousseau's "classical" debt in his *L'Influence...*, p. 52.

ROUSSEAU'S *IDYLLE DES CERISES*—A METAMORPHOSIS OF THE PASTORAL IDYLL

By Mark J. Temmer

"Que j'aime à tomber de tems en tems sur les momens agréables de ma jeunesse! Ils m'étoient si doux; ils ont été si courts, si rares, et je les ai goûtés à si bon marché! Ah leur souvenir rend encore à mon cœur une volupté pure dont j'ai besoin pour ranimer mon courage, et soutenir les ennuis du reste de mes ans." *(Confessions)*
"La poésie lui rappelait le temps pastoral." *(Fragments sur J.-J. Rousseau,* Bernardin de Saint-Pierre)

"Chante moy d'une musette bien résonnante et d'un fluste bien jointe ces plaisantes ecclogues rustiques, à l'exemple de Théocrite et de Virgile, marines, à l'exemple de Sennazar, gentilhomme néapolitain." That du Bellay's poetical imperative went unheeded is history. No French pastoral in the Italian tradition, be it Marot's *Complaincte de Madame de Loyse de Savoye* or Racan's *Bergeries* can rival Garcilaso's first *Egloga* or Tasso's *Aminta*, while d'Urfée's *Astrée* has received honorable mention in default of worthy competition in Italy, Spain, and England. And should this affirmation seem unjustified, one may quote by way of *Deffense* Mia Gerhardt's conclusion to her general survey of the pastoral genre: "En France... la pastorale ne réussit pas à s'implanter dans le roman, et reste fort médiocre dans la poésie; la pastorale dramatique apparaît comme la forme la plus en accord avec les tendances de la littérature française et la plus goûtée du public, mais elle n'a pas abouti à une œuvre de premier ordre."[1] Are we to conclude that there is no "lusignolo /Que va di ramo in ramo /Cantando: Io amo, io amo" in the gardens of French literature, and that we have to content ourselves with Mallarmé's version of the *Sicilian Muse?* Should we agree with Bernardin de Saint-Pierre that "malheureusement, nous n'avons pas eu de poètes épiques ni bucoliques"?[2] If one allows an exception to this rule, it would surely have to be Saint-Pierre's friend, Rousseau, who, as a matter of principle, fancied himself different from all men. However this may be, it is the sense of this essay that Rousseau was the first European writer to have succeeded in modernizing the pastoral idyll[3] which had been for the most part patterned on the graeco-italian and to a lesser extent on the Christian pastoral ideal.[4]

Jean-Jacques leaves little doubt that, as a boy, he was passionately involved with *Le Grand Cyrus* and *L'Astrée*, only to abandon them for Plutarch's *Lives*: "Le plaisir que je prenois à le [Plutarque] relire sans cesse me guérit un peu des Romans, et je préférai bientôt Agésilas, Brutus, Aristide à Orondante, Artamène et Juba."[5] Although the influence of pastoral novels on Rousseau has been studied, his role as an innovator in the pastoral genre has been disregarded by scholars, with the notable exception of the late Renato Poggioli whose views approach our own.[6] Rereading the libretto of Rousseau's *Devin du Village* this neglect seems quite understandable: "Mon chalumeau, ma houlette, /Soyez mes seules grandeurs." This doggerel summarizes his early aspirations; and with such lines in mind, Jules Marsan may have been justified in ending his *Pastorale dramatique française* with a commentary on le *Berger extravagant*, 1627: "Nous pouvons arrêter ici cette histoire de la pastorale dramatique: son rôle est terminé, et, si son influence persiste, la plupart de ceux mêmes qui la subissent—très indirectement— sont les premiers à la mépriser."

Just as Rousseau's mediocrity as an author of traditional pastorals lends no support to our thesis that he is the creator of the modern idyll, so his avowed lack of classical training ("je ne sais point le grec et très peu de latin"[7]) would seem to invalidate our basic argument. And while it is true that a good deal has been written on the impact of Plato, Socrates, Lucretius, Plutarch, Tacitus, and Seneca on the ideology of the Citizen of Geneva, still, if one compares him to Voltaire and Diderot, who were excellent classical scholars in their own right, one would have to conclude that in his case it is unwarranted to speak of well-defined graeco-literary influences. The question of indirect classical literary influences is more difficult to resolve. Although there exists a fairly complete inventory of Rousseau's library, it is evident that we cannot limit the number of Greek authors he read in translation to those in his possession; the list compiled by M. Reichenburg, for example, does not mention either Theocritus or Longus. In view of the fact that Rousseau's early works teem with pastoral stock-characters we may assume that he had read Amyot's translation of the celebrated Alexandrian tale.[8] But in regard to indirect classical literary influences transmuted and transmitted by Italian literature, one is less dependent on conjecture, since studies by Culcasi, Bendetto, and Beall suggest the extent of Rousseau's indebtedness to the *cinquencento* and *settecento*.[9] He knew and loved Italian; his preference was for Ariosto, Tasso and Metastasio; his favorite work was *La Gerusalemme liberata*; and he was acquainted moreover with *l'Aminta*—the point of confluence of the classical pastoral tradition and the apogee of the Renaissance pastoral ideal—which may have exerted a subtle influence upon the composition of *l'Idylle des Cerises*.

Rousseau's originality in reformulating the traditional pastoral can best be shown by means of a preliminary analysis of the thematic components of *l'Idylle*.[10] Its beginning refers specifically to Midsummer Eve, "the turning point of the year," as Frazer remarks "when vegetation might be thought to share the incipient though still almost imperceptible decay of summer, [and which] might very well be chosen by primitive man as a fit moment for resorting to those magic rites by which he hopes to stay the decline, or at least to ensure the revival, of plant life."[11] Thus Rousseau:

> L'aurore un matin me parut si belle que m'étant habillé précipitamment, je me hâtai de gagner la campagne pour voir lever le soleil. Je goûtai ce plaisir dans tout son charme; c'étoit la semaine après la St-Jean. La terre dans sa plus grande parure étoit couverte d'herbe et de fleurs; les rossignols presque à la fin de leur ramage sembloient se plaire à le renforcer: tous les oiseaux faisant en concert leurs adieux au printemps, chantoient la naissance d'un beau jour d'été, d'un de ces beaux jours qu'on ne voit plus à mon âge, et qu'on n'a jamais vus dans le triste sol où j'habite aujourd'hui.

In melodious prose the *Idylle* evokes the universal grief of nature and the lament of the nightingales on the passing of Spring with a graceful stylistic chute suggestive of exile and death. One might note in passing that this feeling of sadness at the destruction of tender life may have engendered the myth of Daphnis, inventor of the bucolic song: "Auch wir suchen die ersten Keime der Daphnissage in uralter Naturanschauung, wir sehen in ihm einen jener zahlreichen schönen, früh verblassten Knaben oder Jünglinge, welche das fröhliche Aufblühen des Naturlebens im Lenze und das von den Menschen betrauerte und beklagte Verwelken der Vegetation in den heissen Tagen der Sommerzeit darstellen (Hylas, Linos, Narkissos u.a.)."[12] Later developments of the myth relate how Daphnis, cherished by muses and nymphs, boasted of being able to withstand the power of Eros, that Aphrodite caused him to love a young girl and that, struggling without hope against this passion, he died despite a vain attempt by the goddess to save him.

Superimposed on these schemas and rituals in *l'Idylle* is the myth of the Golden Age which had first been integrated into the pastoral tradition in Virgil's fourth *Eclogue*. Whereas the latter's Golden Age is about to return (*redeunt Saturna regna*) and Tasso's is voluptuously present (*E veramente il secol d'oro questo*), Rousseau's *Idylle* shimmers with the light of a Golden Age long since past: "Und Strahlen aus der schönern Zeit/Haben die Boten dein Herz gefunden."[13] Whether Virgil believed in his Arcadia must remain a matter of conjecture; it is certain, however, that Jean-Jacques wanted to believe in his Alpine Arcadia, and that the discrepancy between his reminiscence of rustic innocence and the miseries of exile in England creates contrapuntal moods. Like Tasso, whom he thought the equal of Homer and Virgil, Rousseau animates his pastoral idyll with powerful feelings. Unlike Tasso, he does not people his world with shepherds, nymphs, goddesses and the like, but fills it with projections of himself and his youthful loves, maintaining all the while the essential patterns that sustain the pastoral. It might be argued that in dispensing with shepherds Rousseau destroys the essence of the pastoral, since its high degree of conscious artificiality represents the very essence of the genre. In the words of Mia Gerhardt: "L'écrivain pastoral est, par définition, un *artifex*, celui qui *fait de l'art*; la pastorale est artificielle, non seulement dans l'acception courante du mot, qui ne présente aucun intérêt, mais dans son sens propre et étymologique."[14] If the pastoral had always been what it became after Virgil transformed it into a vehicle for allegory, our interpretation of *l'Idylle des Cerises* would not be defensible. But the Theocritan tradition preempts the Virgilian, and we hope to show that Rousseau drew on both traditions by way of Italy in order to fashion the modern idyll.

The first sentence after the prologue illustrates the technique of modernization through the elimination of some, although not all, Virgilian and Italian Renaissance literary devices. This allows him to render his version of the pastoral more *vraisemblable*—a *vital* necessity for Rousseau, since the credibility of the *Moi* he wishes to project must not suffer through overt mythopoeic artifacts: "Je m'étois insensiblement éloigné de la Ville." As in Longus' *Daphnis and Chloe*, contrasts between city and country life function as a device to permit urbane readers to peek into a utopian garden where hero and heroine play at love without understanding the game. That Rousseau added a second heroine renders the situation the more piquant, and it takes little insight to recognize in this *idylle à trois* a reversal of the Madame de Warens-Claude Anet-Jean-Jacques triangle.[15] Less apparent, perhaps, is the fact that this supposedly fortuitous meeting of a commoner with two aristocratic girls reflects an unusual reversal of a pattern characteristic of the *pastourelle* which usually relates with more or less irony how a knight encounters a "gentil pastorele, / les eux verz, le chief blondel," with varying degrees of success. If one assumes that the French pastoral tradition of the seventeenth century resulted from a fusion of a national tradition *en langue d'oïl* (typified by the prevalence of a strong caste system and disdain towards peasants with the consecrated exception of the *Jeu de Robin et Marion*) with the graeco-italian tradition in turn characterized by democratic attitudes,[16] *l'Idylle des Cerises* offers a fascinating example of a thematic metamorphosis. In *l'Idylle* Rousseau avails himself of a native pattern (the knight versus the *pastoure*), assumes the role of the *pastoure*, and halves the figure of *li chevaliers* into two *cavalières*. He also appropriates egalitarian beliefs from Tasso's *Aminta* and obviates at the same time any possible accusation of being a *paysan parvenu* by being delightfully shy after having led the horses across the stream.

"Vous vous êtes mouillé pour notre service; nous devons en conscience avoir soin de vous sécher: il faut s'il vous plaît venir avec nous, nous vous arrêtons prisonnier... montez en croupe derrière elle, nous voulons rendre compte de vous. Mais Mademoiselle, je n'ai point l'honneur d'être connu de Madame votre mère." Thus, the two amazons seduce on a level as virtual as virtuous Jean-Jacques who does not content himself with being a latter-day *pastoure*, but assumes the role of the satyr as well as the function of the autobiographer. But whereas Tasso's *satiro* is an eloquent spokesman for the libido ("...queste mie vellute cosce son di virilità, di robustezza indizio") young Jean-Jacques rather creates the impression of a *petit satyre* in need of wine to hold his own with *Mlles les bacchantes*. Obviously, the interlude is not devoid of erotic implications; but, as usual, Rousseau mutes sensuous effects, and readers disinterested in courtship *more Platonico* will have to wait for the idyll of Monsieur Dudding and Mme de Larnage before meeting a *satiro* and *Dafné* worthy of Tasso.

Closer to the subject-matter is the problem of the structure of *l'Idylle des Cerises* and its relation to the structure of the pastoral. That the eclogue is inherently dramatic has become a critical commonplace. In the words of W. W. Greg: "Of the Idyls of Theocritus only about a third contains more than one character; of Vergil's Bucolics at least half; of Calpurnius' all but one; of the eclogues of Petrarch and Boccaccio all without exception."[17] How the dramatic pastoral developed from the recited eclogue still remains a matter of controversy. It is certain, however, that the pastoral dramas and novels of the sixteenth and seventeenth centuries came to be characterized by a rigid organization of human relationships. This equilibrium, this changelessness, results from the fact that interaction among "la chaîne des amants" as for instance, in *Il Pastor Fido* or *La Diana*, is governed by abstract principles determined by myths and traditions. That Tasso, Jonson and Shakespeare were able to dramatize these principles, to breathe new life into stereotypes, can only be ascribed to their genius. This supremacy of essentially static principles over psychodynamic principles of the sort which animate, for example, *El Burlador de Sevilla* or *La Princesse de Clèves*, accounts for the eventual failure of the pastoral drama and novel. *L'Idylle des Cerises* exhibits the characteristically static quality of the pastoral without being lifeless, since the lack of overt action by the *dramatis personnae* is compensated by a powerful flow of energy emanating from the narrator. Having suppressed all excessive developments in terms of intrigue, allegory, and pastoral conventions, and having reduced the number of characters to three, Rousseau organized his confessional data according to the canons of French classical drama. The *Idylle* consists of five parts framed by a prologue and epilogue and strictly observes the rules of the unities.[18] By virtue of this remarkable simplification and by making himself the source of feeling, Rousseau succeeded two thousand years after Theocritus in creating a *modern* idyll woven of sunlight and shade, resounding with laughter and echoing with an ancient strain of happiness and love.

It is noteworthy that the *mise en scène* of *l'Idylle des Cerises* conforms to Curtius' definition of Virgil's *Ideallandschaft* rather than to Theocritus' landscape. The latter's setting, studded with precise details, trembles in the heat of summer: "On the shady boughs the dusky cicadas were busy with their chatter, and the tree-frog far off cried in the dense thornbrake. Larks and finches sang, the dove made moan, and bees flitted humming about the springs. All things were fragrant of rich harvest and of fruit-time."[19] Virgil, while drawing on Theocritus "makes no attempt to match his model in visual richness, in the full scale of sounds and odors. Augustan classicism does not tolerate Hellenistic colorfulness."[20] The parallel between Rousseau and Virgil is obvious—both lived in an age that looked askance on realistic elaboration in favor of stylized outlines. Flowers, trees, summer heat, shade and a brook—these constitute the *locus amoenus* and Rousseau's little picture (*eidyllion*)[21] exhibits a surprising degree of correspondence with this nature *topos*. But whereas in most of his eclogues Virgil escapes to a far away Arcadia he had never seen, Rousseau returns, like Theocritus, to the landscape of his boyhood. We should add that

l'Idylle des Cerises unfolds exclusively in daylight in contrast to *l'Aminta,*
Favola Boscareccia which, according to Tortoreto: "è tutta idillio
(purissimo idillio). "[22] In it, attention is focused on the sylvan setting where
sunlight filters through leaves and branches allowing Tasso to suggest
visions that defy illumination: "Silvia t'attende a un fonte ignuda e sola."
However tempted Rousseau might have been by such *voluttà idillica,* he
conceived his idyll in praise of purity: *la volupté morale réclame la*
lumière.

"Nous nous aimions sans mystère et sans honte et nous voulions nous
aimer toujours ainsi." This triad of "amour-mystère-honte" invites
pleasing meditations on *la pudeur à la chrétienne* that stress the polarity
between spiritual and sensuous love—a contrast which dovetails with other
pastoral oscillations between town and country, the Age of Gold and that
of Iron, reality and unreality. In Tasso's *Aminta,* dynamic tension results
from the dramatic juxtaposition of the chaste Aminta and Silvia (Vossler
calls her "ein sprödes Nymphchen")[23] with the experienced and dis-
enchanted twosome of Tirsis and Dafne flanked by the satyr. In
Garcilaso's first *Egloga* a similar polarity develops out of a lyrical
monologue fashioned of dialectical conceits and allusions: "O más dura que
mármol a mis quejas, al encendido fuego en que me quemo más helada que
nieve, Galatea." But whereas the Italian and Spaniard achieve tension
through reliance on pre-existing mythopoeic value-systems, Rousseau
dispenses with overt references to tradition in favor of a referential system
based solely on *his* Ego. We suggested that in his *Idylle* he is a man of
many parts; it should be manifest that he is also a man of many values,
specifically, of purity and impurity and that his role of value-giver,
although non-Christian, poses thorny problems. It is relatively simple for a
Dante or a Claudel to conjure up the immaculate silhouettes of Beatrice or
La Jeune Fille Violaine since these figures represent poetic fantasies for
authors and readers. One's Ego, however, is not a fantasy, and to declare
that it is pure is to contradict the realities of life in which Egos are
inextricably involved and determined by value-systems (cultures) and
value-makers (parents) over which they have no control. "Or la pureté est
une qualité morale qui ne tolère pas le Je," states Vladimir Jankélévitch:
"Comme Dieu, dont nul ne peut nommer le nom ni supporter la vue, la
pureté exige en quelque sorte un regard oblique."[24] How does Rousseau
resolve psychologically the twofold problem of (1) projecting the presence
of a pure, absolutely independent Ego, "transparent comme le cristal,"
(2) establishing an oblique point of view *on* himself *by* himself, permitting
the process of individuation, the *sine qua non* of autobiography? Most
students of Rousseau, friendly or hostile, will immediately suggest
Rousseau's solution: self-deification.[25] If his absolute purity and goodness
necessitate his being God, he will be God, and, in order to achieve an
oblique viewpoint concerning "himself" (*i.e.,* the inner distance between
the *Moi* that writes in an incessantly evanescent present and the *Moi*
that lived happily and purely in a past far removed), Rousseau postulates
that he *was* the Son of God who lived and died in times that bear no
relation to a sorrowful present.[26] Thus, in regard to value judgments,

Rousseau's *Idylle* is a serene reminiscence of a god contemplating his childhood, and it is evident, we hope, to what degree Rousseau's concern to have been a youthful god correlates with the myth of Daphnis.

It is, of course, possible to relate directly Jean-Jacques' "amour sans mystère et sans honte" to Calvinist and Catholic dogmas as well as to sixteenth-century platonism as formulated by Leo Hebreo's *Dialoghi d'Amore* and Castiglione's *Cortegiano*—doctrines that reached Rousseau through *l'Astrée* by way of *La Diana*. Montemayor's doctrinal pronouncements on "la limpieza del amor" offer some of the ingredients of Rousseau's formula, but none of its charms, since the trinity of "amour-mystère-honte" also revives delightful memories of forbidden fruit on the tree of knowledge which Jean-Jacques wastes no time in climbing:

> Je montai sur l'arbre et je leur en jettois des bouquets dont elles me rendoient les noyaux à travers les branches. Une fois Mlle Galley avançant son tablier et reculant la tête se présentoit si bien, et je visai si juste, que je lui fis tomber un bouquet dans le sein; et de rire. Je me disois en moi-même: que mes lèvres ne sont-elles des cerises! Comme je les leur jetterois ainsi de bon cœur!

Flawless lines with anacreontic overtones lead to the climax of *l'Idylle* whose end—*Auflösung* would be a more fitting term—is more in the tradition of Virgil's *Eclogues* than of Theocritus' *Idylls* which owing to their unsentimentality avoid grief or melancholy. The ransom of feeling is sadness: "iam summa procul villarum culmina fumant /maioresque cadunt altis de montibus umbrae."[27] The light of day fades: "Enfin elles se souvinrent qu'il ne falloit pas attendre la nuit pour rentrer en ville... En marchant nous disions que la journée avoit tort de finir." Through a series of gradations the inner distance between Jean-Jacques the boy, and Rousseau the writer, increases to the point where the adventure becomes a luminescent moment outside of time, a source of consolation to himself and others: "Pour moi je sais que la mémoire d'un si beau jour me touche plus, me charme plus, me revient plus au cœur que celle d'aucuns plaisirs que j'aye goûtés en ma vie." And *l'Idylle* ends on a note of finality that severs the dream from reality lest it be destroyed by it: "Quoiqu'il en soit, il me sembloit en les quittant que je ne pourrois plus vivre sans l'une et sans l'autre. Qui m'eût dit que je ne les reverrois de ma vie, et que là finiroient nos éphémères amours?"

Up to now we have interpreted *l'Idylle* in the light of classical, medieval, and Renaissance antecedents, particularly theme, structure, and intent. Before considering Romantic and post-Romantic idylls derived from. and influenced by, *l'Idylle des Cerises*, we should refer to neo-classical theories on the pastoral genre by Rapin, Fontenelle and Samuel Johnson. Rapin admits his perplexity with disarming candor: "But tis hard to give *Rules* for that, for which there have been none already given; for where there are no footsteps nor path to direct, I cannot tell how any one can be certain of his way. Yet in this difficulty I will follow *Aristotle's* Example, who being asked to lay down Rules concerning *Epicks*, propos'd *Homer* as a Pattern, from whom he deduc'd the whole Art: So I will gather from *Theocritus* and *Virgil*, those Fathers of *Pastoral*, what I shall deliver on this account." But unlike the Stagirite, the Jesuit priest contents himself with formulating axioms that appear quite self-evident: "But as a glorious *Heroick* action must be the Subject of an *Heroick* Poem, so a *Pastoral* action of a *Pastoral*."[28] Fontenelle, rationalist *par excellence*, directs his *Discours sur la Nature de l'Eglogue*, 1688, generally against *les Anciens* and specifically against Rapin "[contre] ceux qui professent cette espèce de religion que l'on s'est faite d'adorer l'antiquité." His criteria are to be "les lumières naturelles de la Raison" and they reveal, like his *Histoire des Oracles*, his enlightened misunderstanding of the poetic power of myth and imagination. His objection that "les bergers de Théocrite sentent trop la campagne" and that their behavior is reprehensible will be echoed by Dr. Johnson's insistence on "Chastity of sentiment . . . and Purity of Manners."[29] In fairness to neo-classical critics, it must be stated that the relative lack of doctrine concerning the pastoral genre invites idiosyncratic views and that, according to Greg, confusion among critics is intensified by the fact that "any definition sufficiently elastic to include the protean forms assumed by what we call the 'pastoral ideal' could hardly have sufficient intention to be of any real value."[30] However, we have to take issue with Greg when he identifies *definition* with *theory* and concludes his valuable treatise on *Pastoral Poetry and Drama* with an *a priori* rejection of the possibility of a theory of the pastoral: "It cannot be too emphatically laid down that there is and can be no such thing as a 'theory' of pastoral, or, indeed, of any other artistic form dependent, like it, upon what are merely accidental conditions."[31] Had he turned to Schiller and Jean-Paul his conclusion might have been less adamant.

Indeed, the essay *Über naive und sentimentalische Dichtung*, 1795, offers a celebrated instance of a theory on the idyll as well as *Hirtenidylle*, and it is somewhat surprising that the indexes of Cararra, Greg, Marsan, Hulubei, and Gerhardt should not mention Schiller, *geschweige* Jean-Paul, although both attempted, aside from analyzing the idyll, to lay a theoretical foundation which makes possible a reformulation of the pastoral to adjust it to contemporary life.[32]

Space does not permit us to outline all aspects of this important problem, and we must limit ourselves to quoting a few passages particularly relevant to Rousseau. Fittingly, Schiller classifies *La Nouvelle Héloïse* as an idyll of the elegiac variety and accuses Jean-Jacques of "betraying a want of physical *repose* rather than want of moral *harmony* . . . of placing the aim nearer the earth, and to lower the ideal in order to reach it the sooner and the safer." After criticizing Longus and Tasso for catering to individual needs of solace instead of to the higher satisfactions afforded to the mind as, for example, by Milton's picture of paradisiac innocence, Schiller exhorts "the modern poet . . . [not] to lower himself to the wants of human weakness . . . but rather to prepare an idyll that realizes pastoral innocence, even in the children of civilization, and in all the conditions of the most militant and excited life . . . an idyll, in short, that is made, not to bring back man to *Arcadia*, but to lead him to

Elysium." That he considered Voss' *Luise* as an approximation of this ideal seems a forgivable error in judgment; what matters is Schiller's emphasis on modernization although his neo-Kantian and to some extent pre-Fichtean orientation led him to relate the idyll to the ideal or vocation of man (*Bestimmung des Menschen*). Less teleological are Jean-Paul's aesthetic considerations on the idyll which he defines as the "epische Darstellung des Vollglücks in der Beschränkung"—a felicitous definition that frees the idyll from traditional pastoral conventions and German Idealistic phraseology and relates it to Rousseau: "Sogar das Leben des Robinson Crusoe und das des Jean-Jacques auf seiner Petersinsel erquickt uns mit Idyllen-Duft und Schmelz." Any serene moment, the holiday of a teacher, the baptism of a first child: "alle diese Tage können Idyllen werden und können singen: auch wir waren in Arkadien."[33] The only conditions that limit his definition are that idylls must not be clouded by passion, nor written by Gessner or a Frenchman.[34]

With these ideas in mind, it is not surprising that Jean-Paul should have turned to Jean-Jacques for confirmation of his theory on the possibility of idylls suitable for modern man. Elsewhere, we have stated that it is Rousseau's greatness to have sought a reevaluation of values— *eine Umwertung der Werte*—in regard to the self, the family, and the state, not by having recourse to transcendental agents, but by exploiting neglected values, employing in the words of Coleridge "the whole of his being to do aught effectually."[35] That these values include *le bonheur* will be disputed by few though many have cast doubt on its reality. Indeed, Rousseau, who often thought himself the most wretched of men, assumes the tragic role of the champion of human happiness and the intention which created *l'Idylle des Cerises* answers this vocation. But whereas his case for "happiness" in *l'Idylle des Charmettes* (weakened by his need to tell things "[comme] elles avoient du être")[36] and to a lesser degree in his *Lettres à Malesherbes* and the *Rêveries*, forms part of a deep and powerful current of feeling, *l'Idylle des Cerises* seems to be shored up, as it were, against the ebb and tide of despair and ecstacy. It is "das Vollglück in seiner Beschränkung" which results from a completely original fusion of the pastoral schema derived from Theocritus, Virgil and Tasso with his personal dream of salvation and peace—a *Vollglück* that is a harmonious reconciliation of classical order and preromantic plenitude.

The historical and literary effects of Rousseau's modernization of the classical pastoral idyll have yet to be studied. A history of *l'Idylle à la Rousseau* would have to take into account three major tendencies: expansion, contraction, integration. It would relate them variously to the narrative and lyrical modes—the resulting idyllic permutations having in turn to be interpreted as representing either *erlebtes*, *erzähltes* and, to complicate matters, *erfundenes Glück*. *Paul et Virginie*, for instance, illustrates colorfully the multiplication of the factors of expansion and *erzählte Rede*, whereas Lamartine's *Jocelyn* portrays in pale and flowing alexandrines Jocelyn and Laurence in their grotto "[épuisant] le bonheur dans toute sa goutte de vie." More rustic than Lamartine's endeavors and certainly more prosaic are, according to Cararra, "gli escritti della

Sand."[37] Her preface to *François le Champi*—Marcel Proust's childhood favorite—reveals clearly that *Lélia* knew what she was doing: "Voyons, le théâtre, la poésie et le roman ont quitté la houlette pour prendre le poignard, et quand ils mettent en scène la vie rustique, ils donnent un certain caractère de réalité qui manquait aux bergeries du temps passé. Mais la poésie n'y est guère, et je m'en plains."[38]

A delightfully ironic example of idyllic contraction *en prose* may be found in Chapter XIII of *Le Rouge et le Noir* graced with the subtitle "Les Bas à jour": "Jamais je n'accorderai rien à Julien, se dit Madame de Rênal, nous vivrons à l'avenir comme nous vivons depuis un mois. Ce sera un ami." Disregarding for the sake of brevity Madame de Mortsauf's *Vollglück in der Beschränkung*, we may surely interpret Proust's meditations on a group of girls on the shores of Balbec as being a derivative of *l'Idylle des Cerises*, integrated in a fresco which like the *Confessions* unfolds in the dimension of time: "Elles étaient, du bonheur inconnu et possible de la vie, un exemplaire si délicieux et en si parfait état, que c'était presque pour des raisons intellectuelles que j'étais désespéré de ne pas pouvoir faire dans des conditions uniques, ne laissant aucune place à l'erreur possible, l'expérience de ce que nous offre de plus mystérieux la beauté qu'on désire, et qu'on se console de ne posséder jamais en demandant du plaisir."

Whether Proust's marine idyll could or should be related to Sannazaro's Latin mythological poem *Salices*, 1517, in which certain nymphs are pursued by satyrs, may be irrelevant to our main argument. More pertinent is Camus' injunction in *l'Homme Révolté*: "Il faut détruire ceux qui détruisent l'idylle." Admittedly his pagan celebrations in *Noces* and happy interludes in *l'Etranger* seem too sensuous to qualify under the heading of *amour sans mystère et sans honte*. On second thought, and after comparing Camus' idylls to raptures by Gide, Giono, and Montherlant, we feel that his artistic powers of *Beschränkung* are so great that they somehow neutralize effects of carnal indulgence, creating an ideal of innocent and "shameless" love which for Camus is but a pretext for idyllic prose.

Antithetical to Rousseau's *Idylle des Cerises* stand Sartre's and Beckett's anti-idylls acted out by Henri and Lulu and Molloy and Edith who, like Meursault, were sired by Dostoyevsky. According to Poggioli, Dostoyevsky subverted the myth of the Golden Age by projecting the idyllic vision into a dream, turning that dream into a nightmare "to prove that the inner necessity of that ideal of perfection by which the revolutionary spirit tempts and threatens the human soul, turns it into its very opposite or into a corruption never dreamed before."[39] But a history of the modern idyll would also have to trace filiations between Rousseau's *Idylle des Cerises* and especially his *Idylle des Charmettes* and the German idyll variously characterized by *Familienglück oder-unglück* (from Voss and Goethe to Hofmannsthal) with the enchanting exception of the Judith and Anna episodes in *Der grüne Heinrich* unquestionably inspired by Jean-Jacques' adventures. It is of interest that in Spain Rousseau's modernization of the classical idyll could have little if no effect, since Gongora's reduction of the dialogued eglogues of Garcilasco and Herrera into *Soledades* precluded any major dramatic expansion of the genre of the idyll. This paved the way for Jimenez's *Platero* as well as allowing García Lorca to find peace in a sunlit courtyard of Granada where "la quietud hecha esfinge se rié de la muerte." [40]

Parallel to the development of the classical idyll as metamorphosed by Rousseau and defined by Jean-Paul, there occurs at the end of the eighteenth and during the nineteenth and twentieth centuries of French literature, a renascence of Hellenism which has been so closely studied by Professor Henri Peyre. [41] Its high points are Chénier's *Bucoliques*, Leconte de Lisle's *Poèmes Antiques*, and Guérin's *Centaure* and, above all, Mallarmé's *Après-Midi d'un Faune*. Yet, despite the consciously graeco-latin nature of these idyllic evocations, the influence of Rousseau's *Idylle* can be detected in these last two works by virtue of their confessional mood which, although masked, animates *faune* and *centaure*. At the risk of courting paradox, which in a discussion of Rousseau may after all be unavoidable, we feel that Jean-Jacques' melodious, warm and serene style is closer to Theocritus' sense of form, his Greek melody and lightness of touch as well as his restraint and love of simple things, than the slightly mannered formalism of Mallarmé and Guérin. "Or, l'essentiel, en littérature," writes Professor Peyre, "presque autant que dans d'autres arts, n'est pas toujours le contenu idéologique de l'œuvre, mais la forme, c'est-à-dire le ton, la chaleur, l'intensité prêtés à certaines pensées par une imagination puissante, une vive sensibilité, un style coloré ou musical." [42] With the advent of Rousseau, "prophet of the new world," the true humanist no longer adorns his work with the details of classical learning, but structures it according to essential principles of the classical tradition.

We should therefore view Rousseau's *Idylle des Cerises* as a necessary moment in a literary tradition which for want of a better term may be called *une petite histoire du bonheur humain*. It is a tradition admittedly problematical in nature and hardly comparable in size and importance to the overwhelmingly tragic and often sadistic implications of European literature. The pastoral genre, on the surface the least desperate of literary modes, by its very obsession with the Hesiodic dream of the Golden Age when men "lived in ease and peace upon their lands with many good things, rich in flocks and beloved of the blessed gods," asks a question that has never been better phrased than by Marvell:

> Thenceforth I set myself to play
> My solitary time away,
> With this; and very well content
> Could so mine idle Life have spent.
> For it was full of sport; and light
> Of foot, and heart; and did invite
> Me to its game: It seemed to bless
> Itself in me. How could I less
> Than love it? ...

And no pastoral poet ever responded more movingly to this question than did Rousseau when he said: "La soif du bonheur ne s'éteint point dans le cœur de l'homme." Could it be that in living as well as writing *l'Idylle des Cerises* he succeeded in quenching that thirst?

University of California
Santa Barbara

Notes

[1] To save space, most bibliographical references (including page references) to works well known to Rousseau scholars and students of the pastoral genre have been omitted. Unless indicated otherwise, quotations from Rousseau are taken from his *Œuvres complètes*, I, ed. *Pléiade* (Paris, 1959). Mia Gerhardt, *La Pastorale—Essai d'analyse littéraire* (Assen, 1950), p. 290.

[2] Bernardin de Saint-Pierre, *Œuvres complètes* (Paris, 1826), VIII, p. 260.

[3] To the best of our knowledge, Francis Gribble was first to refer to *l'Idylle des Cerises* as being a pastoral idyll. In his hostile commentary, he devotes one sentence to the idyll: "The incident as described by him is quite a pastoral idyll, but it has no importance. Nothing came of it either at the time or afterwards...," *Rousseau And The Women He Loved* (New York, 1908), p. 68.

[4] On the relatively small contribution of the Christian pastoral ideal to the pastoral genre, consult W. W. Greg, *Pastoral Poetry and Pastoral Drama* (London, 1906), p. 21 ff. Also consult Renato Poggioli, "Naboth's Vineyard or the Pastoral View of the Social Order," *JHI*, XXIV, 1963; "Dante Poco Tempo Silvano: Or a 'Pastoral Oasis' in the Commedia," *80th Annual Report of the Dante Society*, 1962; and "The Oaten Flute," *Harvard Library Bulletin*, XI, 1957. Concerning Rousseau's *le Lévite d'Ephraïm*, see footnote 6.

[5] Consult the *Confessions* where Rousseau describes his visit to the landscape of *l'Astrée* as well as his analysis of his *état d'âme* preceding his love affair with Mme d'Houdetot: "J'allois malheureusement me rappeler le dîné du Château de Toun et ma rencontre avec ces deux charmantes filles dans la même saison et dans des lieux à peu près semblables à ceux où j'étois en ce moment... Mon sang s'allume et pétille, la tête me tourne malgré mes cheveux déjà grisonnans, et voilà le grave Citoyen de Genève, voilà l'austère Jean-Jacques à près de quarante-cinq ans redevenu tout à coup le berger extravagant." Throughout his writings, Rousseau stresses his love for pastoral ideals and novels, and Seillière and Faguet only amplify Rousseau's succinct statement concerning his mother's bequest: "Ma mère avoit laissé des Romans." *A propos*, Starobinski declares: "...ces romans (ceux de Rousseau) sont un vestige de la mère perdue," *Jean-Jacques Rousseau: La transparence et l'obstacle* (Paris, 1957), p. 6.

[6] Renato Poggioli, "The Pastoral of the Self," *Daedalus*, Fall, 1959, p. 687: "One should, however, never forget that the ultimate representative of the pastoral self was bound to be another and less fictitious Jacques (the other being Shakespeare's Jaques)—the greatest literary figure of the eighteenth century, Jean-Jacques Rousseau...." In his article "The Oaten Flute" Poggioli asserts "that the pastoral longing is but the wishful dream of a happiness to be gained without effort, of an erotic bliss made absolute by its own irresponsibility. This, rather than a sense of decency, is the very reason why the pastoral often limits the sexual embrace to mere kissing, so as to escape the danger of parenthood, and the nuisance of birth control. In this connection nothing is more in a pastoral sense than the episode of Rousseau's *Confessions* that goes under the name of *l'Idylle des Cerises*," p. 159. This view strikes us as an over-simplification. Daniel Mornet dwells at length on Rousseau's fondness for idylls and comments on his attempt to emulate Gessner by writing a biblical idyll *le Lévite d'Ephraïm*. He concludes his *Sentiment de la Nature en France:* "Rousseau parle en son nom, non sous le déguisement des bergers d'idylle et du ton compassé des poètes descriptifs," p. 463. However, it seems to us that Mornet disregards Rousseau's originality in creating the modern idyll as defined by Schiller and Jean-Paul.

[7] Rousseau, *Corresp. gén.*, ed. Théophile Dufour (Paris, 1925), III, p. 13, Lettre à Tronchin, 17 janvier, 1957. Concerning Rousseau's knowledge of latin authors, specifically Virgil, see *Conf.*, pp. 238-39.

[8] Concerning the historical importance of Longus' *Daphnis and Chloe*, cf. pp. 11-13, 39. Did Longus influence Rousseau's conception of *l'Idylle des Cerises?* There exist undeniable analogies to which we refer below. Bernardin de Saint-Pierre relates that "J.-J. Rousseau avait également composé la musique de Daphnis et Chloé..." in *Fragments sur J.-J. Rousseau, op. cit.*, XII, p. 31.

[9] On the relationship between Rousseau and Italian authors, there exist three studies of which L. F. Bendetto's essay is most pertinent to our subject-matter. His analysis deals mainly with Rousseau's interpretation of Tasso's personality and the influence of *La Gerusalemme liberata* on *La Nouvelle Héloïse*. Especially pertinent to our argument are the following comments: "...il Rousseau ha talvolta la penna voluttuosa come il Tasso, il suo poeta favorito, ma si può ravvisare nella sua forma più lenta e più realistica la torbida attività incui il poeta italiano metteva la sua fantasia lussuriosa," "Jean-Jacques Rousseau Tassofilo" in *Scritti varii di erudizione e di critica in onore di Rodolfo Renier* (Torino, 1912), p. 373. Also interesting is Bendetto's remark that «L'autore del *Devin du Village* aprí certo la sua anima con compiacimento infinito al lacrimoso sorriso di voluttà che splende nell'incomparabile *Aminta...*,» p. 374. Chandler B. Beall summarizes Bendetto's arguments and situates Rousseau's predilection within the larger context of his study *La Fortune du Tasse en France* (Eugène, 1942), chap. x. To be consulted lightheartedly is Carlo Culcasi's *Gli influssi italiani nell'opera di G. G. Rousseau* (Roma, 1907). In this somewhat unscholarly investigation, one finds repeated affirmations rather based on flair than on proof (we suspect that Culcasi may have been right) that *l'Aminta* has played a decisive role in the shaping of Rousseau literary imagination: "Il Tasso è il poeta la cui utopia è più affine a quella del Rousseau, e *l'Aminta* è l'opera che mostra più visibili quelle tendenze che svolse e sviluppò il ginevrino," *op. cit.*, p. 105. Furthermore, he bases his airy arguments on a book by Charlotte Banti, *L'Amyntas et l'Astrée* (Milan, 1895). Bendetto limits the influence of *l'Aminta* to two passages in *La Nouvelle Héloïse, op. cit.*, p. 374.

[10] Concerning the historical background of *l'Idylle* consult François et Joseph Serand, *Un épisode de la vie de J.-J. Rousseau—l'Idylle des Cerises* (Chambéry, 1928). Arsène Houssaye believes that Rousseau's inspiration came from a gouache by Baudouin, Boucher's son-in-law. It was exhibited in 1760 and bears the title "Les cerises et les amoureuses." Houssaye asserts that it is "un petit chef-d'œuvre d'esprit et de volupté. Or, c'est mot à mot celui de Rousseau. Voyez plutôt la gravure qui est partout: ces deux belles filles qui attendent les cerises, gorge entrouverte et bras demi-nus, ne sont-ce pas les visions de Jean-Jacques? Et ce galant qui cueille les cerises et qui les jette avec intention, n'est-ce pas Jean-Jacques lui-même? C'est-à-dire que Jean-Jacques, au lieu de se souvenir d'une page de sa vie, s'est souvenu d'un tableau de Baudouin.—A moins qu'il n'ait conté son histoire au peintre; mais alors n'eût-il pas dit cela, en écrivant les *Confessions*" *Les Charmettes—J.-J. Rousseau et Madame de Warens* (Paris, 1863), p. 45.

[11] J. G. Frazer, *The Golden Bough* (New York), 1956, abridged ed., I, p. 371.

[12] Roscher, *Ausführliches Lexikon der Griechischen und Römischen Mythologie* (Leipzig, 1884-1886), I, p. 962.

[13] Hölderlin, "Rousseau," *Sämtliche Gedichte* (Berlin, 1942), pp. 244-45, quoted by Starobinski, *op. cit.*, p. 16.

[14] *Op. cit.*, p. 301.

[15] A similar *idylle à trois* will be that of Saint-Preux and his "deux charmantes amies." Cf. footnote 5.

[16] On this point, it is worthwhile to quote Vossler: "Es ist sehr bezeichnend, dass die Pastourelle auf italienischem Boden nicht recht gedeihen wollte. Es fehlte die gesellschaftliche Voraussetzung: der Gegensatz zwischen Feudalität und Bauernstand. Italien war ein demokratisches Land—und als das hochtrabende Ritterrepos über die Alpen herabstieg, da ging es auch mit seiner Würde, je tiefer es ins Land kam, abwärts." "Tassos *Aminta* und die Hirtendichtung," *Studien zur vergleichenden Literaturgeschichte*, Berlin, 1906, Vol. VI, pp. 28-29.

[17] Greg, *op. cit.*, p. 169.

[18] The epigraph of our essay constitutes the prologue. Act I ends with the passage: "mais l'absente revenoit bien vite...." Act II consists of the next two paragraphs which conclude with "pour la sensualité." The third act is limited to the delightful scene of the cherry tree. The ensuing paragraph contains the fourth act. The fifth act begins with "Enfin elles se souvinrent qu'il ne falloit pas attendre la nuit..." and ends with "nous trouvâmes que nous avions su le secret de la (journée) faire longue par tous les amusemens dont nous avions su la remplir." The

epilogue begins with "Je les quittai à peu près au même endroit où elles m'avoient pris," and ends with "nos éphémères amours?"

[19]Theocritus, *Idyll*, VII, ed. and trans. A. S. F. Gow (Cambridge, 1952), I, p. 65.

[20]Ernst Robert Curtius, *European Literature and the Latin Middle Ages* (New York, 1953), p. 191 ff.

[21] For a summary of problems pertaining to the etymological and historical development of the words "idylle" and "églogue" consult Alice Hulubei, *L'Eglogue en France au XVe Siècle* (Paris, 1938), pp. xi-xiii.

[22] Torquato Tasso, *Aminta*, ed. A. Tortoreto (Milano, 1946), p. 12.

[23] *Op. cit.*, p. 37.

[24] Vladimir Jankélévitch, *Le pur et l'impur* (Paris, 1960), pp. 7, 14.

[25] Consult Starobinski's analysis of Rousseau's value system: "... la norme n'est plus transcendante, elle est immanente au moi," *op. cit.*, p. 21; also "L'imitation de Jésus-Christ, chez Rousseau, est l'imitation de l'acte ' divin' par lequel une conscience humaine solitaire devient source de vérité...," *ibid.*, p. 85. On the question of self-deification, see also M. Temmer, *Time in Rousseau and Kant* (Geneva, 1958), chap. i.

[26] Starobinski's commentary on Rousseau's *Morceau allégorique* relates to our viewpoint: "Le dieu-homme (comme ailleurs Rousseau lui-même) s'offre à tous les regards non pour être vu lui-même, mais pour qu'une source sacrée soit reconnue dans l'acte même par lequel il parle et se communique sans restriction," *op. cit.*, p. 83.

[27] Cf. Panofsky's essay "Et in Arcadia Ego," *Meaning in the Visual Arts* (New York, 1955): "In Virgil's ideal Arcady human suffering and superhumanly perfect surroundings create a dissonance. This dissonance, once felt, had to be resolved, and it was resolved in that vespertinal mixture of sadness and tranquillity which is perhaps Virgil's most personal contribution to poetry," p. 300.

[28] René Creech's translation of the *Idylliums* of Theocritus (1684), (Ann Arbor, The Augustan Reprint Society, 1947), p. 52, p. 26.

[29] Samuel Johnson, *The Rambler*, quoted by Greg, *op. cit.*, p. 416.

[30] Greg, *op. cit.*, p. 2.

[31] *Ibid.*, p. 417.

[32] Cf. William Empson, *Some Versions of Pastoral* (Norfolk, 1950).

[33] Jean-Paul Richter, *Sämtliche Werke—Vorschule der Aesthetik* (Weimar, 1935), XI, paragraph 73, "Die Idylle," pp. 241-44.

[34] Concerning the influence of Gessner, see Paul Van Tieghem, "Les Idylles de Gessner et le Rêve pastoral dans le Préromantisme Européen," *Revue de Littérature Comparée*, 1942, pp. 41-72, 222-69: "On sent confusément que le genre pastoral porte en lui des possibilités presque infinies de développements," p. 46. Van Tieghem also comments at length on Rousseau's reaction on reading Huber's translation of Gessner's *Idyllen* which Usteri had brought to his attention: "Ah! c'est un auteur charmant que M. Gessner. Je voudrais qu'il écrivît toutes les années trois cent soixante-cinq idylles et que je pusse en lire tous les jours une nouvelle." Quoted from *Corresp. de J.-J. Rousseau avec Léonard Usteri*, ed. Usteri and Ritter (Zurich and Geneva, 1910), lettre du 6 juin, 1764.

[35] Coleridge, *Philosophical Lectures* (London, 1949), p. 308.

[36] *Rêveries*, IVe Promenade, p. 1035.

[37] Enrico Carrara, *La Poesia Pastorale* (Milano, 1904-08), p. 474.

[38] George Sand, *François le Champi* (Paris, 1999), pp. 16, 17. Proustians, remembering Maman's careful expurgation of all love passages in *François le Champi* when reading it to little Marcel, may find George Sand's preface to her novel *Les Maîtres Mosaïstes* quite amusing: "J'ai écrit les *Mosaïstes* en 1837, pour mon fils, qui n'avait encore lu qu'un roman, *Paul et Virginie*. Cette lecture était trop forte pour les nerfs d'un pauvre enfant. Il avait tant pleuré, que je lui avais promis de lui faire un roman où il n'y aurait pas d'amour et où toutes choses finiraient pour le mieux," p. 10.

[39] Renato Poggioli, "Naboth's Vineyard or the Pastoral View of the Social Order," *op. cit.*, p. 24.

[40] Quoted by Enrique Martinez-Lopez in his excellent article "Aljibe y surtidor o la Granada de Frederico García Lorca" in *La Torre*, 1962, pp. 11-45.

[41] Henri Peyre, *Bibliographie critique de l'hellénisme en France de 1843-1870* (New Haven, 1932).

[42] Henri Peyre, *L'Influence des littératures antiques sur la littérature française moderne* (New Haven, 1941), p. 3.

II

THE NINETEENTH CENTURY

The 19th century is an extremely rich and fecund time in French literary history, but for purposes of our discussion it is possible to group the writers of the period into roughly three large groups: the Romantics, properly speaking; the Realists and Naturalists (primarily novelists) who evolved in one direction from Romanticism; and the Parnassians and Symbolists who represent the main post-Romantic movement in poetry. In somewhat different ways, all of these groups were deeply influenced by the heritage from classical antiquity, but as we shall see from the three representative essays here—on Vigny, Zola, and Mallarmé—there are certain distinctions that may be made regarding the character or direction of this influence.

The importance of the ancient world—or rather of a certain view of it—for the writers who dominated the first half of the 19th century has long been recognized. Indeed, from Chateaubriand onward the current is so strong that Peyre has called it a veritable "redécouverte de l'antiquité."[1] To a certain extent, of course, this interest was a prolongation of the spirit of inquiry that had so characterized the intellectuals of the preceding century. Like the *philosophes* before them, the Romantics were deeply interested in learning about the classical civilizations, particularly Greece, because they had an active intellectual curiosity. The 19th century popularity of travel accounts, of books on archeological discoveries, and of learned re-examinations or re-interpretations of classical texts all bear witness to a great and almost "scholarly" interest in the past on the part of a large segment of the contemporary reading public.

But there was another, even more important reason for the Romantics' great interest in antiquity; in the ancient world they found satisfaction for some of their deepest emotional needs and desires. As Peyre has put it,

C'étaient la perception du nouveau et de l'étranger, dans le temps et dans l'espace, chez les Grecs qu'interprétait historiquement le relativisme du siècle; un élan éperdu, dans les cœurs des enfants du siècle, pour calmer leur nostalgie de la jeunesse du monde, leurs soupirs et leurs regards d'envie devant la santé harmonieuse de ces adolescents, nés plus tôt dans un monde moins vieux ... surtout peut-être, un sens rajeuni de la vie des choses, la faculté d'émerveillement recouvrée avec joie, et le désir d'éprouver comme les primitifs, dans une puissante effusion panthéiste, la communion entre l'homme et la nature, entre l'homme et les dieux.[2]

In this sense, of course, the Romantics were clearly the spiritual descendants of Rousseau, and scholars have come to characterize this particular aspect of their spirit as Romantic Hellenism.

Two of the major early specialized studies of the role that antiquity played in Romanticism in France are René Canat's 1911 volume on *La Renaissance de la Grèce antique* (which presents the views that French archeologists, scholars, travellers, and intellectuals had of Greece during the high period of the Romantic movement), and the more literary and philosophical inquiry by Charly Clerc, *Génie du paganisme* (1926). More recently, books by other scholars have explored this general problem further. There has also been a large—almost bewildering—number of essays examining the influence that the classical world exerted on the life and works of individual Romantic authors, particularly such major figures as Mme de Staël, Constant, Chateaubriand, Lamartine, Hugo, and Musset, to name but a few. Clearly, the ancient world nourished the whole movement to such an extent that what a close friend of Chateaubriand once said of him is applicable to all the other writers of the period as well, almost without exception: "Jamais l'amour des classiques et de la belle antiquité n'avait consumé un cœur humain d'une plus vive flamme."[3]

However, for a long time specialists of French literature—particularly in France—tended to define Romanticism primarily in terms of its opposition to Classicism, and this sometimes limited their understanding of certain elements in the movement (the role of antiquity, among others). Professor Peyre notes that in view of our ever-deepening awareness of the complexities of this literary period, it is time for a number of points to be re-examined "dans un esprit neuf" so that they may be brought into better focus. In this connection, he specifically calls attention to Alfred de Vigny's preoccupation with Julian the Apostate.[4]

This Emperor of late Hellenistic times (361-363 A.D.) has long been an enigmatic and mysterious figure to those interested in antiquity, but Vigny was particularly fascinated by him. Indeed, as early as 1839, he notes that "Je ne puis vaincre la sympathie que j'ai toujours eue pour Julien l'Apostat. Si la métempsychose existe, j'ai été cet homme. C'est l'homme dont le rôle, la vie, le caractère m'eussent le mieux convenu dans l'histoire."[5] Twenty years later he is still preoccupied with this personnage: "Julien fut grand surtout à mes yeux parce qu'il défendait la Foi en un monde surnaturel et mystique, sans laquelle il n'y a pas de Religion et la terre retombe dans le matérialisme... Julien dut se dire: Plutôt le paganisme qu'un Dieu dont les serviteurs disent: C'est un homme et un philosophe."

Most scholars would agree with the position of a specialist like Citoleux that sentiments such as those cited above give Vigny an important place in the "curieux réveil de l'idéalisme platonicien"[6] which is an important element in the Romantic movement (and which in a certain way culminated in Mallarmé). However a renewed examination of *Daphné*, Vigny's tale centering on Julian, makes it clear that the problem is somewhat more complex than Citoleux would suggest. In his essay here, Professor Bowman points out that the various critics who have studied the story have been unable to agree either on its meaning or its aesthetic value. He further suggests that this disagreement is perhaps due in large part to their unawareness of some of the broader aspects of the intellectual and artistic currents of which Vigny was a part.

Although all the French Romantics underwent a certain influence of the Greco-Roman world, Vigny's case was particularly striking because he was unusually "scholarly". Not only was he familiar with the writings of the Greek and Latin authors at first hand (he translated Homer and Plato, and read Ovid, Horace, and Virgil in the original Latin), but he also studied various serious works in order to learn more about different aspects of the history and culture of the classical past. Most of his contemporaries were interested primarily in Greece and Rome at the height of their glory, but Vigny was drawn to the Hellenistic period, that time during the first few centuries of the Christian era when Greek culture—somewhat altered, but increasingly more widely diffused—mingled with Christianity to form the major cultural tradition of the modern West. As critics have long pointed out, to a large extent the age of transition in which Julian lived appealed to Vigny because the philosophical ideas of the classical Greek thinkers (notably Plato and the Stoics) which gave Man an exalted place in the universe were being re-elaborated, re-interpreted, and integrated into a Christian world-view where Man was a being whose primary glory was simply that he was linked to God in a very special way. Professor Bowman's study makes it clear that Vigny was attracted to Julian and his times for certain more subtle intellectual and aesthetic reasons as well, and his discussion further illuminates an important aspect of the relationship between the Romantics and antiquity.

Notes

[1] Henri M. Peyre, *L'Influence des littératures antiques sur la littérature française moderne* (New Haven-Oxford, 1941), p. 56.

[2] *Op. cit.*, pp. 57-58.

[3] Cited by Peyre (*op. cit.*, p. 62), from Marcellus, *Chateaubriand et son temps* (Paris, 1859), p. xvi.

[4] Peyre, *op. cit.*, p. 62.

[5] Alfred de Vigny, *Œuvres complètes* (Pléiade, Paris, 1948), vol. II, p. 769. The second quotation in this paragraph is from page 770.

[6] Marc Citoleux, *Alfred de Vigny, persistances classiques et affinités étrangères* (Paris, 1924), pp. 508-546.

A ROMANTIC VIEW OF THE HELLENIST PAST: VIGNY'S *DAPHNE*

By Frank P. Bowman

In 1912, Fernand Gregh published a manuscript of Alfred de Vigny entitled *Daphné*.[1] The unfinished text was to be part of a *Deuxième consultation du Dr Noir*, a project which is mentioned very frequently in Vigny's journals. *Daphné* contains an "anecdote illustrative," similar to that in *Chatterton*, but centered this time on the last days of Julian the Apostate. This anecdote is framed by a prologue and epilogue in which Stello and Dr. Noir witness the destruction of the archbishop's palace in Paris in 1831 and then go to visit a dying poet. There they find a crucifix crumbling into dust, a statue of Julian, and the manuscript of the anecdote, which they finish reading only at dawn. Once more they witness new scenes of revolutionary violence, and finally a Saint-Simonian parade. This framework is unfinished, and the present study is concerned only with the anecdote, which seems complete.

This anecdote consists of four letters from the Jew Joseph Jechaïah to a friend, in which he gives an account of his sojourn in the turbulent town of Antioch and of his subsequent visit to the neighboring village of Daphne with its famous temple to the Greek goddess. In the first and by far the longest of the letters, Joseph tells of finding his old professor Libanius in Daphne, and of the arrival shortly afterwards of two other former students, John Chrysostom and Basil of Caesarea. The four men begin discussing the anarchy of the period, and then the life of the Emperor Julian, who has recently rejected Christianity. Julian himself appears, accompanied by Paul of Larissa (another former student of Libanius) who has accepted to become Julian's slave in order to transmit to the emperor his enthusiasm for philosophy. The group engages in a kind of platonic dialogue in which they examine the question of whether or not Julian was right in trying to rid the Empire of Christianity and to reinstate the worship of the pagan gods. The central problem they seek to resolve is whether pagan religion possesses the poetic power necessary to ensure enthusiastic belief. Libanius finally succeeds in convincing Julian that men no longer have enough emotional strength to feel any true zeal for the pagan gods, nor enough intellectual force to understand a divinity stripped of symbolic trappings.

The second and third letters—only a few short paragraphs in length—briefly recount the loss of the battle of Ctesiphon and the joy of the Antioch Christians over the victory of the Barbarians. The fourth one tells how the Genius of the Empire predicted this defeat to Julian and gives an account of the Emperor's death from a wound, including his final apostrophe to the "Galiléen". Shortly afterward a Christian mob, seeking to bring back to Daphne the relics of St. Babylas which Julian had had removed, is castigated and insulted by Paul of Larissa, who praises the dead Emperor as "le plus religieux des hommes." The furious Christians turn upon him as he stands upon the steps of the Daphne temple, stone him to death, and set fire to the building. The letter ends as the Jew Joseph takes advantage of the chaos to buy and hide under the earth a number of pagan statues, including the Venus of Milo.

Daphné is evidently intended to be a didactic work, but critics who have studied it have not been able to define its message in a satisfactory way. In the anecdote itself, Christianity wins out—even though it is presented as an inferior religion—but in the larger framing story Christianity is actually dying. According to Canat, Vigny intended the anecdote to be an attack on Julian for neglecting the need for myths (i.e., Christian legends) in making truth known to men.[2] For Citoleux, the "faculté maîtresse" esteemed by the author was no longer the imagination (as in *Stello*) but rather the reasoning intelligence; Julian, as poet, is presented as being inferior to Libanius, a philosopher, and the story itself seeks to refine Christianity into a "platonisme toujours vivant."[3] Georges Bonnefoy explains the work's ambiguity by Vigny's own evolution; he had begun the story at a time when he still had hope that man could eventually free himself from his humanity but, after the events of 1831, he began to have increasing fears about the dangers inherent in any such freedom.[4] In this view, Vigny's fundamental idea would be that man must turn his back on history or politics if he wants to pursue the truths of religion and philosophy. There is also disagreement among critics regarding the author's attitude toward Julian's neoplatonism; according to Bonnefoy, Vigny regrets it, whereas Citoleux implies that he accepts it. After examining various aspects of *Daphné*, Baldensperger wisely concludes that it would be "imprudent de donner un sens définitif à l'œuvre." However, such a position raises a much more fundamental problem, i.e., the esthetic value of a didactic work which is basically ambiguous or contradictory.[5]

Indeed, critics have been just as divided on the question of *Daphné*'s esthetic value as they have been about its meaning. When it was first published, Ernest Dupuy suggested that it added nothing to Vigny's glory, whereas Paul Souday found in the work a kind of richness, a picturesque quality normally absent in Vigny's writings. Since then, if *Daphné* has above all been a center of contention in Vigny scholarship, many readers have also found in the book a kind of mysterious beauty. The purpose of the present discussion is to define that attraction and in so doing to clarify somewhat the meaning of the work.

The problem of the sources of *Daphné* is a complex one which has been carefully examined. As always, Vigny read everything. First, the Greek and

Latin sources, for he was one of the few Romantics who knew both languages. Then, not only the famous authors who discuss Julian—Montaigne, Gibbon, Voltaire, Chateaubriand—but also relatively obscure historians who had studied the Hellenist period of antiquity, such as Lebeau, Beugnot, Tourlet, and La Bléterie. Vigny enjoyed scholarship, and his fascination for the person and period of Julian was a deep and long-standing one. But while one can easily find sources of almost everything in *Daphné*, it is just as easy to note an almost scandalous indifference toward historical truth, and a novel rejection of the traditional treatments of the figure of Julian. One example of this indifference toward history will suffice. Vigny knew perfectly well that in late antiquity the temple at Daphne was not at all a center of faithful worship, but rather that it suffered from total neglect and that it was burned before Julian's death, not afterwards.[6] Of course Vigny always shared Dumas's conviction that one could "violer l'histoire pourvu qu'on lui fasse un enfant," and he demonstrates the same indifference toward historical facts in other works, such as *Cinq-Mars*.

Some of the changes Vigny makes in the materials he found in his sources can be explained by esthetic concerns, but others reveal a certain attitude toward the meaning of the anecdote. For instance, he suppresses anything from the sources which might make Julian or Libanius antipathetic.[7] Julian was notoriously superstitious, almost an adept of black magic, but Vigny says nothing of this. Historically, Julian was small, hairy, ugly, and washed as rarely as possible, yet in this story Vigny presents him as handsome and dynamic. Most Romantic writers would have seen in Libanius's autobiography the portrait of a vain, proud, self-satisfied man, who was more a sophist rhetorician than a true platonic philosopher. However Vigny's Libanius is a profound and subtle thinker who—far from being arrogant—sincerely regrets the conclusions that his reason forces on him.

There is another significant change from history which to my knowledge is unique in Vigny. In *Daphné* he suggests that the young Julian had been a sincere and enthusiastic Christian who had lost his faith only when the Arian Bishop Aetius denied the presence of the logos in Jesus. "Qu'avez-vous fait du Dieu?" (106), exclaims Vigny's Julian, plunged into despair. Historical sources reveal that Julian actually encouraged the Arians, and that he even made Aetius the gift of a villa on Lesbos. If, on the one hand, Vigny embellishes paganism by suppressing the disagreeable traits of Julian and Libanius, on the other he claims that his hero also went through a sincere Christian period. Finally, it is noteworthy that in his story Vigny does not seek to emphasize any of the "romantic" traits of Julian—his unfortunate youth, his years as a Bohemian student, his military prowess; these are details on which such contemporaries as Chateaubriand and Jouy dwell at length in their portrayals of the apostate Emperor.

It should be remembered that Julian was a center of controversy in the Romantic age as he had been during the eighteenth century. Apologists for the Christian faith saw him as an intellectual ancestor, an iconoclast like

Voltaire, but this is a tradition which Vigny refuses. While the author of
Daphné shares Chateaubriand's thesis that Julian rejected Christianity
because of the heresies which divided the early Church and agrees with his
view of the importance of Julian's neoplatonism, he does not accept
Chateaubriand's protrayal of a Julian who is trying to believe in myths
which his reason rejects and who is attracted by the esthetic spectacle of
pagan ceremonial. Nor, clearly, does he share his attitude in *Les Martyrs*,
where Julian is accused of all sorts of crime and madness.

Vigny also gives the historical material relating to this moment in late
classical times a different interpretation from Gibbon and Voltaire. He
echoes Gibbon's thesis about the bad influence of Christianity on politics
and the arts, and especially the parallel Gibbon draws between the decline
of Rome and the modern age, but he does not repeat Gibbon's
condemnation of Libanius as a proud sophist, nor his attacks on Julian as
a superstitious dreamer. He shares Voltaire's enthusiasm for Julian, and
he even borrows several details of the story from him. But Voltaire denies
that Julian was ever a sincere Christian, and thus claims that he does not
deserve the title of Apostate. Voltaire also suggests that if Julian had lived
long enough, he could have won his victory over Christianity, which is
quite contrary to what Vigny says. [8]

If there is any precursor who shares Vigny's general attitude toward
Julian, it is surely the early 19th century writer, Pierre-Simon Ballanche,
who wrote in *La Vision d'Hébal* (1831): "Et Julien veut rétrograder, et il
entreprend un labeur au-dessus des forces humaines. Et un beau génie et
un grand caractère tombent dans l'opprobre et dans l'absurde."[9]
Ballanche and Vigny share an admiration for Julian, and a conviction that
he was the victim of historical necessity. If one excepts Ballanche, Vigny
differs from his predecessors in three important ways. No one, before,
presented Julian as a sincere Christian who had lost his faith. All previous
writers were concerned with a kind of historical truth which Vigny treats
with indifference. And, finally, no one had accused Julian of being a bad
judge of history for wishing to revive paganism.

If *Daphné* is to be understood, it must be placed less in the traditional
polemic about Julian and his apostasy than in certain intellectual currents
of the romantic period itself.[10] Gibbon is not the only one to have drawn a
parallel between Rome of the last emperors and modern Europe; the
parallel is so widespread that it is almost an "idée reçue." As is, of course,
the notion that there were close links between Christianity and platonism—justified either by a platonic interpretation of the Johanine logos, or
by the theories of "universal revelation." (In Vigny, as in others, this
notion was reinforced by a reading of Malebranche.) Finally, the
Romantic period is greatly concerned with the meaning of myth, and most
Romantics reject Euhemerist or naturalist theses in favor of a Stoic
definition of myth as a structure which simultaneously veils and preserves
profound truths. Such is Libanius's thesis in *Daphné*; but he, like Vigny,
shares Victor Cousin's notion that an elite may know the pure truth,
without the help of symbols. Thus, *Daphné* should be read as a commentary
on four central Romantic problems: the cyclical nature of history, religious

syncretism, the myth as vehicle for truth, and platonism or neoplatonism (with the various platonic theses about the nature of poetic inspiration).

But what attitude does Vigny take in *Daphné* on the above points? To answer this question, one must look at the form and style of the anecdote. For the Romantics' interest in religious syncretism, the respect for myth, the platonist revival, and the cyclical conception of history provoked an esthetic revolution as well as an intellectual one. One need only think of Victor Hugo and Gérard de Nerval...

The long conversation of the first letter imitates the platonic dialogue. But, as Citoleux has shown, if Vigny does keep the irony, the definition, the maieutic form and especially the silence which characterize the Socratic method, his imitation is nonetheless superficial. It is primarily a matter of local color, for Vigny rejects the central element of the method, the dialectic division of questions.[11] He resorts to the dialogue, not to profit from the dialectic mechanism, but in order to preserve ambiguity and contradiction. I have tried to show elsewhere how the ambiguous, subjective traits of Romantic thought led to a revival of the dialogue form, and such is the case here.[12] Vigny imitates the platonic banquet in order that both Libanius and Julian may be speakers of the truth.

In this respect, the form of the work is significant. The anecdote is an old manuscript, discovered by chance. However this manuscript is basically an epistolary novel, and the letters are written, not by important characters, but by an innocent, naive, and not too bright narrator—a kind of narrator Vigny had already used in *Servitude et grandeur militaires*. Joseph does not always understand what is going on, and he refuses to get involved in the questions being discussed. Thus for the overall story we have a dialogue between Stello and Dr. Noir, who read aloud a manuscript containing letters written by a naive, indifferent observer who recounts a dialogue. To borrow a metaphor from Georges Blin, this is a "reversed telescope" structure whose series of frames distance us from the subject and the action. Vigny multiplies those structures which separate the reader from the matter of the text. Such an esthetic distance can serve two ends; it may create a kind of indifference in the reader, or it may surround the work with an aura of mystery. Several stylistic traits of the anecdote demonstrate that Vigny is seeking the latter effect.

Take, for instance, the work's exoticism. Vigny evokes, not the familiar world of Rome or Athens, but the mysterious Near East of the late Hellenistic period. The pages are filled with proper nouns that are quite sonorous for the "good" people (Basile de Césarée, Paul de Larisse) and less beautiful for the "bad" ones (Aetius, Eunape). The geographical names are also rich and mysterious: la vallée de Bet-Rimon, les provinces de la Ceinture de la Reine, la Robe de la Reine, le Voile de la Reine. The exotic common names are equally striking and resonant, and Vigny often chooses oriental rather than classical words. However he makes no effort to explain the meaning of such terms (amra, madhavi, ingudi) or of local color expressions such as "il a humecté ses lèvres du vin noir de Pramnie mêlé d'eau de mer" (95). This exoticism differs from that of a Chateaubriand in that Vigny does not try to paint a picture, nor does he explain; rather, he simply underlines the strangeness. Moreover, *Daphné*'s style is not luxuriant; the exotic words come in rare groups, and serve primarily to emphasize that the world of the anecdote is not our world, but a distant one.

Vigny frequently evokes silence in order to create this same effect of distance and mystery. Thirty-six times in the anecdote he mentions the absence of noise, the moments of silence in the dialogue, the refusal to speak because someone is thinking, or dreaming, or does not want to say what he has to say. This is in part an imitation of the silence of the Socratic dialogue, but there is also an association between silence and the sacred. Antioch is characterized by tumultuous noise, whereas at Daphne "Tout était paisible dans ces silencieuses demeures... le silence était profond" (p. 73).

The novel also frequently evokes an unwillingness—or incapacity—to look or to understand, which somewhat blurs reality. This is not limited to Joseph; in the dialogue, the participants refuse to penetrate the mystery, and Vigny augments the reader's incomprehension by postponing explanations, as for instance in the case of the suppliants. "Les trompettes résonnaient dans l'éloignement" (57), and everything seems to take place at a distance. This technique becomes more evident when one notes the recurrent theme of veils and mantles. Sometimes, the theme is purely metaphoric: "La vérité se voile de plus en plus à ses yeux et aux miens" (141); elsewhere, the image possesses symbolic meaning. Pagan women are veiled, whereas the shameless Christian women unveil themselves, even in church. The mantle is the masculine equivalent of the veil. In the statue found by Dr. Noir, Julian is draped in an imperial mantle which leaves one breast bare. Joseph says Libanius does not consider him worthy to be covered with the flap of his mantle. Paul enters a Christian church, "le front enveloppé dans son manteau" (93)—in part to disguise himself, in part in contrast to the unveiled women. Julian and Paul arrive in "des manteaux longs, blancs" which cover their feet although Paul's, "entr'-ouvert," reveals the slave's sash (123). Several times, imitating Plato, Libanius "prenant un pan de son manteau, le jeta sur ses cheveux blancs et sur son crâne découvert, et se voila la tête et le visage entièrement" (126). Julian, wounded to death, "ramena son manteau sur lui de sorte que personne ne pût voir sa blessure" (172); the vanquished soldiers return to Antioch, "la tête enveloppée" in their mantles (165). Finally Paul, inviting death, twice opens "son manteau blanc pour découvrir sa poitrine au soleil" (179, 182). Clearly, for Vigny this is a symbolic detail. But before defining its meaning, we should note that at times it is bad to cover or veil. Characters cover their faces from shame or despair, and the destructive process of history is described as a flood which gradually covers bridges, statues, and roofs. On the other hand, the temple at Daphne is hidden by laurels. In short, veils themselves are ambiguous.

A total analysis of the thematic structures of *Daphné* is not possible here. For instance, the association perfume-mystery-the sacred is carefully developed. Religious inspiration is associated with images of whiteness, gold, fire, sun, stars. The temple is of white marble, and is first seen as "les rayons rouges du soleil se plongeaient dans l'ombre comme des épées de feu" (68). During the dialogue, "les étoiles éclairaient le ciel par de si larges feux qu'il nous semblait que nous étions placés au milieu d'eux" (122) and Julian contemplates these "constellations brillantes" before explaining his cultus of the Sun-God. Julian is identified at his first appearance as the son of the Sun: "ses yeux bleus touchés par un rayon échappé des voûtes du temple... son teint blanc, animé, enflammé... ses dents blanches éclairées par un rayon, ses blonds cheveux" (96-99). His eyes are blue, burning, bold, whereas those of Libanius are heavy, dark, reddened; the eyes of the Christian mob, at the end of the anecdote, are "à demi fermés, et comme endormis et alourdis" (179).

To sum it up, *Daphné* is bathed in an exotic atmosphere of distance, veils and mystery, ordinarily associated with the sacred but which may also evoke shame and destruction, or simply stupid incomprehension. On the other hand, images of light, sun and stars are associated with religious inspiration.

The "lesson" of *Daphné*, whose style is generally sparse but in which metaphoric language plays an important role, is presented in three central images, and our thematic analysis clarifies the meaning of these images. The most beautiful pages of the book are surely those in which Julian describes the flight of the soul towards celestial Beauty; he offers a complete cosmogony for inspiration with the Sun-King, the solar angels, the nocturnal visions. These pages are of course an adaptation of the historical Julian's *Hymn to the Sun-King*, and Vigny does in fact shorten this neoplatonic work. But he keeps its essentials in order to create, in the middle of *Daphné*, a passage whose tonality makes us think of Nerval; the passage is in any case carefully prepared by the themes of light as inspiration, of perfume and ecstasy, of sacred mystery.

Libanius answers Julian with the image of the mummy, embalmed with the treasures of moral philosophy in its head and in its breast, covered with a thick but transparent crystal which gleams from the light of the torches and the stars. The sense of this image is clear; the crystal of religious beliefs must veil the truths of moral philosophy. But the paradox is that the crystal must both veil and remain transparent, must change with time and yet receive its light from the skies, that it must, despite its transitory nature, be of divine inspiration.

The third image is offered by the narrator Joseph, and comes at the end of the anecdote when he buries under ground the statue of Venus-Urania. (The theme of the cultus of Venus returns several times in the work.) Joseph, who is thoroughly materialistic, is incapable of comprehending the religious significance of the statue; he buries it twenty feet under the earth in order to sell it at some future date. Here again religion is being veiled, but the veils are opaque; they prevent vision and resemble the frightening barbarian flood which is covering the earth.

There are two other points that critics of *Daphné* have perhaps not emphasized enough. The anecdote attacks Christianity much less than it attacks Arianism. If Christianity can become platonist, it will offer a new crystal for revealing essential truths; this will be the task of SS. John

Chrysostom and Basil of Caesarea, whom Libanius orders to become Christians. And Libanius reproaches Julian not for his neoplatonism, or his cult of the Sun-King and the pagan deities, but for his rejection of poetry, that faculty which always demands divine inspiration and which creates those veils of crystal that essential truth needs.

In short, the anecdote contains no criticism of platonism, nor indeed of neoplatonism. Vigny sees in Christianity nothing more than a fairly adequate and surely transitory way of preserving and yet rendering transparent the truths of the ancient gods. If Christianity becomes sufficiently platonist, the elite can become committed to it. If truth is light and inspiration, truth also needs veils; it requires a crystalline poetic form and that mysterious distance which Vigny manages to create in his anecdote. But there is always the danger that veils may be too opaque or too material and thus conceal the truth and beauty which man needs.

The historical significance of *Daphné* then becomes clear. Written around 1835, the book is part of a lengthy polemic begun a decade before by the publication of Saint-Simon's *Nouveau christianisme* and by Théodore Jouffroy's articles in the *Globe* on "Comment les dogmes finissent," and rendered all the more pertinent by Lamennais' evolution, by the publication of *Les Paroles d'un croyant* in 1833, of Lerminier's "Débats sur le christianisme" in the *Revue des deux mondes* in July, 1835. As paganism had died and given way to Christianity, so Christianity was dying and a new religion had to be invented. The efforts to do so were many: Châtel, Gleizes, Fabre-Palaprat, and above all the cultisation of the Saint-Simonian movement evoked in the frame of Daphné. Just as Julian came to recognize, according to Vigny, that paganism was no longer a viable religious form, so the modern Julian, Lamennais, had come to abandon the Church. *Daphné* is Vigny's statement that a new religious form is needed, and his contribution to a definition of the requirements of that form.

This analysis of *Daphné* also coincides with what Pierre Moreau and others have said about the nature of poetic inspiration in Vigny, with what François Germain has noted in his brilliant thesis on Vigny's imagination.[13] It is clear that—like almost all the Romantic writers—Vigny was fascinated by antiquity, but his particular intellectual and aesthetic needs caused him to be drawn to the rather special times of Julian the Apostate. In conclusion, one might cite the work of another 19th century author which expresses comparable interests and a similar concern with mystery:

> La connais-tu, Dafné, cette ancienne romance,
> Cette chanson d'amour qui toujours recommence?
> Reconnais-tu le Temple au péristyle immense?
> Ils reviendront, ces Dieux que tu pleures toujours!
> Le temps va ramener l'ordre des anciens jours;
> La terre a tressailli d'un souffle prophétique...
> Cependant la sibylle au visage latin
> Est endormie encor sous l'arc de Constantin.

Although Vigny's vision of antiquity is closer in color and spirit to Nerval than to Renan, his *Daphné* remains a fine example of the extent to which (as Citoleux put it) "son œuvre entière, en prose et en vers, par le fond et par la forme, éveille la comparaison des chefs-d'œuvre de l'Hellénisme" (p. 546).

University of Pennsylvania

Notes

[1] *Daphné, Deuxième consultation du Docteur-Noir*, Paris, 1913. Page references in the text are to this edition.

[2] René Canat, *L'Hellénisme des Romantiques*, Paris, 1951, sq, II, 241, 358-360.

[3] Marc Citoleux, *Alfred de Vigny, Persistances classiques et affinités étrangères*, Paris, 1924, pp. 232, 250.

[4] Georges Bonnefoy, *La Pensée religieuse et morale d'Alfred de Vigny*, Paris, 1946, pp. 124, 173, 218 sq. V. idem Maxime Chastaing, "L'Atticisme d'Alfred de Vigny" in *Revue philosophique de la France et de l'étranger*, CXXXIX (1949), 333-347, a quite perceptive study and Paul Arnold, "Vigny et la tradition socratique," *Cahiers Hermès*, I (1947), 128-143, an important article which grasps the significance of Romantic neoplatonism from Vigny. On the other hand, Maurice Lebel, "Alfred de Vigny et l'antiquité grecque," *Revue de l'Université Laval*, XI (1956), 132-143 is of no help. One is astonished to read that "on a relativement peu étudié jusqu'ici l'aspect de l'antiquité grecque dans son œuvre," especially in an article which plagiarizes every valid point it makes from Citoleux.

[5] Vigny, *Stello*, ed. F. Baldensperger, Paris (Conard, 1925), p. 429.

[6] *Idem*, p. 452.

[7] *Ibid.*

[8] Chateaubriand, *Etudes historiques*, in *Œuvres complètes*, Paris (Garnier), s.d., IX, 207-267; Voltaire, art. "Apostat" in *Dictionnaire philosophique*. v. also C. H. Gillies, "Julian the Apostate in Montaigne and Vigny" in *MLR*, LV (1960), 578-579 but Montaigne is hardly an important source.

[9] Ballanche, *La Vision d'Hebal*, Paris, 1969, p. 208.

[10] Though a history of Julian through the ages, going down to Ibsen and Gore Vidal, would be of considerable interest.

[11] Citoleux, *op. cit.*, pp. 508-516.

[12] "Notes towards the definition of the Romantic theater" in *L'Esprit créateur*, V (1965), 121-130.

[13] Pierre Moreau, ed., *Les Destinées d'Alfred de Vigny*, Paris, 1936; François Germain, *L'Imagination d'Alfred de Vigny*, Paris, 1962. On distance, see the astute study of G. Clancier, "Vigny ou la distance" in *Mercure de France*, CCCXLV (1962), 613-616.

As Professor Peyre points out, the middle period of the 19th century—
the years following the high point of Romanticism——is one of the most
studied epochs of French literary history, and there are numerous books
which examine the importance that the classical world had for authors like
Baudelaire, the Parnassians, Flaubert, the Hugo of the years of exile and
after, Taine, and Renan.[1] However these are all writers for whom such
evidence is most patently obvious. To shed new light on the role antiquity
played among the post-Romantics, Philip Walker has chosen to center his
attention on Emile Zola. Zola is not at all known as a Hellenist, and
indeed at first glance his spirit may appear to be fundamentally opposed to
any veneration of the classical past. However, Professor Walker's essay—
based on a huge number of source materials and on a painstaking
inquiry—reveals the extent to which even a very "realistic" novelist like
Zola was an integral part of the broad Hellenist tradition that has
characterized so many periods of French literary history.

Notes

[1] Henri M. Peyre discusses the most important of these studies in his *L'Influence des littératures antiques sur la littérature française moderne* (New Haven-Oxford, 1941), pp. 62-73, but he surveys the subject in depth in his *Bibliographie critique de l'hellénisme en France de 1843 à 1870* (New Haven, 1932). This is the sixth volume in the Yale Romanic Studies.

ZOLA'S HELLENISM

By Philip Walker

Zola's place in the history of modern European Hellenism has generally been considered a very minor one at best. However, to my knowledge the question has never received the close attention it deserves, and careful examination may prove that here, too, our inherited assumptions about Zola will have to be revised. After all, he grew up in a period marked by an extraordinary revival of interest in Greece, and he received a largely classical education, including two years of Greek. He tells us he quickly lost whatever proficiency he had acquired in this language, and so—unlike Flaubert, for example—he doubtless had little direct acquaintance with the Greek classics. But even if Zola had never opened Burnouf's grammar or read a single verse of Homer in the original, over the years he would probably have come to absorb much more about the culture of ancient Greece than most of our leading novelists do today.

Professor Peyre has noted that during the middle years of the 19th century the influence of Greece was reflected everywhere in the French intellectual environment. It reached Zola through his physical sur-roundings, his friendships and acquaintances, the conversations that he overheard along the boulevards, the plays he went to, the fashionable journalists that he read, and the works of the great French authors he admired. It is significant, for example, that one of the most vivid memories of his youth in Aix was of religious processions passing between houses hung with tapestries "à grands personnages mythologiques, tout l'Olympe païen, nu et blafard, venant regarder passer l'Olympe catholique."[1] While still in his late adolescence, in Paris, he wrote Cezanne that he had fallen in love with the naiads adorning a fountain by Jean Goujon (*Cor.*, I, 51). Later on that same year, 1860, his artist friend Chaillan was painting his portrait, as he wrote Baille, "nu, quelque peu drapé, tenant une lyre antique et les yeux au ciel" (*Cor.*, I, 88). Cézanne and Baille, his two closest confidants, were both profoundly molded by classical culture, and Cézanne's letters to Zola are full of Latin quotations, Latin verses of his own making, and poems in French composed on mythological themes.[2] Baille—who could find no more eloquent way to express a disappointment in love than to write Zola, "J'ai perdu mon Euridice, j'ai perdu mon idéal"

(*Cor.*, I, 36)—in his youth wanted to become another Homer. Flaubert was particularly preoccupied with Greece at the time Zola knew him, and more than one of their most animated conversations must have been on that subject.[3] (Zola does not tell us whether or not they ever talked about the passages inspired by Greece in *La Tentation de saint Antoine*, which Flaubert had taken up again the year they met. But we do know that they argued about the question of Homer's modernity and that Flaubert confided to him at some length his plans for a *nouvelle* about Leonidas at Thermopylae.) Among Zola's wider circle of acquaintances were several other men who had played leading roles in reinstituting the cult of Greece in nineteenth-century France, including both Henri and Arsène Houssaye and Théodore de Banville.

Among other indirect sources of Zola's Hellenism, one would certainly have to include such writers as Ronsard, Montaigne, and the great French classical dramatists, especially Racine. He knew and loved the poetry of Chénier, and of several other Romantic authors whose verses were filled with the spirit and culture of Greece—above all Hugo. Zola read a large proportion of everything Hugo wrote and he analyzed many of Hugo's works in detail, including *Les Chansons des rues et des bois*, with its strongly bucolic qualities, *La Légende des siècles*, with its powerful evocations of the Creation, War of the Titans, and other classical myths, and that curious novel, *L'Homme qui rit*, with its parallels—as Hugo points out and Zola was quick to note (*Le Gaulois*, April 29, May 4, 1869)—with the idyl of Daphnis and Chloe. Zola was also almost certainly acquainted with Hugo's *William Shakespeare* (1864), which contains celebrated pages on Homer and Aeschylus, and he very probably read with some care Michelet's *La Bible de l'humanité* and some of the essays on Greek subjects scattered throughout the works of Taine, Renan, and Sainte-Beuve (notably Taine's "Jeunes gens de Platon" and Sainte-Beuve's "Essai sur le roman dans l'antiquité").

Given Zola's passion for the theatre, it is unlikely that he was entirely indifferent to the attempts made by his contemporaries to revive the Greek dramatists in translation or to present plays inspired by Greek mythology. During 1859 (the year after he moved from Aix to Paris), there were at least two such productions—Jules Lacroix's *Oedipe Roi* and Louis Ratisbonne's *Héro et Léandre*, not to mention Crémieux and Offenbach's light opera, *Orphée aux enfers*. In 1864 Zola reviewed for the provincial press a lecture given under the auspices of the Emperor at the rue de la Paix on "Le Peuple dans Shakespeare et dans Aristophane" (*Cor.*, I, 240). During his years of employment as chief of publicity at Hachette, the firm published a significant number of Greek translations, including P. Mesnard's *Orestie* (1863), Auguste Salmon's *Les Travaux et les Jours* (1863), Giguet's *Homer* (1863), F. Jacobs' *Anthologie grecque* (1863), Bouillet's translation of Aeschylus (1865), and Talbot's Plutarch (1865). During the same period, Hachette also issued a number of books about Greece or inspired by Greece, notably Louise Ackermann's *Contes et Poésies*, which contained five poems on classical themes. All of these works undoubtedly passed through Zola's hands. However, his correspondence indicates positively that he read Laprade's *Psyché* (*Cor.*, I, 192), Henri Houssaye's *L'Armée dans la Grèce antique* (*Cor.*, I, 301), Anatole France's *Les Noces Corinthiennes* (*DL*, 140). There are also some books by relatively obscure authors dealing in whole or in part with Greek subjects with which Zola was familiar; e.g., Eugène Pelletan's *La Mère* (*MH*, 89), Eugène Paz's *La Santé de l'esprit et du corps par la gymnastique* (*MH*, 49), and, above all, Victor Chauvin's *Les Romanciers grecs et latins* (1862), which he studied in detail.[4]

Zola's own writings contain many passages touching either on the classical world or on French Hellenism. Taken altogether they shed a remarkable amount of light on his knowledge of the Greeks, his conception of his own relation to them, and his attitudes with respect to the cult of Greece in the art and literature of his day. In my opinion, the most important of these texts are the following: his letters to Baille of June 15, 1860 (*Cor.*, I, 94-99, meditations on Chénier and the imitation of the ancients, reactions to Hugo's *La Légende des siècles*) and early September, 1860 (*Cor.*, I,133-139, in which he expresses his ambition to create a new epic); *Du Progrès dans les sciences et dans la poésie* (1861?—a crucially important early essay, republished twice in revised form, providing numerous insights into Zola's concept of poetry, aesthetic relativism, ideas on how poetry could be rejuvenated, reflections on the classical genres and the use of classical mythology[5]); "La Littérature et la gymnastique" (1865, *MH*, 47-53, revised, 1872, *M*, 119-122, reflections on Eugène Paz, descriptions of ancient Athens, contrasts between Greek and modern civilization); *Salons* (ed. Hemmings and Niess, Droz, 1959, *passim*, especially "La Sculpture," June 17, 1868); "Causerie" of June 28, 1868 (*Atelier*[6], 154-159, meditations inspired by Michelet's *L'Oiseau, L'Insecte,* and *La Montagne,* on the epic of the future and the comparative poetic value of science and mythology); "Chronique" of July 15, 1868 (*Atelier*, 90-92, a vigorous defense of the attempt by Victor Duruy, Ministre de l'Instruction Publique, to make Greek an elective subject); "Causeries" of September 19, 1869 (*Atelier*, 199-202, on the Parnassians); "A M. Armand Silvestre" (1878, *RE*, 240-245, a polemical article including reflections on the nature of immortality in literature—whether poets have a greater chance to achieve enduring fame than novelists); "Les Poètes contemporains" (1878, 1879, *DL*, 129-152, comments on Hugo, Auguste Barbier, Gautier, Baudelaire, Banville, Leconte de Lisle, Mendès, Anatole France, Dierx, Armand Silvestre, and others); "Théophile Gautier," Part I (1879, *DL*, 107-115, containing an interesting passage on the Hellenism of Gautier and his disciples); "Sainte-Beuve" (1879, 1880, *DL*, 209-254, including reflections on Sainte-Beuve's Hellenism and on the "querelle des anciens et des modernes"); "Adieux" (1881, *UC*, 319-327, with a definition of what constitutes progress in poetry); and *Mes Voyages*, Part II, *Rome* (1894, ed. René Ternois, Fasquelle, 1958, containing several references to Greece and the author's reactions to the Greek sculpture in the Vatican).

Finally, in this connection one must not fail to mention the long paper entitled *Deux Définitions du roman*, which Zola submitted in 1866 to the Congrès Scientifique de France.[7] Part I, "Le Roman dans l'antiquité et dans les premiers temps du christianisme," begins with a description of ancient Athens inspired chiefly, I suspect, by Chauvin's *Romanciers grecs et latins*[8] and by a passage in Taine's introduction to his *Histoire de la littérature anglaise*. Then, borrowing heavily from Chauvin (who, in turn, had plagiarized Villemain[9]) Zola traces the early history of novels, summarizing in some detail the plots of two classical works, Heliodorus' *Theagenes and Charicleia* and Longus's *Daphnis and Chloe*. Part II of the essay deals with "Le Roman au XIXe siècle." Likewise paraphrasing Chauvin as well as Taine and Sainte-Beuve, it begins by contrasting Paris and Athens, and then proceeds to define the modern realistic novel, suggesting how it differs from the Greek epic and the Greek romance.

Much in these and other writings by Zola would seem to support the conventional view of him as an aggressively modern author who turned his back on the past and encouraged others to do likewise. But it should be noted at the outset that the principal object of his criticism is not the Greeks themselves, but certain forms taken by modern Hellenism. When, for example, he says of Balzac's characters: "Auprès de ces créations géantes et vraies, les héros grecs ou romains grelottent, les héros du moyen âge tombent sur le nez comme des soldats de plomb" (*NAT*, 24), he is comparing them with personages in classical French tragedies and in Romantic drama on medieval themes, not with the heros of the *Iliad* or the *Song of Roland*. His unfavorable judgments on Greek art itself—and they are rare—occur in newspaper articles composed in the heat of battle during his campaigns in support of Impressionism or Naturalism. In one such instance, he refers to "l'art grec, cette idéalisation de la forme, ce cliché pur et correct, cette beauté divine et impersonnelle"—adding, "Je n'aime ni les Egyptiens, ni les Grecs, ni les artistes ascétiques, moi qui n'admets dans l'art que la vie et la personnalité" (*MH*, 26). But this passage is part of a violent attack on Proudhon in which he is really rejecting Proudhon's conception of Greek art, and not Greek art itself (of which he knows little at the time). The same holds true for the similar remarks made by him in "La Sculpture"; like any good iconoclast, he tries to weaken his enemies by smashing their idols.

But if Zola is repelled by the Greece of Proudhon, Gérome, or Offenbach he is attracted by the Greece of Taine. In an article in praise of one of the latter's books, he writes, "Le professeur triomphe lorsqu'il examine les grandes époques et les indique à larges traits: la Grèce divinisant la chair, avec ses villes nues au soleil et ses nations fortes et souples, revit tout entière dans le peuple de ses statues" (*MH*, 171). Interestingly, it is in this same essay that he makes a heroic attempt to reconcile his definition of art as nature seen through a temperament and his concept (which he got from Proudhon) of Greek art as a collective creation: "Car j'accorde que souvent l'artiste est fait de tous les cœurs d'une époque; cet artiste collectif, qui a des millions de têtes et une seule âme, crée alors... l'art grec ou l'art gothique; et... les belles chairs pures et puissantes, les saints blêmes et maigres sont la manifestation des souffrances et des joies de l'individu social" (*MH*, 173-174). These remarks are, needless to say, highly theoretical.

As a result of his readings, Zola develops a few fixed general ideas about Greek art which he repeats with minor variations on every appropriate occasion. Here, too, as in so many other areas of his thought, we find tension, contradiction, ambivalence. But it is interesting to note that when he is actually confronted by classical sculpture, he is filled with admiration. When he visits the Capitoline Museum in Rome in 1894, for instance, the Dying Gaul and some black marble centaurs strike him as "pièces hors ligne." He is most impressed, it is true, by the realistic Roman portrait busts: "Ce sont les hommes du temps qui ressuscitent. Comme ceci vous prend autrement que l'histoire classique qui vous fait exécrer l'antiquité, et comme on comprend, comme on sympathise!" (*Mes Voyages*, 161). Yet this does not keep him from noting that the best Roman sculptures are copies from the Greek (*M*, 156). During his visit to the Vatican, he writes in his notebook:

Ce qui me frappe, c'est toute cette antiquité retrouvée à la Renaissance, admirée, déifiée par l'art, entourant la papauté. Elle y baigne. Ils ont eu beau mettre des feuilles de vigne aux statues, c'est le triomphe splendide de la chair, l'épanouissement magnifique de la vie, c'est Vénus tout entière, et c'est Pan, et c'est Jupiter tout-puissant. La nudité y clame la toute-puissance de la nature, l'éternelle matière. Et ce pape qui passe tous les deux jours au milieu de ces Vénus, de ces Apollons qui le regardent, de toute cette chair nue.

He concludes with words that might have been spoken by a Louis Ménard or a Leconte de Lisle: "Comme nous sommes loin du christianisme pauvre, ignorant, tout âme, méprisant la chair, maudissant la nature complice de l'amour et de la joie. Comme la vie frissonne et s'étale là. Comme il y ferait bon de vivre et d'aimer, sous la caresse du beau ciel" (*Mes Voyages*, 229-230). In the final analysis, for Zola it is of course Taine's vision of Greece which wins out, and not Proudhon's.[10]

As for Greek literature, here also Zola has very few adverse criticisms, and most of these relate to the Greek romance. In *Deux Définitions du roman*, he repeats the negative conclusions of Chauvin almost verbatim, but like Chauvin and Villemain before him he makes an exception of Daphnis and Chloe. His other unfavorable observations reflect his positivism and have to do chiefly with the inferiority of mythology to science. Otherwise, he shares the admiration of his contemporaries for the Greek classics. Not long after reading Montaigne, he expresses respect for the wisdom of Epicurus (*Cor.*, I, 92). He regards Aristotle as a forerunner of modern times (*RE*, 91), places Aeschylus on the same plane as Shakespeare and Corneille (*Atelier*, 136), and lauds Aristophanes as one of the "grands farceurs" of literary history, worthy of comparison with Shakespeare, Rabelais, and Molière (*T*, I, Preface, *Les Héritiers Rabourdin*, p. IV). Above all, Zola shares in the vast cult of admiration for Homer, to whom he refers again and again—often as a symbol of Greek literature in general. In one of the most extreme of all his naturalist articles he concedes that "la colère d'Achille, l'amour de Didon, resteront des peintures éternellement belles" (*RE*, 50). But what he admires above all in Homer and Virgil is not so much their style as their creative genius, the humanity and life that he finds in their verses: "Nous ne sentons plus la perfection technique d'Homère et de Virgile; ce qui les fait vivre dans les âges, c'est le souffle vivant dont ils se sont animés, c'est l'humanité qu'ils ont mise en eux. Avant l'arrangeur de mots il y a le créateur" (*DL*, 77). Unlike some other students of Zola, I do not think that we can dismiss these comments—and the others he makes on these great authors—as purely conventional. Indeed, they are the very highest praise that he can bestow on any writer, and whether they imply an original or profound knowledge of Greek literature or not, they cannot be passed over lightly. After all, an artist may be as profoundly influenced by the *image* he has of another great artist as by the actual reality of that artist.

As has been suggested above, Zola's animosity was reserved not for the masters of antiquity, but for certain aspects of modern Hellenism. He never lost a schoolboy's distaste for the classical disciplines *qua* disciplines. We may see this in the ironic article he wrote for *L'Evénement illustré* of May 30, 1868, commenting on the "generosity" of the English, who, after driving the Emperor of Ethiopia, Theodorus III, to suicide, planned to make their victory complete by sending his young son to a British boarding school in Bombay to study Greek and Latin: "On a bâillonné le lionceau avec un exemplaire du *De Viris*, on l'a enfermé dans l'étroite et dure prison des études classiques. C'est généreux et c'est habile" (*Atelier*, 76). But his most violent attack on the teaching of Latin and Greek is in the article that he wrote that year in defense of Victor Duruy. In it he says, among other things:

> J'ai contre le grec une haine toute personnelle. Je l'accuse d'une infinité de crimes. Je le rends d'abord responsable de notre manque complet d'originalité. C'est lui qui coule tous les esprits dans le même moule, c'est lui qui nous enferme étroitement dans une antiquité où nos arts étouffent. Nous sommes fils des temps modernes, nous devons vivre dans un âge savant et positif, et nous recevons une éducation de lettrés, mettant leur joie à discuter un accent doux ou rude" (*Atelier*, 91).

Elsewhere, he objects to the pedantry, affectedness, snobbishness, and bookishness of many Hellenizing poets; e.g., Autran (*Atelier*, 74). He evokes the Academy of the *ancien régime*, where they loved "ces parlottes où l'on se chamaillait au nom des oracles de l'antiquité. On se jetait alors son grec et son latin à la tête... Pendant deux siècles, des hommes d'Etat tombés du pouvoir, des poètes bilieux, enragés de vanité, des hommes de bibliothèque, la tête farcie de bouquins, sont venus là se soulager" (*RE*, 133). He pours even greater scorn on certain classicizing Second-Empire salons: "On y lit de petits vers, on s'y pâme aux noms de Rome et d'Athènes, on y affecte une nostalgie de l'antiquité, on s'y attarde dans toutes sortes d'admirations de sous-maîtresse qui a lu ses classiques, comme d'autres ont appris le piano; et, naturellement, on nie la littérature vivante de l'heure actuelle" (*RE*, 150).

Furthermore, there are several reasons that convince Zola of the impossibility of continuing to use the classical genres. In the first place, the great Romantics have exhausted all their possibilities: "Oui, la poésie est morte, en ce sens qu'il vient une heure où une forme s'épuise, où un mode d'être poète s'use et ne peut plus servir. Qui osera, de nos jours, faire des

odes après Hugo et Lamartine, qui touchera à l'élégie après Musset"
(*Atelier*, 179). Another reason is that modern times are basically different
from the past and, like Baudelaire, he prefers to speak with a
contemporary voice: "Pour mon compte, si j'étais poète, voici ce que je
ferais. Je dirais adieu aux beaux mensonges des mythologies; j'enterrerais
la dernière naïade et la dernière sylphide avec le respect dû à leur grand
âge; je dédaignerais les mythes et n'aurais plus d'amour que pour les
vérités" (*Atelier*, 180). He feels that imitations of the past often are
incongruous, even ridiculous in a modern setting:

> Regardez dans nos jardins publics l'étrange effet que font les marbres antiques sous un ciel
> étranger, au milieu d'une civilisation pour laquelle ils ne sont pas nés. Rien n'est ridicule,
> selon moi, comme des habits noirs entourant le *Discobole* ou la *Diane à la Biche*. Et encore
> ici l'œuvre à sa grandeur particulière. Mais si vous groupez des bourgeois modernes
> autour de la statue maigre d'un de nos artistes, imitation plate et prétentieuse de quelque
> idole grecque, le spectacle devient navrant: cette idéalisation bête de la nature en face des
> vérités contemporaines paraît un enfantillage, un entêtement grotesque et mesquin"
> (*Salons*, 142).

Moreover, much classical subject-matter strikes him as basically uninter-
esting:

> Eh! bon Dieu! quel intérêt veulent-ils que nous prenions à Jupiter ou à Brahma... S'ils
> désirent nous intéresser, nous tirer des larmes et des rires, qu'ils nous parlent de nous, de
> nos passions, de nos mœurs, qu'ils écrivent les poèmes de la génération présente. En art,
> tout ce qui n'est pas vivant est mauvais. La vie seule féconde une œuvre, la rend éternelle
> de vie et d'intérêt. Les poésies du cénacle contemporain sont mortes; elles exhalent des
> senteurs de momie, elles ont des rigidités de statue" (*Atelier*, 200).

Zola also believes that an excessive concern with the past will distract
the poet from his true mission, which has to do with the present and
future. "Un peuple viril," he says on the final page of his notes on his trip
to Rome, "doit revivre dans son temps et pour son temps" (*Mes Voyages*,
292), and he often associates the enthusiasm for Greece of many of his
contemporaries with a cult of form, chill perfectionism, aesthetic
absolutism, escapism, and hatred of the modern age. But, above all, he is
opposed to the imitation of the Greeks because he is opposed to imitation
per se. Few men have given more thought to the problem of originality in
art or prize it more highly. His ideal artist is the creative giant who resumes
an entire epoch while molding it in his own image, dominating all his
rivals. The major sources of originality are, in his opinion, a unique
temperament and the fresh, distinctive forms which the eternal themes and
truths of art assume at any particular historical moment. It is significant
that when he goes to Rome he is overwhelmed by Michelangelo. For Zola,
imitation is the hallmark of the second-rate artist—an "Autran, élève de
Virgile qui n'aurait jamais vu une vague ni une motte de terre" (*Atelier*,
74). As he puts it in the preface to *Mes Haines*:

> Les sots qui n'osent regarder en avant regardent en arrière. Ils font le présent des règles du
> passé, et ils veulent que l'avenir, les œuvres et les hommes, prennent modèle sur les temps
> écoulés... Autant de sociétés, autant d'œuvres diverses, et les sociétés se transformeront

éternellement. Mais les impuissants ne veulent pas agrandir le cadre; ils ont dressé la liste
des œuvres déjà produites, et ont ainsi obtenu une vérité relative dont ils font une vérité
absolue. Ne créez pas, imitez.

Zola accuses the Parnassians of just this kind of weakness:

> La large expansion de la science, le souffle d'analyse exacte qui a fécondé la littérature,
> passe sur leurs têtes avec des bruits d'ouragan. Et ils se coulent, pris de terreur, se disant
> que cette tempête doit briser les anciennes idoles et que le grand Pan va mourir... Ah! s'il
> y avait, parmi ces messieurs, un homme intelligent et fort, nous entendrions vite d'autres
> accents... Cet homme jetterait au feu toute la défroque grecque et barbare (*Atelier*, 200-
> 201).

He formulates similar criticisms in a number of his comments about
contemporary neo-classic painters and sculptors, and it is hardly surprising
that in an 1880 article on Sainte-Beuve he vigorously identifies himself with
the Moderns in the famous Quarrel, which he does his best to revive—
"cette querelle, que le romantisme a soulevée de nouveau en 1830, et que
nous soulevons, nous aussi, avec le naturalisme" (*DL*, 238).

Nevertheless, we would be gravely mistaken if we were to infer from
this that Zola ever seriously contemplated making a complete break with
the Greek tradition. Although, as we have just seen, he had nothing but
contempt for the pedantry, servile imitation, and flight from the present
which was too often associated with the cult of Greece, he was by no
means impervious to the charms of certain kinds of modern Hellenism.
This was particularly true when he was confronted by some artist of
genius. We may, if we wish, explain away his approval of Cézanne's boyish
poem on Hercules (*Cor.*, I, 147) as a concession to friendship. His
admiration for the Hellenism of Chénier was more serious and dated back
to 1860. "Son vers est si gracieux," he writes Baille, "que je lui passe
toutes les allusions possibles, même celles que je ne comprends pas, moi
l'ignorant, moi qui n'ai entendu parler de Virgile que par ouï-dire." And
he adds, "Chénier est le dernier homme de talent qui ait parlé sur ce ton, et
encore, si je puis m'exprimer ainsi, ce n'est pas l'antiquité qui l'a servi, c'est
lui qui a servi l'antiquité" (*Cor.*, I, 95). In 1865, reviewing Hugo's *Les
Chansons des rues et des bois*, he comments, "Je suis heureux que Victor
Hugo se soit décidé à se faire berger, et pour rien au monde je ne voudrais
que le livre fût autre" (*MH*, 85).

Later on in his life, after his philosophy of art has matured and taken
more definite shape, he is still capable of such reactions. At a performance
of Banville's *Deidamia* in November, 1876, the year he finished *L'Assommoir*, he does his best to object to the unrealistic setting in the name of
naturalism, but he is utterly delighted by the poet's fantasy:

> Il est si haut dans son ciel bleu, dans sa sérénité d'Olympien, que je me ferais un crime de
> vouloir le ramener à la prose. Non! lorsqu'un écrivain vit les yeux sur les étoiles, en pleine
> extase du rêve, il ne faut point l'éveiller, il devient sacré, même pour les révolutionnaires
> qui cassent à coups de marteau les vieilles idoles... Je pouvais croire que j'étais endormi,
> que ma fantaisie elle-même vagabondait dans mes souvenirs classiques... Oui, vraiment,
> c'était l'Olympe qui ressuscitait, non pas l'Olympe dont on grelotte au collège, mais un

Olympe tout ensoleillé, doré d'un reflet romantique, amusant comme une montagne
ciselée par un orfèvre moderne. Il faut entendre la danse ivre des hémistiches, les césures
imprévues faisant sauter les vers comme des chèvres au flanc d'un coteau grec (*NAD*, 298).

At the Exposition Universelle of 1878 he is troubled, irritated, almost
seduced by Gustave Moreau's *Le Sphinx deviné*. He returns to it despite
himself, and finally concludes: "Voici mon pronostic. Il servira à l'honneur
de Gustave Moreau" (*Salons*, 219).

It should also be pointed out that Zola's own philosophy of literary art
grows to a considerable extent out of his meditations on Greek literature
or on the poets, dramatists, and novelists who had been influenced by
Greece. He even goes so far as to habitually define the modern realistic
novel by contrasting it with the Greek epic or the Greek romance. His two
important early essays, *Du Progrès dans les sciences et dans la poésie* and
Deux Définitions du roman are obvious examples of the spirit of these
meditations. But the same tendency may be observed in many other places
in his writings, including «Le Roman expérimental» itself, which ends with
a paragraph contrasting the methods of the experimental novelist with
those of Virgil and Homer. Over and over again Zola links the ancients
and the moderns together by contrast and analogy. In making such
distinctions, he equates contemporary artists, novelists, statesmen, and
institutions with their Greek or Roman counterparts. For example, in a
major article on Balzac written in July, 1877, he refers to "César Birotteau,
qui est aussi grand dans sa boutique de parfumeur que les héros d'Homère
devant Troie" (*RN*, 52). And he says with respect to Flaubert: "C'est un
Titan, plein d'haleines énormes, qui raconte les mœurs d'une fourmilière,
en faisant des efforts pour ne pas céder à l'envie de souffler des chants
héroïques dans sa grande trompette de bronze. Un poète changé en
naturaliste, Homère devenu Cuvier" (*Atelier*, 206-207). There is much
more here, we may be sure, than a simple comparison; it is the recognition
of a definite evolution leading from the Greek epic via the Greek and
Roman romance to the modern novel. One genre does not replace the
other. It *is* the other in a new form. Or, as Zola says in *Deux Définitions du
roman*, "L'épopée, lorsque le génie de la Grèce a décliné, est devenue le
conte; le conte, sous les tendances scientifiques des temps modernes, s'est
transformé de nouveau et s'est changé en roman d'observation et
d'analyse. La filiation est évidente."[11]

Despite the enormous emphasis Zola places on originality, he never
forgets that he is working within an ancient tradition deeply rooted in the
classical imagination. "On parle d'Alexandre, de César," he says in an
essay on war written in 1899, "mais tout ce qu'ils avaient créé, tout leur
empire, tout cela a été emporté, ce ne sont plus que des ruines, que des
sables que le vent soulève et emporte, tandis que les œuvres d'Homère, les
œuvres de Virgile, tous les monuments de la civilisation demeurent et sont
encore nos richesses. Nous en sommes les enfants, nous ne vivons que sur
ce passé, que sur ces ancêtres de la pensée humaine" (*M*, 178). This helps
to explain still another tendency in Zola's thought which would seem to
run counter to some of his most publicized theories but which is not really

as contradictory as it might at first appear if a distinction is made between *imitation* and *emulation*, and between *servile* imitation and *inspired* imitation. For the better we know him, the more apparent it becomes that Zola is intrigued all his life by the idea of equalling or surpassing the great masters of antiquity. And if, in order to do so, it is necessary to borrow from the same fund of ideas, themes, images, and plots from which they borrowed—or model himself on their works—he is, whatever he may tell the public, quite as willing to do so as any other great European writer before him.

This is already apparent in his early correspondence, as for example in the letter to Baille dated July 18, 1861, in which he says, "Je veux dérober aux grands poètes, les raisons de leur grandeur, et dans l'idée et dans la forme, pour établir des règles qui puissent faire naître des grands poètes." His ideal poet, he tells his friend, would be "en quelque sorte tous les grands poètes du passé, comparés et fondus en un seul, autant qu'ils le permettraient." In the same passage, he leaves no doubt that Homer (and by extension Greek literature in general) would be included in their number—Homer "qui vivait dans les premiers siècles et qui cependant, au dire de tous, est le plus grand des poètes" (*Cor.*, I, 208-211). Nor must we overlook, in this connection, his comments on Victor de Laprade's *Psyché* in a letter to Baille written two or three months earlier. On the whole, he says, he finds Laprade's work boring. Nevertheless he admires Laprade, approves of his dream of a new Golden Age, and is far from viewing with disfavor his using the Greek fable of Psyche.

Obviously Zola is more susceptible to the influence of Greece than most critics have supposed. However, it is only by turning to his creative works and projects that we can gauge the full extent of his Hellenism. For in them will we find not only attitudes very similar to those that have been discussed above with respect to his nonfictional writings, but we shall also see that his debt to the Greek tradition is far greater than anything we have said up to now would suggest.

We know, for example, that in addition to a tragedy in three acts to be entitled *Annibal à Capoue* during his early years in Paris he considered writing *Les Héroïsmes*, a series of *nouvelles* based on the lives of the great heroes of humanity which would have included fictionalized studies of Archimedes and Socrates. He also was intrigued by the idea of writing a modern *Andromache*, based on Racine and Euripides, but set in a working-class or peasant milieu.[12] There is no record of when the idea first occurred to him, but we know that he actually did study Euripides' *Andromache*, probably with this end in mind, sometime before November 27, 1876. The article on Banville which he published on that date contains an excerpt from a dialogue between Andromache and Menelaus. In the accompanying commentary, among other things Zola expresses his belief that the closest modern equivalents to the heroes of the Greek epic are peasants and workers:

    Mais supposons qu'un écrivain, aujourd'hui, veuille remettre le sujet d'Andromaque au
    théâtre et le place dans le monde moderne. Eh bien! s'il veut garder la scène, il ne pourra

pas la mettre dans les classes supérieures, où les passions n'ont plus cette franchise; tandis que, s'il la met dans le peuple, il lui sera permis de tout conserver...

Oui, l'ouvrier qui serre les poings et qui provoque un camarade, sur nos boulevards extérieurs, est un véritable héros d'Homère, Achille injuriant Hector. J'oserai dire que le langage a dû être le même. On ne sait point encore quel cadre vaste et puissant peuvent être les mœurs de nos faubourgs; les drames y ont une force et une largeur incomparables; toutes les émotions humaines y sont, les douces et les violentes, mais prises à leurs sources, toutes neuves (*NAD*, 301).

Whether or not Zola ever went so far as to plan, or even begin writing, this work is perhaps not very important. It is enormously significant, however, that he expressed these ideas just at the time that he was completing *L'Assommoir* and before he wrote *Germinal* and *La Terre*. If nothing else, it indicates the extent to which he believed himself to be working within the Greek epic tradition when he composed his greatest masterpieces.

If we turn to those works which he completed or was at least able to begin, we may be impressed, first of all, by the overt, intense Hellenism of some of his early verse. Part III of *L'Aérienne* makes a passionate comparison of Provence with Italy and ancient Greece—

O Provence, des pleurs s'échappent de mes yeux,
Quand vibre sur mon luth ton nom mélodieux.
Terre qu'un ciel d'azur et l'olivier d'Attique
Font sœur de l'Italie et de la Grèce antique;

. . . .
. . . .

(*M*, 351)—

The evocation of gods, nymphs, and satyrs, quiet, shady woods, boulders, fields, and flowers in this poem is as Greek in spirit as anything by Banville or Leconte de Lisle. The first eight verses of *La Genèse*—the only ones Zola managed to compose for this projected epic—may recall in certain respects part of *Chant I* of Chénier's *Hermès*, but there is an even closer resemblance to the section in Book One of *De Rerum Natura* in which Lucretius informs Memmius of his poetic ambitions (beginning with the verse "Nam tibi de summa caeli ratione deumque").

Zola the short-story teller is also deeply rooted in the Greco-Roman tradition. A good example is in the first pages of the *Contes à Ninon* where he depicts Ninon, that marvelous creature, part incarnation of Provence, part projection of his youthful erotic fantasies, in the form of Hermaphroditus: "Ainsi tu réalisais le rêve de l'ancienne Grèce, l'amante faite homme, aux exquises élégances de forme, à l'esprit viril, digne de science et de sagesse" (*CAN*, 55). "Simplice," the first piece in the volume, is an adaptation—or possibly an unconscious recreation—of the myths of Pyramus and Thisbe or Hero and Leander,[13] both of which were popular with the public of Zola's time. "Les Aventures du grand Sidoine et du petit Médéric," one of Zola's longest tales, contains a glowing summary of the history of ancient Greece and a bit of dialogue expressing the same distaste

for Greek as an academic discipline that we have already encountered in
Zola's journalistic writings. It also includes a curious chapter—"L'Aimable
Primavère, Reine du Royaume des Heureux"—which would seem to
suggest at least a superficial acquaintance with Ovid's descriptions of the
Golden and Silver Ages and his presentation of the philosophy of
Pythagoras.

One of the best shorter pieces in the *Nouveaux contes à Ninon* is "Le
Forgeron" with its epical descriptions of a blacksmith, a powerful figure
which Zola compares to a Michelangelo sculpture and transforms into a
gigantic symbol of modern labor. One of the descriptions includes a
sentence ("Je trouvais, à le regarder, la ligne sculpturale moderne, que
nos artistes cherchent péniblement dans les chairs mortes de la Grèce")
which is reminiscent of the Zola of the *Salons*. Another piece, "Souvenirs,
III," ridicules popular Second-Empire Hellenism by contrasting the
bathers in the bathing establishments on the Seine with the ancient
Greeks. It contains a highly amusing evocation of a fat man:

> J'ai vu, pendant toute une saison, aux bains du Pont-Royal, un gros homme, rond
> comme une tonne, rouge comme une tomate mûre, qui jouait les Alcibiades. Il avait étudié
> les plis de son peignoir devant quelque tableau de David. Il était à l'Agora; il fumait avec
> des gestes antiques. Quand il daignait se jeter dans la Seine, c'était Léandre traversant
> l'Hellespont pour rejoindre Héro. Le pauvre homme! Je me souviens encore de son torse
> court où l'eau mettait des plaques violettes. O laideur humaine! (*CAN*, 389)

"Les Quatre journées de Jean Gourdon," the last story in the *Nouveaux
Contes à Ninon*, reads like an illustration of Ovid's account of the four
seasons of human life in Book XV of the *Métamorphoses*. (*Madeleine
Ferat* [1868], the last of Zola's pre-*Rougon-Macquart* novels, should
also be mentioned in passing here because it contains an obvious
and quite deliberate use of the myth of Pyramus and Thisbe from
Ovid, which is introduced at a climatic moment through the device of a
series of eight popular prints based on the story that decorate a hotel-
room setting).

La Fortune des Rougon, the first *Rougon-Macquart* novel, presents the
origins of the family and the historical events at Plassans resulting from the
coup d'état of December, 1851, in a dramatic framework that is
reminiscent of more than one Greek romance. I am referring, of course, to
the youthful love and tragic death of Silvère and Miette. Zola is himself
aware of these analogies, which are certainly quite deliberate, and twice
draws the reader's attention to them: "Les jeunes gens, jusqu'à cette nuit
de trouble, avaient vécu une de ces naïves idylles qui naissent au milieu de
la classe ouvrière, parmi ces déshérités, ces simples d'esprit chez lesquels
on retrouve encore parfois les amours primitives des anciens contes grecs"
(188); "Leur idylle traversa les pluies glacées de décembre et les brûlantes
sollicitations de juillet, sans glisser à la honte des amours communes; elle
garda son charme exquis de conte grec, son ardente pureté, tous ses
balbutiements naïfs de la chair qui désire et qui ignore" (228). Zola
undoubtedly had this novel as well as others in mind when he remarked to

the Félibres in 1892, "J'ai bien, pour ma part, cinq ou six idylles sur la conscience et toujours la même, Daphnis et Chloé, Paul et Virginie, Estelle et Némorin" (*M*, 278). Moreover there is also a parallel here with the myth of Pyramus and Thisbe as well as other mythological reminiscences. Miette is compared to "la Bacchante antique" (25), Sicardot to Hercules (91). The jealous one-eyes man who kills Silvere is a kind of Polyphemus. Zola's epic imagination sometimes invades and merges with his lyricism. Evocations of the Greek love idyl mingle with more epical mythological allusions. The Provencal setting is transformed very early in the book into a gigantic amphitheatre across which the band of insurrectionists "reprit sa marche héroïque." The whole scene is invested with a certain classical quality: "La lune faisait de chaque rocher un fût de colonne tronqué, un chapiteau écroulé, une muraille trouée de mystérieux portiques. En haut, la masse des Garrigues dormait, à peine blanchie d'une teinte laiteuse, pareille à une immense cité cyclopéenne" (180). There is here an obvious attempt to evoke something of the sacred horror of a classical tragedy, to create a mood of cosmic catastrophe. (Of course, this is not the only time Zola employs the adjective "cyclopéenne". It seems to be one of his favorite words, and recurrs from time to time throughout his works.)

La Curée, the second novel in the *Rougon-Macquart* series, may well have grown out of Zola's desire to succeed where his friend Pagès du Tarn—the author of a notoriously unsuccessful *Nouvelle Phèdre*—had failed. In any case, Zola wrote in his *ébauche*, "Décidément, c'est une nouvelle *Phèdre* que je vais faire," and he included a synopsis of Racine's play in his preparatory notes.[14] Although numerous other French authors have treated the theme of Hippolytus and Phaedra, it is undoubtedly more than a mere coincidence that Zola's friend Ludovico Marguéry also did so, in *Le Fils de Thésée*, a one-act *opera-bouffe* produced at the Théâtre d'Aix in February, 1864.[15] In *La Curée*, a second myth—Narcissus and Echo (which is also recounted by Ovid)—is introduced and ingeniously interwoven with the myth of Phaedra.In each case Zola employs the theatrical device of a play within a play. Renée, Zola's Phaedra, is shown attending a performance (in Italian!) of Racine's *Phèdre*. At a costume ball that takes place towards the end of the novel, Renée poses as Echo and Maxime, her stepson, poses as Narcissus, in a succession of *tableaux vivants* entitled *Les Amours de Narcisse et de la nymphe Echo*. Much of the interest of the novel is to be found in the way Zola combines these two classical themes and creates contrasts and analogies with the original myths in the dramatic action, character development, and setting. In the process, he expresses both his strong aversion for the Second-Empire cult of Greece in its sillier and more vulgar forms and his own profound fascination with the classical mythology.

Winifred Newton, in a valuable study, compares Zola's development of the Phaedra theme with Racine's but does not suggest the full extent to which the traditional myth is reflected in the novel.[16] Zola's technique in some respects anticipates James Joyce's *Ulysses*. Everywhere we look we find curious analogies; e.g., between Renée's father, a retired presiding judge, and Phaedra's father, Minos, one of the judges in Hades. When

Renée's husband, Saccard, visits the old gentleman's house on the Ile Saint-Louis there is a shadowy parallel with the descent of Theseus into the Underworld: "Saccard, que rien jusque-là n'avait décontenancé, fut glacé par la froideur et le demi-jour de l'appartement, par la sévérité triste de ce grand vieillard, dont l'œil perçant lui sembla fouiller sa conscience jusqu'au fond" (79). The extensive sun imagery in the novel is also undoubtedly inspired by the myth of Phaedra, whereas the mirror and water imagery is almost certainly suggested by the story of Echo and Narcissus. (In the first chapter, for example, the lake in the Bois is described as "ce miroir clair.") We are reminded in some ways, of the art of the fugue. The modern and the ancient stories, the realism and the myth, tend to reinforce each other, to create a constant relief. The old myths end up by with a certain enhanced beauty and nobility. The sordid, decadent Second-Empire society that Zola is portraying is seen in all its ugliness. It is, all in all, much the same technique that Zola tried out in "Souvenirs, III."

A number of the other *Rougon-Macquart* novels possess many of the same qualities, and there is hardly one that does not contain at least some indication of Zola's debt to the classical tradition. In *Le Ventre de Paris*, for example, he set out—as he wrote in his preliminary notes—to transform himself into a "Théocrite aux Halles."[17] The scheming, dominating Abbé Faujas with whom Marthe falls desperately in love, in *La Conquête de Plassans*, bears the given name of Ovid. *La Faute de l'abbé Mouret* and *Son Excellence Eugène Rougon* are, to a greater or lesser degree, adaptations of Biblical stories (Adam and Eve, Samson and Delilah).[18] However, it is in *L'Assommoir* that the filiation with the Greek epic once again becomes clearly evident. I am thinking not only of the comparison that Zola makes, for example, between Goujet, the smith (a descendent of the smith that we have already encountered in *Le Forgeron*) and Hercules,[19] or of the way Zola's mythopoeic imagination transforms inanimate objects into terrifying monsters, but of the filiation which we know existed in Zola's mind between his proletarians and the heroes and heroines of the Homeric epic. The next *Rougon-Macquart* novel, *Une Page d'amour* (1878), poetically transforms the city of Paris into a kind of Greek chorus: "Eh bien! dès ma vingtième année, j'avais rêvé d'écrire un roman dont Paris, avec l'océan de ses toitures, serait un personnage, quelque chose comme le chœur antique," he says in a *Lettre-Préface*. "Il me fallait un drame intime, trois ou quatre créatures dans une petite chambre, puis l'immense ville à l'horizon, toujours présente, regardant avec ses yeux de pierre rire et pleurer ces créatures. C'est cette vieille idée que j'ai tenté de réaliser dans *Une Page d'amour*" (ed. Pléiade, 1605). In *Nana*, the myth of Mars and Venus plays much the same complex and central role that the romance of Daphnis and Chloe and the story of Pyramus and Thisbe do in *La Fortune des Rougon*, or the myths of Phaedra and of Echo and Narcissus do in *La Curée*.[20] Octave Mouret, the hero of *Au Bonheur des Dames*, is quite as much as Shaw's Dr. Higgins a modern incarnation of Pygmalion.[21]

However, in my opinion it is in *Germinal*, Zola's masterpiece, that he most brilliantly achieves his desire to be utterly of his own historical moment while at the same time exploiting to the greatest possible degree the poetic legacy of the classical past. The dramatic subject of the book—a major industrial strike—is at once intensely new and extremely old, for it is nothing other than a recent historical form of the ancient epic theme of war. The mines (particularly as Zola describes them) suggest numerous parallels with the classical Underworld as well as with the Christian hell. The book is haunted throughout by myth, especially the myths of the creation, the wars of the gods, and the flood. There are more or less veiled allusions to Tartarus, the Furies, Ceres, and the Golden Age, among other classical references. As for Zola's other novels, mention should be made of *L'Oeuvre* (in which all the criticisms of the *Salons* are repeated), and of *La Terre*, with its profoundly pagan Nature poetry, its vision of Mother Earth, of the great cycles of history and of individual human lives. Nor, finally, should one forget *La Bête humaine*, of which Banville wrote:

> Je suis encore tout brûlant de l'admiration que m'a inspirée *La Bête humaine*. Oui, cette effrayante épopée, au-dessus de laquelle planent les Fatalités cruelles comme les Dieux, m'a fait songer à ce qu'il y a de plus grand dans le passé. Mais il n'y a ni passé ni présent; il y a une nuit sombre, où passent çà et là les étincelles d'une torche que secoue le génie. Portez-la longtemps, vous qui êtes jeune! Moi, je vous acclame au passage.[22]

It would be appropriate to conclude with mention of one of Zola's dramatic works which no student of his Hellenism can ignore. *Violaine la Chevelue* is a "Féerie lyrique" in five acts and nine tableaux, apparently composed shortly before his death in 1902 and dedicated to his children.[23] Here, once again, we find the youthful poet of *L'Aérienne* and the earliest *Contes à Ninon*, and the admirer of Banville and Chénier. One of the characters is named Léandre, and a member of the ballet troupe is called Lycidas. The four elements are represented by fairies with the classical names of Floriane, Nerée, Célie, and Luce. There are also numerous *bergères*, *sylvains*, and *faunes*, a choir, Coryphee, and even an orgy. And in the concluding speech by the chorus of Le Peuple there is a touching evocation of the Golden Age of the classical past which suggests the deep emotional appeal that ancient Greece still had for Zola, the "scientific" literary explorer of our rather seamy modern world: "*Le Peuple*—Miracle, miracle! L'âge d'or est revenu. Plus de chômage, tous au travail! Et que la terre enfin fleurisse, dans la joie et dans la fraternité!"

Thus it is clear that Zola's roots extend much more deeply into the Greek tradition than most critics have heretofore suspected. His art grows out of the Hellenism—as well as the modernism—of his times. The young lovers of Theocritus and Longus, the gods and heroes of Euripides and Homer survive in his imagination. The Greek idyl, the Greek tragedy, and the Greek epic, are only half disguised under their modern trappings. Like so many writers before and after him, Zola had a vision of Greece as the ideal representation of the great destiny to which men had been called—at least once in their long history on this earth. Something of the eternal

Greek spirit and even—as Banville intimated—something of the Greek
genius live on in his work.

University of California
Santa Barbara

Notes

[1] «Souvenirs, II,» *Contes à Ninon*, ed. Maurice Le Blond (Paris: Bernouard, 1927), p. 383.
Subsequent references to Zola's works will be to the various volumes in the Bernouard edition
(1927-1929), unless otherwise noted and wherever possible the references will be given in the
text. The following abbreviations will be used: *CAN (Contes à Ninon); T (Théâtre); Cor.
(Correspondance); MH (Mes Haines); RE (Romanciers naturalistes); DL (Documents
littéraires); NAT (Naturalisme au théâtre); NAD (Nos Auteurs dramatiques); UC (Une
Campagne); and M (Mélanges).*

[2] Paul Cézanne, *Correspondance*, ed. John Rewald (Paris: Grasset, 1937).

[3] See Zola's essay on Flaubert, in *Les Romanciers naturalistes*, passim.

[4] See Guy Robert, "Trois textes inédits d'Emile Zola," *Revue des sciences humaines*, fasc.
51 (1948), 181-207. Robert indicates Zola's debt to Chauvin on p. 192. Readers of this essay
may also be interested in Professor Robert's "Zola et le classicisme," in the same review,
fasc. 49 (1948), 1-24, and fasc. 50 (1950), 126-153. However this long and illuminating study
has to do almost entirely with Zola and French classicism. Professor Robert's conclusions with
respect to Zola's knowledge of and interest in the Greeks and Romans are largely negative and,
in my opinion, somewhat misleading. I find Robert's assertion that Zola's classical education
"paraît l'avoir peu marqué" very debatable.

[5] The earliest version has been reproduced by Robert in "Trois textes inédits d'Emile
Zola."

[6] *L'Atelier de Zola. Textes de journaux, 1865-1870*, ed. Martin Kanes (Genève: Droz,
1963). Subsequent references to this collection will be given in the text.

[7] A complete version is included in Robert's "Trois textes inédits d'Emile Zola."

[8] I have in mind the passage beginning: "Pareillement, quand nous lisons une tragédie
grecque, notre premier soin doit être de nous figurer des Grecs, c'est-à-dire des hommes qui
vivent à demi-nus, dans des gymnases ou sur des places publiques, sous un ciel éclatant, en face
des plus fins et des plus nobles paysages, occupés à se faire un corps agile et fort, à converser, à
discuter, à voter."

[9] *Etudes de littérature ancienne et étrangère* (Paris: Didier, 1846).

[10] It is interesting that the *Catalogue des objets d'art et d'ameublement...* printed at the
time Zola's effects were sold at the Hôtel Drouot in 1903, the year following his death,
mentions numerous classical sculptures as well as several 18th century bronzes on classical
themes (Jupiter, Pan, Hercules, etc.).

[11] "Trois textes inédits d'Emile Zola," p. 204.

[12] For information on the incompleted projects just mentioned, see Denise Le Blond-
Zola's *Emile Zola, raconté par sa fille* (Paris: Fasquelle, 1931), pp. 23, 31-32, 185. The *ébauche*,
together with the synopses of Racine's *Andromaque* and Euripides' *Andromache*, is now in the
possession of Zola's grandson, Jean-Claude Le Blond-Zola.

[13] Cf. F. W. J. Hemmings, *Emile Zola* (Oxford: Clarendon Press, 1966), p. 15, and Rodolphe Walter's article, Pyrame et Thisbé à l'Hôtel du Grand-Cerf," *Nouvelles de l'estampe*, No. 9 (Nov. 1963), 238-241.

[14] *Bibliothèque nationale, MS Nouv. acq. fr.* 10282, fols. 298, 374.

[15] Winifred Newton, *Le Thème de Phèdre et d'Hippolyte dans la littérature française* (Geneva: Droz, 1939), p. 131.

[16] *Le Thème de Phèdre et d'Hippolyte*, pp. 68, 132-134, 137-138; cf. also Lawson A. Carter, *Zola and the Theater* (Yale Univ. Press, 1963), pp. 50-51, and Hemmings, *Emile Zola*, pp. 91-97.

[17] BN, MS. *Nouv. acq. fr.* 10338, fol. 71: "Il me faut l'idylle parisienne, très pimentée... Je mettrai, en un mot, Théocrite aux Halles." See also foll. 34, 35, where the phrase "Théocrite aux Halles" is repeated.

[18] Yet Mouret's sister, Desirée, is compared with Cybèle, a precious indication of the symbolic value of this character. See Roger Ripoll, "Le Symbolisme végétal dans *la Faute de l'abbé Mouret*," *Les Cahiers naturalistes*, No. 31 (1966), 18. In the same novel there is a reminiscence of the war of the gods, in Zola's description of oaks as "arbres titans, foudroyés, renversés dans des poses de lutteurs invaincus" (Livre Deuxième, ch. xi).

[19] It has been suggested that Goujet may be modeled on a statue that Zola had perhaps seen during visits to the Louvre with Cezanne—the *Hercule Gaulois:* "... il semblait un colosse au repos... des épaules et des bras sculptés qui paraissaient copiés sur ceux d'un géant, dans un musée" (Bernouard ed., pp. 171-175). Both Goujet and the central character in "Le Forgeron" may, furthermore, reflect the influence of Michelet's *Bible de l'Humanité* (1864), which Zola must have read not long before he became acquainted with the smith at Gloton on whom these two characters are probably based. In this work Michelet presents Hercules and two Persian heroes, both of them smiths, as archetypal symbols of Labor: "Chose étrange et qui stupéfie! La Grèce a un bon sens si fort, une raison si merveilleusement raisonnable que—contre ses préjugés même, le mépris des labeurs qu'elle nomme serviles—son grand héros divinisé, c'est justement *le Travailleur*" (*La Bible de l'Humanité*, III, iv).

[20] See Frances Leonard's illuminating essay, "Nana: Symbol and Action," *Modern Fiction Studies*, IX (1963), 149-158.

[21] BN, MS. *Nouv. acq. fr.* 10278, fol. 350 bears the cryptic notation: "Lutte avec Pygmalion" (included in a list of what appear to be research topics and themes that Zola intends to develop in this novel).

[22] Eileen Souffrin, "Banville et Zola (avec des lettres inédites)," *Les Cahiers naturalistes*, Nos. 24-25 (1963), 56.

[23] The text is reproduced in the Bernouard edition of Zola's theater.

The poetry of the second half of the 19th century (contemporary with Zola) was dominated by two movements—Parnassianism and Symbolism—and by three giants who really transcended any movements: Baudelaire, Rimbaud, and Mallarmé. All of these writers were influenced by antiquity in various ways and to varying degrees, but as Peyre points out the question is a complex one and a great deal of study remains to be done before it is clarified. However it is clear that as the century advanced, increasingly "tout ce qu'il y avait dans l'antiquité de mysticisme et d'occultisme [a] séduit les modernes."[1]

One of the poets who is generally considered to have been most indebted to Greece and to have made the most original and resourceful use of the mysterious resonances of classical elements in his works was Stéphane Mallarmé. Not only did he "dans quelques poèmes célèbres, revêtu d'une musique nouvelle quelques mythes antiques," as Peyre puts it, but he also formulated the task of the poet in very Hellenist terms as "l'explication orphique de la terre."[2] However, as Robert Greer Cohn points out in the following essay, the mature Mallarmé's assimilation of the Greek mythological materials was so complete that in his major poems they have virtually no meaning except that which he gives them. In this sense, he was strictly speaking no longer part of the Hellenist tradition. However, in other parts of Mallarmé's works there are certain Hellenist elements which do retain their identity and provide revealing insights into his relationship with the classical tradition. It is these that Professor Cohn sets out to examine in his illuminating discussion.

Notes

[1] Henri M. Peyre, *L'Influence des littératures antiques sur la littérature française moderne* (New Haven-Oxford, 1941), p. 73.

[2] *Op. cit.*, p. 86.

MALLARMÉ AND THE GREEKS

By Robert Greer Cohn

The mature Mallarmé's relation to Greek art and thought is conditioned by one prime fact: he aimed, not (as some, like Marinetti, believed) to discard tradition in favor of a pure modernity, but rather to subsume it all, the ancient and the contemporary alike, to his own total view and expression of reality from the ground up.

Although Mallarmé is sometimes thought of as being in a classic tradition—by Claudel, for one, who saw him as the "couronnement" of that tradition in France—nevertheless in his late manner, because of the sought-after wholeness, we find very little that can be deemed derivative or imitative, hence neo-classic in the strict sense of the word. To a certain extent, this is also true of much of his earlier writing as well. For example, in the "Après-midi d'un faune," which represents a sort of middle stage in his evolution, there is surprisingly little left from the archetypal eclogue of Theocritus, Bion, Moschus, or from pagan *décor* generally: only the faun himself as an ambiguously pastoral creature, the nymphs, the syrinx, and a single reference to Venus. (One might add to this the tacit homage to the seventeenth century implied by his use of the alexandrine verse-form.) The rest is made up of the intense crystallizations of his own inner-outer world and a subtle verbal music. By way of illustrating his position, through contrast, even Valéry—representatively, in the sequence of "Narcisses"—keeps more of the automatically inherited in his lines, which at times read almost predictably with something of a decorative and melodious eighteenth-century prettiness.

Despite Mallarmé's quest for purity in this sense, we come upon some interesting vestiges of the Hellenic tradition scattered throughout his writings. These are mainly to be found in the earliest poetry and prose, which are naturally more derivative and youthfully rhetorical; occasionally in the critical pieces on theatre (including his musings about a "Grand'-Oeuvre", which he at times envisioned as a dramatic presentation or ritual and which is related to some aspects of the "Coup de dés", the fullest recorded attempt at the work); and finally, in the miscellaneous references to Greek culture in his *Dieux antiques* and *Mots anglais*. It is on these three groups of works that the present discussion will center.

The collection of adolescent poems entitled *Entre Quatre Murs* is adorned by various of the standard allusions to antiquity which Mallarmé inherited, chiefly via Lamartine, Banville, and Gautier. "Loeda" (subtitled an "Idylle antique") is characteristic of this manner and, incidentally, strikes exactly the juvenile, scholarly and lush mood of Rimbaud's "Soleil et Chair," written a decade later:

> La brise en se jouant courbe les jeunes fleurs,
> Le myrte de Vénus embaume les prairies,
> Et l'onde s'enfuyant dans sa rive fleurie
> Murmure son amour aux herbages en pleurs.
>
> . . . .
>
> Jupiter!... à ce nom, mollement son sein rose
> Plein d'amour se noya dans le sein ondoyant
> Du cygne au col neigeux qui sur son cœur riant
> Cueille d'ardents baisers. Sous son aile il dépose
> La nymphe frémissante: ils ne forment qu'un corps.
> Lœda se renversa, la paupière mi-close,
> Les lèvres s'entrouvrant... sourit dans cette pose...
> — Et la nuit tomba noire et voila leurs transports.[1]

Reality offers only so many truly privileged images to the poet, be he Greek or French, images vibrant with possibilities in all directions, *convergent* ones that are apt to be called "symbols" when used for these virtualities. The swan is certainly one of the most powerful of these *topoi*. Mallarmé will remain true to this enduring creature in his fashion—as well as to the faun, who puts in a fleeting appearance, with his pitiless prey, in the line here: "Les nymphes en riant fuient un faune lascif..."

"Pan," another long poem from this early collection, contains a lament for the passing of the naive wholeness of pagan nature, which is now, alas, contaminated by Christianity:

> La nature, riant sous le pied radieux
> Du printemps qui semait l'amour avec les roses.
> Or, ce soir-là, j'entrai dans leur temple poudreux
> Pour voir leur Christ béni par leurs hymnes moroses

(p. 181).

This reminds one again of Rimbaud's "Soleil et Chair," or of the Christ, "éternel voleur des énergies," whom he portrays in "Les Premières communions," or in "l'Homme juste." In his correspondence with Lefébure, Mallarmé observed how the simple smile of Venus became the twisted mouth of the Mona Lisa, bitten by the serpent of original sin. Such generalizations ran rampant in the nineteenth century, encouraged in particular by the German Romantics with all their exaggerated praise for the Golden Age and their pagan past; with Spengler they spilled over into the twentieth. Of course, certain Greek authors, notably Hesiod, encouraged this penchant for pastoral sentimentality. At their best, of course, they were every bit as messy as we are; nostalgia, it seems helps make some fine art— and some dreadful theorizing.

Mallarmé's poem "Pan", written in 1859 (his seventeenth year), marks a provisional turning point in his religiosity: many of the previous poems are frankly pious, though occasionally bitterly questioning. The term "provisional" is used because elementary prudence should dictate more caution than some critics have shown in pinning down such delicate and evanescent matters. Nevertheless, despite Mallarmé's having more or less formally rejected the cult of Catholicism ("Oublions..." etc.) at an early date, there are certainly Christian overtones to many of his later utterances. This is scarcely a unique case: we think of Joyce, who refused to have his children baptized but who on occasion was unable to resist plunging into some inviting nave he was passing, pushed to such an action by more than a merely aesthetic compulsion.

The other Greek references in Mallarmé's early verse ("A Une Petite Laveuse blonde," "A Un Poète immoral," etc.) need not detain us here, for they are no more than frivolous little echoes. More rewarding are certain parts of "La Symphonie littéraire," a youthful prose poem praising his favorite contemporaries—Banville, Gautier, and Baudelaire—which takes especially from the first two its Hellenic flavor of afflatus:

Je lis les vers de Théophile Gautier aux pieds de la Vénus éternelle. Avec lui [Banville] je bois le nectar dans l'Olympe du lyrisme... Tout ce qu'il y a d'enthousiasme ambrosien en moi et de bonté musicale, de noble et de pareil aux dieux, chante, et j'ai l'extase radieuse de la muse... Ainsi dut être celui qui le premier reçut des dieux la lyre et dit l'ode éblouie avant notre aïeul Orphée. Ainsi lui-même, Apollon.

Dans une apothéose... Ronsard chante des odes, et Vénus, vêtue de l'azur qui sort de sa chevelure, lui [au Poète] verse l'ambroisie... la grande lyre s'extasie dans ses mains augustes.[2]

In the later collection, *Poésies*, there is nothing like the foregoing: all becomes airy concision. We have previously mentioned the pastoral over-tones of Theocritus and others like him in the "Faune" poem: moreover, there is something of the Phèdre-Oenone duo (via Racine) in the dialogue between Hérodiade and her nurse, with not a few declamatory lines recalling the eloquent past. Gautier's pagan belief gives the unsentimentally Greek tragic mood to "Toast funèbre," with its "pur soleil mortel." In the final image of Mallarmé's 1885 "Prose (pour des Esseintes)," there is—as I have surmised elsewhere—a reminiscence of the Venus Anadyomene, a stunning female standing before the sea she rose from (cf. "Le Phénomène futur:" "jambes lisses qui gardent le sel de la mer première"). But the famous and puzzling pair, Anastase and Pulchérie, appear to be vaguely Byzantine rather than Hellenic and, more probably, neither.

Mallarmé's sonnet "Ses Purs Ongles" (p. 68-69) depends on some antique terms for two of its main effects: the bric-a-brac of a 19th century salon—*lampadophore* and *amphore*—and more importantly, the crisp and stark qualities of classic austerity, sustained particularly by the letter x in six of the poem's end-rhymes: *onyx, Phénix, ptyx, Styx, nixe, fixe*. Most of this, for etymological and other reasons, is decidedly Greek.

In "Le Tombeau d'Edgar Poe," (p. 70), the *hydre* faintly recalls the hydra of Lerne, but it has been generalized here into a universal monstrosity in the spirit of *Les Dieux antiques* wherein all myths are related back to a total tragedy between light and darkness. But certainly the term echoes back down the corridors of tradition, as does much else in the poem, *sub specie aeternitatis.*

Two other sonnets in the collection, "Surgi de la croupe" (p. 74) and "Quelle soie," (p. 75) feature a Greek-like *Chimère*, symbol of the "Glorious Lie" which is art and eventually all reality. A comparably seductive Attic cousin is the *sirène* of "Salut" and, much later, of the "Coup de dés." Allusions of Heine, Gautier, Redon, Debussy, and Régnier indicate that this creature was very much in the air—or in the surf—during this period. Moreover, perhaps the *talon nu* of "M'introduire" (p. 75) can be attached to a sort of Achilles, at any rate a pagan hero.

Curiously, the sonnet Mallarmé chose to come last in his collection is transparently Attic in mood. The poem opens with the following evocative stanza:

> Mes bouquins refermés sur le nom de Paphos,
> Il m'amuse d'élire avec le seul génie
> Une ruine, par mille écumes bénie
> Sous l'hyacinthe, au loin, de ses jours triomphaux.

(p. 76)

Elsewhere there is an allusion to the Greek funeral chant, *nénie*, and to a "sein brûlé d'une antique amazone," an image which joins with various others in his canon—like the "casque guerrier d'impératrice enfant" of "Victorieusement fui"—to refer amusedly to the challenging qualities of the fair sex, or to the larger sense of androgyneity which also came down from the sophisticated ancients. Altogether the poem seems to owe something to "To Helen," the best-known piece of his mentor, Poe. Paphos, the place name which started the poet's meditation, occurs in a bit of verse by Alexis Piron which the adolescent Mallarmé copied into a personal anthology.[3] It also appears in Keats' *Sleep and Poetry*, which is a far likelier source, as Wais has indicated. And Mallarmé himself said of Keats: "[In him] la plus splendide imagination d'à présent revêt à la fois la grâce et la solennité antique."[4]

As has been indicated above, Mallarmé's ideal of a theater was a "total" ritual, synthesizing modernity and antiquity in time, the various arts in simultaneous space. Hence the ambivalence of his attitude toward various theatrical manifestations as expressed in *Divagations*. His sincere admiration for many aspects of the Greek theater is qualified by inevitable reservations. For example he strongly praises the Greek tradition (along with its rejuvenation in the play *Erechtheus* by his friend, Swinburne) in the following passage: "A la tragédie [*Erechtheus*] de la maturité spirituelle [de Swinburne] restait donc la fortune nouvelle d'une inspiration savante, pure quoiqu'enthousiaste, conforme davantage à quelque chose de grec... l'auguste nudité des sentiments antiques et leur délicatesse suave. Odes maintenant, à strophes et antistrophes, puis épodes de chœurs ajoutés à tout ce long hymne" (pp. 701-702). In his autobiographical letter to

Verlaine, Mallarmé alluded to his vision of a Great Work as an "explication orphique de la Terre... ce rêve, ou Ode" (p. 663), and something of this has undoubtedly remained in his own Work; the tripartite division of the "Coup de dés" corresponds roughly to the initial phase of brute reality, followed by an artistic evolution, and finally a synthesis of these elements in the Poem.

More praise for the Greek theater emerges in passing from the essay on Wagner. Mallarmé begins by pointing out that Wagnerian opera is not fully either theater or music, but rather a mixture of the two. Therefore, "chez Wagner... je ne perçois, dans l'acception stricte, le théâtre (sans conteste on retrouvera plus, au point de vue dramatique, dans la Grèce ou Shakespeare)" (p. 335). His reservations about this type of theater are somewhat amplified in the following passage, from the above-mentioned essay on Swinburne:

"Nous voulons un théâtre quotidien et national (diront les bien-intentionnés) et non une résurrection, même égale à la vie, de l'art grec", soit: mais, tant que ce théâtre ne se produit pas chez vous à l'heure qu'il est, jubilez, aux reprises du XVIe siècle; ou de ce qu'il y a eu de notoire auparavant, c'est l'antiquité (évoquée surtout par l'heure actuelle). Tracée avec d'impeccables lignes sur le modèle ancien, mais s'inspirant d'un souffle de maintenant, la pièce de Swinburne... peut devant tous ceux-là qui la lisent se jouer et les ravir (p. 703).

It is evident in the foregoing that Mallarmé is trying to honor the work of his friend—as well as its Renaissance and pagan antecedents—but also that he understands the *bien-intentionnés* modern critics who would prefer something more original and contemporary. We also are aware from all we know of him that he has in mind something even more ambitious, which the *bien-intentionnés* would hardly welcome. This is a characteristic example of how a gifted mind could go beyond both sides of a debate, and we are reminded of Baudelaire, who—in the *Salon de 1845*—seemed to be siding with the bourgeoisie against false artists or bohemians, but who *in petto* was wishing "a plague on both your houses."

As is clear in the following quotation, from Mallarmé's special viewpoint the shortcomings of the Greek tragedies are present in Wagner as well. True, both kinds of theater go toward the sources of life: "Il [le héros wagnérien] n'agit qu'entouré, à la Grecque, de la stupeur mêlée d'intimité qu'éprouve une assistance devant des mythes... un public, pour la seconde fois depuis les temps, héllenique d'abord, maintenant germain, considère le secret, représenté, d'origines" (p. 544). But they fail to make it all the way—"pas jusqu'à la source"—and hence emerge with something less-than-lucid, "la légende": "Voici à la rampe intronisée la Légende... Si l'esprit français, strictement imaginatif et abstrait, donc poétique, jette un éclat, ce ne sera pas ainsi: il répugne, en cela d'accord avec l'Art dans son intégrité, qui est inventeur, à la Légende" (*ibid.*).

Mallarmé applies similar strictures to Zola's resurrection of the neoclassical mood of the seventeenth century. First he pays homage to the universal—the abstract or philosophical—qualities of the *grand siècle:* "... l'intention, quand on y pense, gisant aux sommaires plis de la tragédie française, ne fut pas l'antiquité ranimée dans sa cendre blanche mais de produire en un milieu nul ou à peu près les grandes poses humaines et comme notre plastique morale." Then he continues, still in reference to Zola, with an allusion to the instinctual depths which spring forth in tragedy, despite all the mitigating efforts: "d'inutiles précautions contre l'acte magnifique de vivre... le drame, latent, ne se manifeste que par une déchirure affirmant l'irréductibilité de nos instincts... ingénus, morbides, sournois, brutaux, avec une nudité d'allure bien dans la tradition française classique, se montrent des caractères" (p. 321).

Finally he concludes with a reservation—and it is a serious one—about "le théâtre classique à l'éloquent débat ininterrompu" that characterizes the era of Racine and Corneille, pointing out that it was too imitative, erudite:

> Statuaire égale à l'interne opération par exemple de Descartes et si le tréteau significatif d'alors avec l'unité de personnage, n'en profita, joignant les planches et la philosophie, il faut accuser le goût notoirement érudit d'une époque retenue d'inventer malgré sa nature prête, dissertatrice et neutre, à vivifier le type abstrait. Une page à ces grécisants, ou même latine, servait, dans le décalque. La figure d'élan idéal ne dépouilla pas l'obsession scolaire ni les modes du siècle.[5]

In contrast, Mallarmé's ideal drama would be "mystère, autre que représentatif et que, je dirai, grec. Pièce, office. Vous sentez comme plus 'objectif', détaché, illusoire, aux jeux antiques, Prométhée même, Oreste, il convenait d'envelopper les gradins de légende, dont le frisson restât certes, aux robes spectatrices mais sans la terreur en ce pli, que telle vicissitude grandiloque affectât quiconque la contemple, en tant que protagoniste à son insu" (p. 393).

Again, the tone is subtly and inevitably ambiguous: the legendary aspect of Greek drama is for the masses, or rather for their bodies ("robes") but the finer minds—and the truer instincts in those same masses, "la Foule (où inclus le Génie)" (p. 383)—vibrate to the original depths expressed in the dramatic "vicissitudes". Hence Mallarmé goes on to say: "Ici [both in the Greek drama and in Mallarmé's own conception of ritual] reconnaissez, désormais, dans le drame, la Passion, pour élargir la conception canoniale [Christian ritual is also assimilated] ou, comme ce fut l'esthétique fastueuse de l'Eglise, avec le feu tournant d'hymnes, une assimilation humaine à la tétralogie de l'An... Sa hantise, au théâtre que l'esprit porte, grandira, en majesté de temple" (p. 393). Here we are squarely on the track of the "Coup de dés" with its "symphonic equation proper to the seasons," taking up the Hesiodic tradition of the Four Ages and the Greek dramatic tetralogy in addition to later Christian equivalents. Moreover, in the "Coup de dés," there are strong hints of the ancient Greeks in the section which portrays the rise of theater as an expression of a fundamental stage in the evolution of human culture. The "hilarité et horreur" of Page 6 of the Poem have their counterparts in Greek comedy and tragedy; the image of the "plume... en opposition au ciel/trop..." is a reference to Promethean hubris. The dice theme itself, in varying expression as a burst of light (p. 1) and military coup (p. 4) may echo the opening speech of Aeschylus' *Agamemnon*, where the beacon signalling victory over Troy is referred to metaphorically as "my lord's dice cast aright" and a "torchlit throw." (Cf. Lattimore translation.)

Almost always when Mallarmé refers to his future Work there are resonances form the past—often Greek; in the essay on Wagner the Work is referred to as "un Poème, l'Ode" (p. 545).

And although he goes on to say that an old myth should not be resurrected—except as "dégagé de personnalité"—nevertheless the feeling is spiral: something radically new and yet very old, and the past echoes wilfully at every turn of his original expression.

In *Les Mots anglais*, Mallarmé offers some highly personal comments on the English language, with etymologies and groupings of "word-families." These include numerous Greek roots, and there are various remarks on the relations between Greek and modern languages. From a conversation with the older poet, André Fontainas has reported the following: "Il dit en être venu à attacher, à l'origine et l'étymologie des mots, une importance telle que dans sa langue, surtout éprise de latin, il n'use de vocables d'autre origine, grecque par exemple, que par exception: seulement en vue d'un effet. Même le mot *idée*, il ne l'emploie pas sans scrupule."[6] This seems generally to be the case—even in the "Coup de dés" the favorite Mallarmean term *idée* is surprisingly absent—but we must immediately add that the exceptions are numerous and important. Among his key terms, beyond *idée*, must be counted: *le Rythme, la Critique, la Chimère* (both in the poems and the prose), and *la Musique*. (The latter word, he observes in a letter to Gosse, he uses in the Pythagorean sense of a universal harmony.) And when he ventures out, mindful of Poe, it is with "Psyche, my soul" (p. 294).

Les Dieux antiques, an adaptation that Mallarmé made of an English scholar's book, needs only a brief mention here. The work is a fairly dutiful one, even a potboiler. True, it contains interesting hints for an understanding of Mallarmé's serious work—such as the tragedy of light and darkness he sees underlying every myth—but it will be enough for our purpose here to say that there is a sizable section devoted to the Greek heroes and gods, and to remind the reader that these occasionally have overtones in the poetry, as we have tried to show in *Toward the Poems of Mallarmé*.[7]

Mallarmé has been called a Platonist by almost everyone who has written on him. Often the term is used as a shibboleth to dispose of the poet in the name of that famous "return to reality" which no dissertation about any post-Symbolist writer, however minor, can do without. Critics like these scarcely stop to consider that a universal dilemma or tension between reality and something else is involved in all expression. What counts is the force of the tension itself, the intensity of the dilemma—which always includes a temporal dialectic of alienation and return, "l'éternel retour de l'exilé," as Mallarmé put it, after Homer—and the concrete resolution of it on the page, not the one-sided entity of Reality. (One suspects that in many of these cases, they never got far off the ground of reality to begin with.) But once we have admitted that there is a problem here, and that the strawman "Platonist" is a half-truth, we can allow that it is a *powerful* half-truth for Mallarmé. His warm and affectionate interest in Greek antiquity might best be summed up in his brief but vibrant allusion—in "La Musique et les lettres"—to "le nom très haut de Platon."

Stanford University

Notes

[1] "Loeda," in Henri Mondor, *Mallarmé Lycéen, avec quarante poèmes de jeunesse inédits*, Gallimard, 1954, pp. 152-155. The poem is dated April, 1859.

[2] "La Symphonie littéraire,"in Stéphane Mallarmé, *Œuvres complètes*, ed. Henri Mondor et G. Jean-Aubry, Pléiade, Gallimard, 1945, pp. 261-265. Except as otherwise indicated, future references to Mallarmé's poems will be to this edition and will be included in the text.

[3] *Mallarmé lycéen*, p. 291.

[4] In "Beautés de l'anglais."

[5] *Ibid.*, pp. 319-320. Mallarmé had cocked a mild snoot at Racine in some juvenile verse: "J'aime le sucre d'orge et les vers de Racine. Le plus fade des deux?... Devine si tu peux." Rimbaud was equally irreverent: "Le divin sot." We need hardly add that this view cannot be ascribed to the mature Mallarmé.

[6] See Henri Mondor's *Vie de Mallarmé* (Paris, 1946), p. 699.

[7] *Toward the Poems of Mallarmé*, Berkeley, University of California Press, 1965.

III

THE TWENTIETH CENTURY

As the 20th century has advanced, it has become increasingly (and more self-consciously) "moderne". Yet, at the same time our era has also witnessed a renewal of a deep interest in the classical past, particularly Greece. For this reason, notes Peyre, "une revue générale des survivances et des influences antiques dans la France [contemporaine] devrait mentionner un très grand nombre de noms."[1] Given the format of this collection of essays, it was obviously not possible to examine all the authors he mentions as having been influenced by antiquity, nor to explore in depth the various classical elements that have marked French literary production since 1900. However, the essays that follow—centering particularly on Péguy, Gide, Giono, Giraudoux, Sartre, and Malraux—are very representative, in that they exemplify the major ways in which antiquity has remained a living force in our contemporary literary world through the works of some of France's greatest authors.

The Catholic Socialist Charles Péguy, one of the dominant figures of the opening years of the 20th century, occupies a major place both in the history of "religious" literature and in that of social commitment. Yet, paradoxically, this modern Christian was also profoundly marked by certain elements from the West's pagan past. As Professor Guy makes clear in the following essay, Péguy was deeply influenced by his "classical" education. Moreover he was virtually unique among modern authors in that his first-hand knowledge of the texts of the ancient authors strongly marked his own use of language and gave him what Peyre has called a "style de pesant hoplite . . . fortement marqué de cicéronianisme."[2] Indeed, Professor Guy's careful and illuminating analysis of several passages clearly reveals Péguy's deliberate and skillful use of an astonishing number of classical rhetorical devices.

In spite of a profound Christian commitment, Péguy considered some figures in the ancient pagan world to be eminently worthy moral guides. Like Voltaire, Zola, and many other French intellectuals of various periods, he saw the timeless human value that certain of the heroes of antiquity had, and he realized—as he once put it—that "c'est souvent d'une âme païenne que l'on fait la meilleure âme chrétienne."[3] In an unusual way, this ardent Catholic "a réalisé harmonieusement en lui la conciliation du paganisme et du christianisme en retrouvant tout ce que la cité antique incarnait de pur, de pieux, et de sacré. "[4] In the concluding section of his essay, Professor Guy makes a provocative examination of this aspect of Péguy's relationship with antiquity, showing the extent to which the moral voice of the classical world may still have meaning for men of today.

Notes

[1] Henri M. Peyre, *L'Influence des littératures antiques sur la littérature française moderne* (New Haven-Oxford, 1941), pp. 73-74.

[2] Peyre, *op. cit.*, p. 77.

[3] Cited by Peyre (p. 78), from Péguy's *Clio.*

[4] Peyre, *op. cit.*, p. 78.

NOTES ON PÉGUY AND ANTIQUITY

By Basil Guy

More than twenty-five years have passed since Professor Peyre suggested (in *L'Influence des littératures antiques sur la littérature française moderne*) that a study ought to be made "de l'imprégnation de Rome et de la Grèce dont Péguy... reste entre 1900 et 1914 le plus frappant exemple."[1] To be sure, there are many references to classical antiquity in Péguy's not inconsiderable production and many indications of its influence on him, but surprisingly Professor Peyre's call to action seems to have gone unheeded, although many another suggestion in his book has borne fruit. Perhaps this is because too many find the particular topic of Péguy and antiquity familiar or self-evident, and so take it for granted.[2] In any case, the present study will attempt to elucidate this problem and hopefully will serve as a spur for further, more probing investigations, particularly of Péguy's style.[3] Indeed, at the risk of vitiating this undertaking by too brief and too narrow a perspective, we would here sketch the known facts of Péguy's classical studies and his continuing interest in Greek and Latin. After some consideration of their pervasive influence on his thought and expression, we would attempt in the last few pages to suggest the extent to which classicism and the classical world were major factors in his formation.

I

"Ce n'est pas mon idée." This blunt statement is supposed to have been the reply of the ten-year-old Péguy to his curé's proposal that he enter the seminary and study to be a priest. For many a later commentator, this declaration of 1883 marks the beginning of his spiritual itinerary—one which would have him begin life as a full-fledged socialist and end a "convert" to Roman Catholicism. While the attitudes represented by these two ideologies are not incompatible and are indeed subsumed in all that Péguy thought and did,[4] the usual point of departure for most of his biographers is his ardent, if uncertain, socialism—with all the term implied under the Third Republic. Such a view is possible because Péguy himself helped to formulate it and keep it alive, just as in *l'Argent* he wrote about his introduction to the world of "l'école laïque":

M. Naudy me rattrapa si je puis dire par la peau du cou et avec une bourse municipale me
fit entrer en sixième à Pâques, dans l'excellente sixième de M. Guerrier. *Il faut qu'il fasse du
latin*, avait-il dit: c'est la même forte parole qui aujourd'hui retentit victorieusement en
France de nouveau depuis quelques années. Ce que fut pour moi cette entrée dans cette
sixième à Pâques, l'étonnement, la nouveauté devant *rosa, rosae*, l'ouverture de tout un
monde, tout autre, de tout un nouveau monde, voilà ce qu'il faudrait dire, mais voilà ce
qui m'entraînerait dans des tendresses. Le grammairien qui une fois la première ouvrit la
grammaire latine sur la déclinaison de *rosa, rosae*, n'a jamais su sur quels parterres de
fleurs il ouvrait l'âme de l'enfant.[5]

Although Péguy started with a certain handicap he quickly made up for
time lost in earlier educational establishments. As early as 1887 he went to
the head of his class and stayed there until he graduated from the lycée. He
shone not only in arithmetic, drawing, religious instruction, and French,
but also—and most important to us here—in Greek and Latin. Meanwhile
the youth rose to appreciate the dignity of intellectualism, even as he drank
from the richest and deepest sources of culture. He would later recall the
happiness he felt when learning from his teachers stories more wonderful
than those his grandmother had taught, stories about Priam at the feet of
Achilles, Prometheus on his craggy mountain-top, Oedipus and Andromache.[6] Yet, here, as Bernard Guyon has said:

Il s'agirait d'établir le bilan de la culture de Péguy. Cette enquête reste à faire. Bien
conduite, poussée à fond, elle aboutirait à des résultats assez inattendus.... Reconnaissons
pourtant le caractère privilegié que les grandes cultures classiques avaient à ses yeux,
conservant jusqu'au bout cette fraîcheur embaumée d'un parterre de roses qu'elles avaient
eue lorsqu'il y fut introduit aux Pâques fleuries de 1885... Le sens de la pureté, de la
fatalité, du sacré dans la vie quotidienne, de la grandeur du héros et du suppliant, de la
Cité, de l'ordre militaire, des réalités temporelles, de la suprématie des lois non-écrites sur
les ordres du tyran, voilà les biens précieux qu'il a reçus des Anciens.[7]

In 1891-1892 Péguy spent a year at the Lycée Lakanal, where he
received first prize in Latin translation, second in Latin composition and an
honorable mention in Greek.[8] At the end of that same year he failed in his
first attempt to pass the entrance examination to that forcing-house of
French intellectuals, the Ecole Normale Supérieure. Whatever the reasons
for this surprising reversal of fortune, Péguy made a fair showing in classics
and received on the written examination 7.5 in Latin composition, 2.5 in
Latin translation, 3.5 in Greek translation, and, on the oral 5 in Latin and
4.5 in Greek. His grades generally, including classics, were less good when
he sat again for the examination in November, 1893, because he had spent
the intervening twelvemonth as a recruit doing his military service at
Orléans. Then, fortunately, he received a scholarship that allowed him to
continue his preparation for entrance to the Ecole while studying another
year in Paris, at the collège Sainte-Barbe.

Among his teachers, both early and late, pride of place is taken by that
M. Naudy mentioned in our first quotation. Although Péguy begins
l'Argent with a paean to this early master, Jules Isaac claims that his
presentation is otherwise calculated, adding that later there would be "le
père Edet" or "pater Edeas," an excellent teacher of Greek, as well as a

professor named Bompard. The influence of these individuals—all of whom were classicists—was most important for the aspiring scholar.[9] Inspired as he was by them, and with a renewed sense of faith in himself, Péguy was no less inspired—if we are to believe the Tharauds' biography— by the associations of what has since become the sentimental symbol of these years, "la cour rose" of Sainte-Barbe. There

> L'antiquité grecque et romaine qui ne se présentait guère à nous que sous les apparences d'un manège où nous faisions nos exercices, était pour Péguy quelque chose d'aussi passionné qu'une grève de mineurs à Carmaux. C'est qu'il aimait l'antiquité comme nous autres, nous ne pouvions pas l'aimer. Nous étions de jeunes bourgeois qui étions bêtement passés de la septième à la sixième, et cela n'avait pas été un drame dans notre histoire d'enfant. D'avance les études classiques étaient inscrites au programme de notre vie. Mais elles ne l'étaient pas du tout au programme de Péguy. Après le certificat d'études, on l'avait mis à l'école primaire supérieure d'Orléans. Son destin semblait réglé. Jamais il ne ferait connaissance avec Homère et Virgile. Par bonheur il y avait [eu] M. Naudy![10]

As a result, not only did Péguy receive excellent grades for his work at Sainte-Barbe, and, on graduation, a second prize for Greek translation and an honorable mention for Latin translation, but in 1894 he also succeeded at last in passing the entrance examination to the Ecole. This time, on the written examination he received 10.5 in Latin composition, 4.25 in Latin translation, 4 in Greek translation, while his scores were more equal on the oral: 7 in Latin and 6 in Greek. Péguy's grand total of 74.25 (written and oral in all subjects) was therefore sufficient for him to be placed sixth on the immatriculation register. While such scores may not be truly relevant, and while they may be differently interpreted, sheding a not-too-glorious light on either the system or the professorate, these records do show that Péguy was sufficiently qualified both to read and write Greek and Latin with some ease.[11] Moreover his competency enabled him to supplement his income (both at Sainte-Barbe and later) by tutoring less-talented students in Latin, and he even introduced his son Marcel to the *Iliad* by translating it with him during 1912.[12] (To be sure, in *Clio* he admits that in this last undertaking he had recourse to the translation of P. Giguet, as elsewhere he acknowledges the revelatory powers of Leconte de Lisle's transliterations;[13] but these admissions should in no way modify our appreciation of the thoroughness of his classical training.) .

Until the year he spent at Sainte-Barbe, Péguy's culture was entirely bookish. Indeed, it would remain largely so throughout his life. This explains why he was so concerned by the touted educational reforms of 1902 that—as he saw it—would lessen the value of classical studies by introducing a "modern" program and relegating the study of Greek to the fourth, from the fifth, form.[14] Nonetheless, there was another aspect of the classical heritage with which Péguy would come into contact during 1893-1894 and by which he would greatly profit in the years to come.[15] During the winter season, on his free days, he frequented the Comédie Française, where Julia Bartet was appearing in *Antigone*. Despite the poor lighting and sets, and Vacquerie's atrocious verse, the Tharauds still felt that Péguy was deeply moved, carried away by the drama, the prestige, and the rhapsody of a distant creation whose sentiments were not new, but were, rather, the timeless expression of constants in the human condition.[16] Certainly, this was for Péguy an exciting period, one in which were mixed pell-mell not only Mme Bartet and Antigone, but also Aeneas, Edet, Oedipus, and Mounet-Sully. The letters which he wrote to Camille Bidault at this time reveal the light-heartedness and joy, the zest for life which is so clearly reflected in his preoccupation with such mundane pastimes as the theatre and music.

> Voici ce qu'on fait: on n'y joue plus *Antigone*. On n'y joue plus *Oedipe-Roi*. Alors, j'entends de la musique. Une ingénieuse combinaison m'a permis d'entendre à l'œil la *Walkyrie* samedi soir, qui m'a plu, mais qui m'a aussi effaré un peu... Dimanche au tantôt, je suis allé au Colonne entendre le *Requiem* de Berlioz... En sortant j'ai rencontré Bartet, rue de Rivoli, et je l'ai regardée marcher avec un sentiment harmonieux d'art parfait que je ne dirai pas aux Barbares.[17]

These preoccupations were still predominant in Péguy's life in the summer of 1894 when he made a kind of pagan "pilgrimage" to Orange—a journey undertaken in almost mystic enthusiasm. In retrospect, this trip to the south of France to see Mounet-Sully play Oedipus in the Roman amphitheatre may have had certain religious overtones, as well as humorous ones (he was concerned about the funds which, for once, his mother was able to provide). Moreover, in a letter to Leon Deshairs in which he referred to this incident as "la bataille d'Orange," he told of his delight and expectations.[18] But for Péguy the trip was evidently to be a sort of commemoration as well, a thanksgiving to Greece and to classical antiquity for all they had done to bring him to the threshold of manhood. The experience at Orange was something he would always remember. And although there were other pilgrimages, only once thereafter was he to travel so far from Paris.

With his involvement in the Dreyfus case, his early politicizing, his editing of the *Cahiers de la Quinzaine*, and ultimately his religious preoccupations, detailed considerations like the foregoing become more difficult; Péguy the man merges with his work. And yet the classical influence remains, forming and informing whatever portrait one would wish to draw. Even though traces of the thematic and stylistic inspiration of Greece remain after, roughly, 1900, there is a much more pronounced and more easily recognized influence of the civilization and language of Rome. The reasons for such a change in perspective are not hard to find, if we realize that, for Péguy, the interaction of the ancient and modern worlds had produced only three cultures worthy of note: Greek, Roman and French (II:180). Such being the case, the latter owed less to Greece than to Rome, and the Latinity of French culture was oriented in a way that could of necessity only underline the debt owed to the Church of Rome and Christianity.

Whereas Péguy's principal (and favourite) Greek inspiration was derived from Homer, Hesiod, Aeschylus and Sophocles, among the Latins it was largely Horace and Vergil. Yet Vergil had early been applauded for expressing sentiments that did not conform too strictly to preconceived notions of ancient pagan thought (particularly in the Middle Ages, when he was frequently mentioned with those prophets who had foretold the coming of Christ) and, as a result, he had not been deemed unworthy to be Dante's guide through the nether regions of the *Divine Comedy*.[19] Péguy makes scarcely any mention of Roman historians and of authors like Lucretius and Cicero,[20] but there are references to texts like Bk VI of the *Aeneid* and the fourth *Bucolic* which point the way to Saint Augustine, and Augustine to Pascal and other writers of 17th century France.[21] In these classical works, Péguy found one more confirmation of the parallel between the ancients and the moderns, its continuity and appositeness for his own purposes, and he was ultimately led to declare:

> Quand on dit les Anciens au regard des temps modernes, il faut entendre ensemble et les Anciens anciens et les anciens Chrétiens... Au regard du temps moderne l'antique et le chrétien vont ensemble... Le chrétien était autrefois antique (II: 1128).

Or again:

> Non seulement la spiritualité latine, non seulement le monde latin a dû prendre la forme du monde romain, mais tout le monde grec a dû prendre la forme du monde romain; et le monde chrétien a dû prendre la forme du monde romain. Et l'autre moitié du monde antique, les prophètes, pour une très grande part et peut-être pour tout, a été forcée de prendre la forme du monde romain (II: 1218).

Thus, in examining Péguy's "classicism", we are brought face to face with the fact that his early schooling had had a deeper, more pervasive effect on him than several of his partisan critics might care to acknowledge. Nor should we forget that Péguy the adolescent and budding classicist was indeed father of the man, and that the catechumen instructed in the (Latin) ways of Roman Catholicism made his first communion on 25 June, 1885. He himself took pains to point out that his predisposition toward the classical ideal—albeit in a religious context—was almost foreordained when he wrote:

> Tout est joué avant que nous ayons douze ans. Vingt ans, trente ans d'un travail acharné, toute une vie de labeur ne fera pas, ne défera pas ce qui a été fait, ce qui a été défait une fois pour toutes, avant nous, sans nous, pour nous, contre nous (II: 1099).

II

As for the way in which Péguy utilized his knowledge of Greek and Latin, a few words are necessary. The next paragraphs will attempt therefore to indicate some of the considerations essential to an understanding of classical influences on his style. It is not our intention to proceed here with a *Stilforschung* in the manner, say, of Spitzer, who has long since made a valuable contribution to this topic with his article *Zu Charles Péguy's Stil*.[22] Rather, by stressing certain rhetorical devices used by Péguy, sometimes to excess, we would suggest how his work might be analyzed before proceeding to explain why his classical sources and their expression are important to our understanding of him and his writings.

Given what has been said above, it would not be excessive to claim that those authors he preferred and whom he quotes most often were an open book to him. Were there any doubt about such statements, we need only recall his analysis of the expression *res publica* at the end (II:653-5) of *Notre Jeunesse*, or glance at the effulgent paragraph of the *Note Conjointe* where (admittedly for a private purpose) Péguy develops one of those antitheses for which he is famous, but humorously, imitating a pedantic classicist:

> *Duellum, bellum,* c'est le même mot. *Duellum,* c'est la forme en *du* qui est celle de *duo;* et *bellum,* c'est la forme en *b* qui a donné *bis.* Et la forme en *du* elle-même est la même forme que la forme en *b,* parce que *b* c'est le *v* qu'il y a en *dv* qui est le même que *du.* Et ceci n'est pas une charade. *Duellum, dvellum, bellum.* "*Duellum,* dit Bréal et Bailly, est encore employé, à côté de *bellum,* par les écrivains de l'époque classique." Horace, *Ep.* I, 2,7. Graecia barbariae lento col lisa duello. Id. *Od.* I, 14, 18. Et cadum Marsi memorem duelli. Le changement de *duellum* en *bellum* (le *v* s'étant changé en *b* et le *d* initial étant tombé) est pareil à celui de *duonus* en *bonus.* Le nom propre Duilius est de même devenu Bilius. Dans *perduellio,* au contraire, le *d* est resté: remarquer le sens particulier de ce mot, qui s'applique au crime de lèse-majesté; *per* est probablement le préfixe péjoratif qu'on a dans *perjurium, perdere, perire.—Bis* est pour *duis;* en grec, c'est le *v* qui a disparu (δίς pour δυίς). Et il avait dit à l'article des Dérivés: "Ils se partagent en deux séries, ceux en *du* (dualis, duellum), ceux en *b* par changement de *du* en *dv-, b-* (b-is, b-ellum)." Et il ajoute: "Un ancien dérivé du nom de nombre "deux" est le préfixe *dis* (voyez ce mot)." De sorte que lorsque nous disons discerner, dissoudre, distinguer, disséquer, nous disons bien résoudre en deux, couper en deux. Et *dissection* est le même mot que *dichotomie* (II: 1422).

There is no need to enumerate, either, the many instances when Péguy has recourse to Greek and Latin expressions in his writings. As an example, one might note the classic inspiration behind the titles of his three "Situations", where an imitation of Caesar or of Cicero (*De Bello Gallico, De Senectute*) is very evident.[23] Some of the other terms Péguy chooses to employ are equally informative, especially when we consider the way in which he twists them to suit his needs in a polemic dictated by circumstance. Yet never is the word or term improper. Whoever has leafed through *Clio* and the "dialogue" entitled *Véronique* in the Pléiade edition, is surely aware of the extent of Péguy's classic vocabulary and of the masterfulness with which he can bring it into play for effects of sarcasm or piety. One possible explanation, particularly of the Latin vocabulary in Péguy's poetry, has been offered by Albert Béguin:

> Sans doute prend-il un plaisir manifeste à enfermer dans ses quatrains français tout le trésor des termes latins qu'il aimait depuis le temps de ses études (et qui lui redevenaient plus présents et plus chers tandis qu'à l'époque même de la composition d'*Eve,* il refaisait du latin et du grec avec son fils aîné). Il y a dans ces accumulations de vocables antiques la candide exaltation du collégien qui aux premières lectures du *De viris illustribus* ou de Tite-Live ou de Virgile, s'émerveille de pénétrer par les mots dans un monde inconnu. Dans la grisaille de l'ennui des classes de latin, dans la morne tristesse que dégage la réalité romaine elle-même, surtout pour ceux qui sont déjà initiés au monde hellénique, n'avons-

nous pas tous connu cette impression d'un mystère malgré tout séduisant? Et l'on sait combien Péguy adolescent fut accessible à ce genre de surprises heureuses et sérieuses. Tout lui revint en mémoire maintenant, dans un jeu interminable d'associations de mots et d'images: le droit romain et l'armature de la cité, les magistratures et les légations, la légion et les mercenaires, le système métrique et les répartitions agraires, la conquête, l'empire, les guerres d'Orient et d'Afrique, les peuples asservis, les routes, les monuments, la prose latine — l'œuvre entière de Rome.[24]

It is rather more interesting, and certainly more informative to consider how Péguy's style (or at least that aspect of his writing composed of repetitions and playing on syllables of like sounds) is created. In addition to a certain indigenous heaviness that characterizes many of his most representative passages, there is also present an element owing more than has been admitted to his imitation of Latin models.[25] This suggests that his work may be somewhat Ciceronian—but in the best sense, free and open, and not restrictive. In order to present our appreciation with some coherence, we would call attention to that passage of the essay "A nos amis, à nos abonnés" (1909) familiarly entitled "O drapeaux du passé," found in volume two of the Pléiade edition, beginning page 20 with "Alors il y avait de la boue..." and ending on page 22 with "—se relevant comme eux." In this passage, Péguy is attempting to describe the flags of the forces before Valmy in order to equate his animistic description of them with those feelings of depression and defiance that characterized the morale of the Revolutionary army and which, in 1909, for various other reasons obsessed Péguy himself.

Beginning with the mud on the fields, Péguy repeats the word "boue" several times, in much the same way, as Danton had used the word "audace" at the very historical moment being described. After a brief lapse into an apostrophe to the reader which is familiar in tone ("vous vous rappelez"), Péguy implicitly personifies the mud, which then speaks to the wagonmasters: "Où sont vos martyrs... héros... ... victimes?" Then the author interrupts with another aside and indulges in an hyperbole of vast proportions that, allied with and applied to the series "martyrs, héros, victimes," strikes us forcibly because of the repetition of several excessive terms: centaines, milliers, centaines de milliers. Then in a sentence some twenty lines long he elaborates that repetition of suffixes in "-ant, -ants, -ent, -ente" so neatly analysed by Spitzer[26] and the paranomasia deriving therefrom, reinforced by the repetition of the word "même". This is followed by a series of rhetorical questions posed either by the animated mud, the author, a combination of the two, or even by the alert reader, and Péguy goes through the same verbal gymnastics with the words "clameurs" and "blés". Suddenly, from the "blés" our attention is turned to the flags of the nearly overwhelmed troops, the pennons and guidons which—as the attack begins—are dragging in the same mud that nourished the "blés". The flags, a symbol of Revolutionary idealism, and the crude reality of the mud are as one. But Péguy's epic imagination takes charge and, with almost the same stylistic means as before, he visualizes the flags as men. Working from one to the other, he fills the page with such a vision of

animated, sentient things, that the last lines of this passage are almost
perfectly interwoven with human discouragement and affective description.
The words "comme eux"—with a pause on the mute *e* of "comme"—are
then introduced at varying intervals like a drumbeat or a heart, wavering
and unsure, before the charge. Not only are the words "comme eux"
repeated, but on occasion other adjectives taken together with them are
repeated too. Thus it is clear that Péguy achieves a powerful, extremely
pathetic effect in this passage because of his very skillful use of a combination of several classic rhetorical devices: alliteration, anaphora, climax,
hyperbole, metaphor, and paranomasia. Further examination would reveal
other such devices.

Shortly before the middle of this last movement, Péguy reverts to one of
those asides to the reader that, in another context, might break the surging
advance of the prose and destroy the effect, not only by reason of its
abruptness, but also by reason of the tone which is both familiar and ironic.
Such at any rate seems the value of the phrase beginning "Parbleu!" and
ending "car c'est très drôle." Yet the pathos is heightened by this
interruption which is not so gratuitous as might at first appear. For again,
in the closing lines, Péguy picks up where he had left off, repeating in more
and more distressed fashion the phrase "comme eux", until the antithesis
toward which his every thought and effort have been tending all the while
(like the flags of the Revolutionaries struggling toward a military objective)
is suddenly stated baldly, beyond the rupture occasioned by the aposiopesis
of "se relevant comme eux."[27]

Now, if in such an unexceptional example of Péguy's prose we can
discern the various elements of classical rhetoric which went to compose his
style, how much more true this must be of the more famous and brilliant of
his verbal displays! Without repeating here the excellent remarks of Spitzer
on Péguy's use of chiasmus (p. 328), high style and low (p. 338), "zweier-
rythmus" (p. 357), etc. we should point out that from a purely technical
point of view, Péguy's work is oratorical in the extreme. Because of the
gradually increasing emphasis which is to be found in almost every text he
wrote, many of the effects of oversimplification and repetition which until
recently have given the impression of uncultured (and unworthy) peasant
imitations may have been written to be read aloud, "gueulés" in the
market-place and not studied in the library. This was of course much the
case with the great orators of antiquity, from Demosthenes onward, who
also happened to be great writers. In other words, classical rhetoric
provided the skeleton for Péguy's thought, leaving him free to embroider
on it with whatever vocabulary seemed best suited to his needs. It is
likewise worth noting in this connection, as Bernard Guyon has pointed
out,[28] that Péguy's favourite form of composition seems to have been the
dialogue. For if his prose works are as speeches, every speech is intended
for an audience. The audience may not be able to reply and take an active
part in the dialogue, but consciously or not, many a text by Péguy was
written with an audience in mind, whence his *ars bene dicendi* is also—and
primarily—an *ars persuadendi*, in the same "classic" sense as that of his
models.

III

We have already suggested the extent to which Péguy's early work was but a prelude to his later writings, that it contained in germ many of the ideas and almost all the technical devices he would exploit at the height of his career. But we should not forget that the devices themselves represented a corpus of thought and attitudes to which Péguy was constantly drawn and which he would develop at length, although adapted and sometimes difficult to recognize. In other words, the mainstay of Péguy's inspiration, inseparable from the man himself, was a constant classical source. Greco-Roman antiquity not only provided him with a frame of reference or form, but it coincided with, governed and buttressed his every mode of thought. For the word Antiquity is writ large in practically everything he undertook. Antiquity, not perhaps as the historians see it, but rather as Péguy himself saw it through his souvenirs and above all as he would reconstruct it to suit his own ideas and the needs of his polemics.

To a great degree, the ancient world of Péguy is highly personal and as little historic as the Middle Ages of Claudel's *l'Annonce faite à Marie*. But though his view of Antiquity is a tendentious one, coloured by the ancient fables told by his teachers at Orléans, nevertheless it enabled him to feel that he was part of a chain linking the modern world with a human reality a hundred times more real and true than the one in which he had to live and work. His preference became even more pronounced as time went on. Not for him Euripides, "ce méprisable" (II:257, 779), guilty of modernism and parlous tendencies; rather, it was Homer, Aeschylus, and Sophocles who continued to hold his interest. In them be pretended he had found the Ancient World, a temple of purity. This purity allowed no half-measures in human comportment, presented no middle ground for understanding the race or men or—indeed—the man Péguy himself. Impelled by the language of the Ancients, Péguy also adopted their moral attitudes, for they were most consonant with his own. The result was, as we have mentioned, a tendency to idealistic intransigence and absoluteness. Péguy would ever show his innermost feelings in those great antitheses by which he is perhaps most readily remembered today: Ancient-Modern, pagan-religious, Antiquity-Christianity, Catholicism-Socialism, and mystique-politique.

His method was the most direct imaginable. No criticism, no glosses; the classical text and nothing but the text would be the basis of his study (cf. II:252f). His intense interest in the text was not the same as that of the philologist or the historian. A few lines suficed for him to savour that purity he so admired and desired. "Une ligne, un mot, éclairent un monde" (II:244). A chorus from Sophocles, a word of two from the poets brought him that certainty which the reader could then interpret for himself. Thus the classics, read, meditated and re-read over fifteen or more years, were newly illuminated for Péguy, and they also served to illuminate the human condition as he saw it.

Without going into detail, one can note four broad stages in this spiritual itinerary toward a total view of Man's condition. These stages are marked by the inspiration of four figures from the classical world: in 1897,

Antigone and the lesson of revolt; in 1905 Oedipus, the man of infinite compassion; in 1912 Achilles with his heroic purity; and, lastly in 1914, Polyeucte and the sense of vocation. It is these that we propose to examine briefly here.

When contemplating the first *Jeanne d'Arc*, Péguy wrote, "Je suis dans un état d'esprit, je ne sais pourquoi, à ne me déranger que pour du théâtre de génie, pour du Sophocle, du Corneille." From this statement Jules Isaac concludes that the "théâtre de génie" was probably at the root of the dramatic form in which Péguy then composed.[29] A further examination of this text would convince us of what Péguy's companion had only surmised. For, if Jeanne d'Arc is Péguy's favourite heroine in modern times, Antigone remained his favourite in antiquity and not without influence on his idea of the former. In his eyes both these women are eternal witnesses to the supremacy of the moral law and of the categorical imperative. They are not only witnesses; they are models and symbols as well. Of the two, Antigone was probably the more powerful evocation of what Péguy saw himself attempting with his 1897 activities in the Dreyfus affair, for she too had disobeyed the Law in order to remain true to Truth and Justice. She was nonetheless the elder sister of Jeanne d'Arc, condemned to death for refusing to compromise. This classical example haunted Péguy, for he seems not only to remember, but at one point even to imitate the dialogues between Antigone and Ismene (v. 1-99, 536-560) when he has Hauviette serve as a foil to the revolt of Jeanne in their conversations (*OPC*, pp. 952-967, 974-988). Undoubtedly Antigone lived as surely for him as her historic counterpart, since in one day her fate was made real and her destiny fulfilled. And so, the impetus toward the theater which moved Péguy at the beginning of his career was spurred by his realization of the ultimate tragedy of man's fate. And nowhere was that tragedy better expressed than in ancient examples of moral revolt such as Antigone (cf. I:195f, II:117f). It is notable that in this context politics provided the next direct inspiration for such reflections by Péguy.

On 22 January 1905, a procession of workers in Saint-Petersbourg, led by an otherwise obscure priest, Father Gapon) was proceeding to the palace to lay grievances before the Tsar when when they were fired on by troops. Péguy, who never lacked compassion, thought fit to comment on this incident by establishing a parallel between the revolt of the Russian people and the chorus of Sophocles' *Oedipus*. Although he believed he had made a successful literary composition, today's readers usually find that this work, *Les Suppliants parallèles*, is marred by the considerable difference in tone which separates the call of a people, touched by a mysterious fatality, to their natural leader and the respectful request which the workers addressed to their sovereign. Péguy is even less convincing when he makes Father Gapon the leader of a classic chorus in order to prove to French socialists that the manoeuvre of 22 January was not a revolutionary movement. A corresponding change in the roles of Oedipus and Nicholas II suggests that for Péguy the purpose of the debate in this tragedy was not to know who was guilty, but rather who would suffer most. This expression of his all-encompassing pity is more like those found in his writings posterior to 1905. It is so deeply akin to them in its religious feeling, that, as Jules Isaac has noted, we would not be amiss in seeing here a "porche du mystère" of Péguy's genius.[30]

By 1912, however, Péguy's thought had evolved so far as to suggest to him an essay "Sur la pureté antique" (cf. II: 250). Although he never wrote it, the very topic is important for understanding the influence of classical culture on him. Simply because the "accidents of the modern world" were for Péguy so upsetting and so devastating, nothing could be more simple, more attractive or more grand than Antiquity with its essential moral refinement, including the contrast of heroes with death, or, of heroism with eternity. The lesson afforded by his interpretation was never much appreciated by Péguy's contemporaries except in regard to some aspects of the Dreyfus case. There, like ancient heroes, certain dreyfusards rose against the inauthenticity of human law and struggled against a "vérité d'Etat," even as Péguy himself disobeyed the socialist party doctrine which pretended to assert itself through official truths. Thus, of all the basic realities of human existence, there was one which daily became more familiar to Péguy and which little by little, gave new meaning to his own struggle: the sacrifice of all, including self, to the greater good of the race. Such a sacrifice meant the struggle of man with man, party with party, nation with nation, and war. But of this last alternative, Péguy was not afraid; he harked back to the early lessons in which he had learned of the death of Achilles. The hero's fate was choice, for there had happened to him "ce qu'il y a peut-être de plus grand dans le monde, et de plus beau et de plus grand dans Homère; d'être tranché dans sa fleur, de périr inachevé, de mourir jeune dans un combat militaire" (II: 260). Such was not only the fate of Achilles, but the fate of thousands of others, the fate of innumerable mortals, the fate which would strike Péguy himself a few years later.

Yet, faced by such a text as this last, we are embarrassed. Are there not implicit in these plaints overtones of the language of salvation, the language of Christianity? Undoubtedly, only one additional step was necessary to change the advancement of his heroes into a saintly ascension—and for the misfortune of mankind to be transformed into an eminent dignity. However, Péguy did not yet take this step (as least not in his published writings), for he still insisted on conducting his examination independently of any reference to Christianity or, more specifically, to the doctrines of the Church of Rome. But as he and his readers penetrated further into the mystery of the universe, Christianity became ever more important.

Nowhere was it so important, though, as in the third "Situation" (1907) and in the *Note Conjointe* (1914), where his by-now famous analyses of Corneille's tragedy *Polyeucte* with its hero (and heroine) reflect faithfully, as in a mirror, a key position in the development of Péguy's own attitudes (I: 1200-1203; II: 1391 *passim*). Not only was the hero transformed into a saint; the pagan became Christian, the Latin Roman, the Ancient Modern, the secular religious—and through the intervention of divine grace, all stood revealed in Polyeucte's vocation. As Péguy attempted to distinguish between these polarities, he underlined their importance to him, especially the second element in every pair, thanks to the dialectic which classical rhetoric had taught him and which had found fertile ground in his own nature. By opposing these elements he was able to synthesize them more easily in the figure of the hero-saint à la Polyeucte, the repentant hero a saint, the symbol of a spiritual victory through which the Cid, in Péguy's eyes, became Polyeucte.

According to Péguy, a hero like the Cid gambles on his life in order to find an ideal, gratuitously, and not necessarily with the intention of realizing that ideal; for the idea of being crowned with laurel and earning a place in history does not even cross his mind. On the other hand, the saint gambles with his life consciously in order to win eternity; or, rather, his every fibre is tense with straining after saintliness in a calculated risk, the expectation of positive achievement. To be sure, this ascetic passion, this most difficult struggle against man, nature, and life itself, which forces the supernatural to be of this world, will ultimately receive its reward. Péguy therefore leans toward and even prefers a military saintliness, an earthly battle waged for God with every opportunity for heroism, but in another context. This rare combination and unique possibility was best realized for him in Polyeucte, about whom he makes this final clear and essential distinction:

> J'aime fort peu cette expression, les saints laïques. Elle est maîtresse de confusion et d'erreur. Mais réduite à la figure, et au sens de la figure, elle est profonde et réelle et vraie. Il y a bien eu dans le monde antique un certain réduit, il y a bien eu dans la philosophie et dans la sagesse antiques une certaine citadelle, il y a bien eu dans le monde laïque et dans le monde profane un certain sacré et c'était le stoïcisme qui avait été chargé de fournir ce sacré, de donner ce qui seul pouvait annoncer laïquement, temporellement figurer le saint et le martyr: le héros et déjà peut-être le martyr.
>
> Comme tous les vraiment grands chrétiens, Pascal se gardait de mépriser l'antique. Il savait trop qu'il y avait eu Rome et la Grèce. Et la philosophie et la sagesse antiques. Et une pensée laïque et une pensée profane. Et même une science antique. Et une véritable figuration temporelle. Il savait trop qu'il y avait eu la cité antique. Et allant, comme il faisait toujours, au cœur même du débat, et allant tout de suite, comme géomètre, aux maxima, il avait bien vu que le stoïcisme donnait, était chargé de donner le maximum de la grandeur antique *sub specie*, au point de vue de la grandeur chrétienne, le maximum de la nature au point de vue de recevoir la grâce, le maximum du héros (et du martyr) au point de vue du saint et du martyr, le maximum de l'homme sans Dieu au point de vue de Dieu, le maximum du monde sans Dieu au point de vue de Dieu (II: 1449).

The true summation of all these tendencies would appear late in 1913, in the poem *Eve*. Péguy considered this enormous work, written in a sort of divine frenzy, nothing less than another *Iliad*.[31] Since it is a work of the imagination and not of criticism, nowhere is the dialectic of his mind more evident nor more complete. He himself was the first to admit as much, notably in the commentary which he published in the *Bulletin des professeurs catholiques* for 1914. As one critic has summed it up:

> Sans être aussi élaborée que dans un dialogue, cette immense question de la vocation temporelle de la Grèce et de Rome est présentée avec tous les caractères d'une extrême gravité et sous une forme particulièrement saisissante dans une des parties capitales de cette *Eve*.

C'est ce que Péguy dans *l'Argent suite* avait déjà nommé le berceau temporel. Il est certain que cette sorte d'insertion du temporel dans l'éternel et réciproquement, du charnel dans le spirituel et réciproquement, de la nature dans la grâce et réciproquement, est l'articulation centrale du mystère de la destination de l'homme.[32]

In effect, such a mingling had been constant in Péguy's life and thought from the very beginning. Just as there was commitment both to socialism and to Christianity throughout his brief existence, so was there an accompanying response to classicism and to the moral lesson of the classical world. As early as 1907, Péguy was declaring that the dialogue between pagan solidarity and Christian charity was ever one, and that grace would be found wherever and however possible—a truly divine manifestation of the ancient classical triumph, but in the modern world.[33]

With his exploration of an increasingly closed religious frame of reference, the path of his future development seemed ever more clear. Little by little he turned to those French authors, especially of the seventeenth century (but we must not omit the name of Hugo from such a consideration) who had come closest to imitating and continuing the classical procedures of the Ancients, and in whom he recognized kindred souls. This is particularly true of Corneille, but it applies as well to La Fontaine, La Bruyère, Bossuet, and most of all to Pascal—all of whom had been visited by the "grace" of classical antiquity and so had become—as we now recognize—classics themselves. In this context it seems highly significant that the last work Péguy is supposed to have written before departing for the front in that fateful August of 1914 is the *Note conjointe*, a text which contains a rather full development on classical qualities. Indeed, we may apply to this text, as characteristic of all those which had preceded it, that judgment which Péguy had formulated earlier about his own work:

En un temps où tant de politiciens de la littérature et tant de politiciens de la politique croient qu'être classique c'est transférer en romantique, c'est dénaturer, c'est traiter *romantiquement* les matières traditionnelles classiques, saluons un classique qui est classique sans le faire exprès, par l'articulation naturelle de son esprit, sans s'en être fait ni un programme ni un exercice, par sa nature enfin, par son être même, organiquement.[34]

Thus, in sketching the development of Péguy's debt to the Greco-Roman tradition, we have arrived at that conclusion which was implicit in our consideration of Péguy and antiquity from the beginning: he is a classicist, but he is also a classic. Further examination would not infirm this conclusion but would simply confirm it in a wider context and in greater detail. It is not our intention to analyse here those traits in Péguy which make him a "classic", but classic he certainly is. Notwithstanding his peasant vocabulary, his inordinate love of repetitions and punning the quasi-liturgical incantations and other anti-classical devices that one may discern in his work, beneath these outward signs of disarray there is an order, a calculation and even a "grace" so organically suited to his nature (and to his material), that one cannot deny the ultimate classicism of the man as he himself defined it:

Cette exactitude classique, cette sorte de ponctualité géométrique, cette probité, cette honnêteté (par suite de cette totale liberté), cette dureté, cette pureté du classique, pour tout dire, cette nudité et pour dire encore plus cette pauvreté dans l'ordre de l'intention première, dans l'initial, dans la première poussée place instantanément l'auteur au cœur de son sujet. Dans le mode elle obtient constamment et du premier coup cette exactitude d'assemblage, cette absence de transition, cette absence de jointure qui fait consister la composition précisément en cette juxtaposition qu'il fallait. Mais elle ne donne pas seulement le germe et le lancement de l'œuvre et elle n'en donne pas seulement le mode. Elle en donne, elle en règle l'être même, car elle en donne ce qui exprime, ce qui manifeste l'être même, ce qui le traduit, ce qui le représente, ce qui est peut-être l'essentiel, elle donne le ton. Le ton étant le règlement de l'être même de l'œuvre.[35]

Péguy himself was ever aware of the great debt which he owed to both Greece and Rome. As the Tharauds long since pointed out, he was fond of saying "Je suis un classique de la première génération, je veux dire Sophocle et Corneille, et non de la deuxième, Euripide et Racine."[36] What more typical expression could they have found than this "Je suis un classique"? What more true?

And yet, at the same time, what more Romantic?

University of California
Berkeley

Notes

[1] *L'Influence des littératures antiques sur la littérature française moderne* (New Haven, 1941), p. 47.

[2] Whatever the reasons, there are, in the ever-growing canon of studies on the publisher-poet, titles by Albert Béguin, Bernard Guyon, Jules Isaac, Jean Onimus and Marjorie Villiers—to name only a few who have mentioned the problem. But in the material of more recondite essays, such as "Péguy et le sens de l'histoire" by Fr. J. Millet (CACP, LXI), where such a reference would seem to be implicit, there is scarcely any notice of Péguy and his relation to classical Greece and Rome. Only in the article by Simone Fraisse (*Esprit*, Nos. 8-9, 1964, pp. 317-330), primarily concerned with Péguy's use of ancient history, is there any attempt to assess the available materials and to interpret them. Although this study is both valid and valuable, the author's intention and point of view necessarily leave the essay on Péguy and antiquity invited by Professor Peyre still very much to be desired, and the relevance of his remarks as undeniable today as in 1941.

[3] There may be references to Péguy's classicism in Fr. J. Barbier's thesis, *Le Vocabulaire, la syntaxe et le style dans les poèmes religieux de Charles Péguy* (Paris, 1957), but this work was unavailable to us.

[4] As we have tried to make clear in *FSt* XV:i (1961), pp. 12-29.

[5] *Oeuvres complètes* (Paris, 1961), II:1130. Hereafter, references to this edition will be given in the text with a Roman numeral indicating the volume and an Arabic numeral the page.

[6] S. Fraisse, *loc. cit.*, p. 321.

[7] Bernard Guyon, *Péguy, l'homme et l'œuvre* (Paris, 1960), pp. 20-21.

[8] Jules Isaac, *Expériences de ma vie*, I (Paris, 1959), p. 45n.

[9] Id., pp. 53 and 302. Cf. Péguy, I:930, II:103, 869, 1099, 1131. The pun "pater Edeas" is noted in the Tharauds' *Notre cher Péguy* (Paris, 1926), I:34. For a sensible and farreaching criticism of this work (and others like it), see J. Isaac, op. cit., p. 337f. If we quote from the Tharauds, however, it is because, despite recent, better biographies, we are most familiar with theirs.

[10] J.-J. Tharaud, *op. cit.*, I:31-32.

[11] As J. Isaac has clearly shown, *op. cit.*, p. 303.

[12] Marjorie Villiers, *Péguy* (New York, 1965), p. 82; Péguy, II:103-104.

[13] Péguy, I:883f; cf. Bernard Guyon, *L'art de Péguy* (Paris, 1948), p. 26.

[14] S. Fraisse, *loc. cit.*, p. 319.

[15] Familiarity with Péguy's work should convince the reader that Péguy was not "visuel" and that he should discount any contact Péguy may have had with classical art at the Louvre and elsewhere.

[16] J.-J. Tharaud, *op. cit.*, I:46.

[17] Quoted by B. Guyon, *Péguy, l'homme et l'œuvre*, p. 28.

[18] The letters to Léon Deshairs have been presented in *FACP*, No. 38.

[19] Cf. the important article by Paul Maury, "Le secret de Virgile," *Lettres d'humanité* (Paris, 1944), III:71-147.

[20] Though cf. Péguy, I:546, II:231.

[21] Cf. the edition of Péguy's *Pascal* by Jules Riby (Paris, 1947).

[22] In *Stilstudien* (Munich, 1961), II:301-364.

[23] For matters involving Latin vocabulary, see for example Péguy's use of "monument" in *Par ce demi-clair matin*, "dévouer" in *Notre Jeunesse*, "obsession" in the *Note conjointe*, and his abuse of incohative forms (flavescente. ardescente) in *Victor-Marie comte Hugo*, as also his rare reference to Caesar in *Entre deux trains* (I:224).

[24] Albert Béguin, *Eve de Péguy* (Paris, 1948), p. 134.

[25] As, for instance, the cases of synesis, or agreement by attraction, in *Un nouveau théologien* (II:960), *L'Argent suite* (II:1200-1243), etc.

[26] Cf. L. Spitzer, *loc. cit.*, p. 323.

[27] "Ces formules détachées, isolées, c'est à l'intérieur même du texte pour lequel elles ont été écrites qu'il faut les replacer si l'on veut en goûter pleinement la saveur. Elles surgissent généralement à la fin d'un développement abondant dont elles relèvent la monotonie, auquel elles donnent sa signification décisive; elles sont comme des paliers qui nous permettent de

respirer. Ce n'est pas dans les entassements des vitrines de joailliers que nous admirons le mieux les bijoux, mais isolés, magnifiques et solitaires sur une poitrine étincelante de blancheur ou sur un sombre tissu de brocart ou de velours.

Quoi qu'il en soit, ces formules nous apportent la preuve que Péguy autant et mieux qu'aucun autre écrivain français, est capable d'un style qui utilise le raccourci et la concision. Le moins que nous puissions en conclure, c'est que, lorsqu'il use d'autres méthodes, en particulier du procédé de la répétition, ce n'est pas par impuissance, par suite de je ne sais quelle infirmité bavarde, mais bien parce qu'il le veut; parce qu'il vise à d'autres effets." Quoted from B. Guyon, *Art de Péguy*, p. 38. And, we might add, because his classical preparation had taught him not only how to make his point, but also what affective advantages might be gained thereby. Common examples of such misunderstanding are to be found in the Tharauds' appreciation of Péguy's style (II:4-15) and in Proust's dictum (or is it a boutade?).

[28] Id., p. 34.
[29] J. Isaac, *op. cit.*, p. 89. See also the letter to Deshairs, 15. viii. 95, *FACP*, No. 38.
[30] J. Isaac, *op. cit.*, p. 335.
[31] Quoted by B. Guyon, *Péguy, l'homme et l'œuvre*, p. 243.
[32] A Béguin, *op. cit.*, p. 218. See also pp. 216-217.
[33] B. Guyon, *Péguy, l'homme et l'œuvre*, p. 193.
[34] A. Béguin, *op. cit.*, p. 210.
[35] Id., p. 211.
[36] J.-J. Tharaud, *op. cit.*, I:35.

As many critics have pointed out, Greece played an important role in the poetic movements of the second half of the 19th century because the classical tradition was a rich source for the myths and symbols which the writers of the period required for their poetic statements. Not surprisingly, young Gide—closely associated with the Symbolists at the beginning of his literary career—was greatly interested in such classical materials. A recent study has presented a detailed account of his Hellenist background and shown the degree to which he remained generally preoccupied with Greek mythology throughout his lifetime.[1] Of course, as Professor Peyre notes, such preoccupations risked being infecund because from one point of view these "reprises de sujets cent fois traités" could stem from "la faiblesse secrète de tant d'auteurs modernes; le manque de fougue imaginative, la crainte de puiser à même la vie, souvent vulgaire et brutale, et la préférence pour la matière déjà épurée, sublimée, et filtrée par maints prédécesseurs."[2]

Peyre would also be the first to agree that in many cases a writer's particular transformation of traditional elements can be as revealing and as "original" as his entirely personal imaginative inventions. Wolfgang Holdheim's provocative essay indicates that this was certainly the case with Gide. In a remarkable way, his study illuminates the meaning of certain tragic mythological materials as used by Gide in three typical forms (a sotie, a play, and a récit), at three widely separated moments in his creative lifetime—1899, 1931, and 1946. We have seen that a man like Péguy was particularly attracted to the Greek tradition because of certain outstanding moral examples it offered, but Professor Holdheim makes it clear that in large part Gide's return to the Hellenist past was motivated by reasons that were essentially aesthetic: i.e., to enrich the language of a wide-ranging intellectual and artistic inquiry. Gide's use of Greek myths enabled him both to make a more resonant statement of his personal quests, and to add dimensions to his various artistic explorations.

Since Gide was a major figure in French literary life during the early years of the 20th century, it is not surprising that in retrospect he appears as a primary factor in what one critic has recently called the contemporary "renaissance of Greek mythological matter, transformed by the imagination of the 20th century."[3] Professor Holdheim's very skillful analysis of

Gide's use of such materials provides particularly meaningful insights into both the man and the literary artist, and makes more understandable how his example could have helped encourage a number of subsequent writers (as different as Giraudoux and Sartre) to see the contemporary meaning and aesthetic possibilities of this particular heritage from the classical past.

Notes

[1] For a recent detailed study of this general question, see Helen Watson-Williams, *André Gide and the Greek Myth: A Critical Study* (Oxford, 1967).

[2] Henri M. Peyre, *L'Influence des littératures antiques sur la littérature française moderne* (New Haven-Oxford, 1941), pp. 80-81.

[3] Watson-Williams, p. 12. See also Professor Peyre's essay, "What Greece Means to Modern France," in *Historical and Critical Essays* (University of Nebraska Press, 1968), p. 101.

GIDE AND THE ASSIMILATION OF TRAGEDY

By Wolfgang Holdheim

I

The Ironic Synthesis: Le Prométhée mal
enchaîné (1899)

Quand, du haut du Caucase, Prométhée eut bien éprouvé que les chaînes, tenons, camisoles, parapets et autres scrupules, somme toute, l'ankylosaient, pour changer de pose il se souleva du côté gauche, étira son bras droit et, entre quatre et cinq heures d'automne, descendit le boulevard qui mène de la Madeleine à l'Opéra.[1]

Prometheus' journey is impressive. One single sentence succeeds in carrying him all the way from his Caucasian rock to Paris. This spatial distance stands for an even greater temporal one, that between ancient Greece and the modern world. And even this does not exhaust Prometheus' feat. He passes from ideal to real space, from timelessness to time, from the universal locus of atemporal myth to a precisely determined spot that is subject to seasons (like "autumn") and other chronological definitions. We are privileged to watch the transition of the tragic spirit, represented by the Aeschylean hero, from its archetypal sphere to the setting of the modern realist novel where (like Valéry's detested marquise) one does trite things exactly at 5 p.m. Tragedy has become unchained, it has awakened. Its rebirth, and the problem of its assimilation: no subject could be more burning for a generation that has heard the voice of the author of the *Birth of Tragedy*. The passage, then, deserves careful scrutiny. How well does Prometheus' descent into the modern metropolis succeed?

Seemingly, it is not meant to be sudden and jolting. The author behaves as if he sought a smooth and natural transition. Why else would he, from the very outset, introduce elements that are foreign to the world of Aeschylus? I am referring to the tools of imprisonment. In *Prometheus Bound*, the hero was riveted to his rock by chains, wedges, nails, steel rings and girdles. The chains have remained, but already the carpenter-like technicality of the second term ("tenons") sounds somewhat strange in an Aeschylean context. The extraneousness grows with the "strait jackets," suggestive as they are of modern alienism. As for the "parapets," their sphere is medieval. Denoting tradition, they are figuratively rather than literally restrictive (in the sense of Rimbaud's line "je regrette l'Europe aux anciens parapets"): the materiality of the old instruments of torture is being diluted into a delicate historical symbolism. Dilution culminates in the last item, the "scruples". It is a favorite term of the Huguenot André Gide, but its significance goes beyond his personal idiosyncrasies. Does it not subjectivize, interiorize, in a sense "psychologize" the objects of torment in a way that is distinctly modern?

Let us think of that other descent in the *Prométhée*, where Prometheus' eagle bursts into the café, destroying a window and Coclès' eye. "Ça ... un aigle! Allons donc!! tout au plus une conscience" (p. 314): this exclamation of the bystanders exemplifies the same interiorization of a material object, its transformation into a moral entity. This time the object is the bird, which embodies the principle of tragedy itself. In fact the general reaction is an attempt to minimize that principle, but actually the qualification "tout au plus" is ill-advised. Dividing man within himself, his conscience contains at least the germ of a predicament that can ultimately assume tragic dimensions. Such a process would be appropriate to the over-subtle mind of a late civilization, sharpened by centuries of questioning and introspection. Besides, we should not forget that the French word "conscience" also means "consciousness"—that other form of self-division and therefore (*in nuce*) self-transcendence. In Prometheus' speech in part II, the eagle is indeed interpreted as the dynamic principle of self-transcendence and progress—that within man which devours him and makes rise above himself. All this is illustrated by the spiritual self-immolation of Damocles, who—starting out with scruples about his involuntary and incomprehensible connection with Coclès' suffering—advances to self-consciousness, metaphysical questioning and tragic death. "Scruples," then, are an authentic starting-point for modern tragedy. And returning to our passage, we find that they are not merely the last in a series: they serve as a collective summing up of all the tools of torture. Therefore does it not appear that this hero who decides to change his posture already has very much of a modern Promethean consciousness, and that he is well prepared to step down into our world?

However, this is not the case, and the preparation for his journey is a failure. The road from chains to scruples is neither smooth nor natural. It does not present itself as a genuine historical development of the tragic spirit but rather as an amusing jumble of irreconcilable spheres (cultural, technical, psychological). This is due to simple enumeration. Enumerative juxtaposition has always been a favorite device for the comical suggestion of absurdity. Here it is used to undermine the ostensible portrayal of an organic evolution. The analytic presentation sabotages the apparent synthetic purpose. And in the ensuing lines, everything is done to enhance the impression of incongruity. The prosaically calculating determination "somme toute" banalizes Prometheus' tragic predicament (as does the adverb "mal" in the title of the book[2]), while the reference to ankylosis propels it into the inappropriate sphere of medical pragmatism. Let us also note the pedestrian manner in which the tragic spirit is pleased to awake. And finally we are jolted to learn of Prometheus' actual arrival amongst us: was a raising of his left side really enough to break his shackles—and what connection is there between a stretching of an arm and a walk down a boulevard? The passage presents an abortive transition, meticulously elaborated. No wonder that Prometheus seems disoriented in his new surroundings. There seems to be no real communication between the world of tragedy and that of the *grands boulevards*.

The clash of incommensurable spheres constitutes the very essence of the humor of this work, an instance of Gide's famous *saugrenu*. Comical incongruity springs from the very appearance of mythological and ancient names in present-day Paris. All those who are essentially connected with tragedy bear Greek names; Cocles, who turn his misfortune to good moral and social use in a most untragic manner, is a Roman. But what happens to the representatives of tragedy? The Aeschylean Zeus becomes a fat financier who grants interviews. When it proves difficult to find a comforting professional label for Prometheus, he is registered as a man of letters—and when the Titanic inventor of fire at last blushingly admits that he used to fabricate matches, he is imprisoned as a manufacturer without a licence. Examples could be multiplied at will. The principle is always the collision between myth and modernity, between tragedy and the well-policed realm of boulevards, and the latter's attempt to gobble up the former. This is most clearly brought out in the previously mentioned scene where the eagle causes havoc in the café. The customers, as we know, do their best to minimize the occurrence. This is no eagle, just a conscience; besides, we all have an eagle, but one just doesn't wear it in Paris, where it is too bothersome; surely one does not show it in public. One should stifle or sell it; at any rate "on s'en débarrasse avant d'entrer," as if it were a hat (pp. 314-315). The tragic phenomenon is thus subjected to the most superficial social categories and relegated to insignificance.

Conversely, we witness the effort of the tragic spirit to get acclimatized in the modern world. In part II, Prometheus first regains an awareness of his heroic past and of his aquiline essence (like a man who, having awakened in an unfamiliar setting, gradually realizes who he is) and then tries to "sell" them to his new contemporaries. He does it by propounding a tragic philosophy of life. Appropriately so: how else would tragedy seek to re-enter this ideological age of ours? However, his enterprise puts him in bizarre situations. He gives a public lecture in a kind of Lunapark and has to employ the crudest tricks of circus demagogy to keep the interest of an unruly public. He shows a talent for acting which had been discreetly foreshadowed by our initial passage: did he not free himself "pour changer de *pose*"? He does overcome the prejudice that good manners forbid the showing of the eagle, but at what cost! To the thunderous applause of the multitude he makes his bird perform pirouettes and displays it gnawing his liver: the Titan of ancient myth has become a romantic exhibitionist and a *fin de siècle* "heautontimoroumenos". This is not an assimilation of tragedy but its comical degradation: Prometheus' efforts result in nothing but a new form of the *saugrenu*. And when the speaker finally concentrates on the serious part of his oration, the listeners leave the hall.

Thus, on the whole, modernity seems to distort the tragic spirit. But what about Damocles, that other bearer of a Greek name which (as he admits) "n'est plus très porté" (p. 309)? Have we not recognized him as one whose fate, in a modern way, is truly tragic? The fact that the profits from Cocles' misfortunes puts him a position of guiltless guilt and makes him ponder the mysterious concatenation of events. His anguished questions finally grow into a hopeless and self-destructive investigation of the ultimate nature of things, partly under the influence of Prometheus' speech. For whereas Aeschylus' Titan knew more than Zeus himself, the new Prometheus is a questioner, desperately asking for the "*cur*" of his eagle. Afterwards he vainly tries to prevail on the divine banker to show himself to the dying Damocles: the upstart lord of the gods has become a Christian *deus absconditus*. Damocles is eaten by his eagle, consumed by his desire for attainable knowledge. He is a tragic character, to be sure—but only in the most formal and schematic way. Qualitatively speaking, his experience is banalized by the familiar procedures of the *saugrenu*. The specific cause of his fatal illness is supposedly a common cold which he caught during Prometheus' lecture. And what is the original event that leads to all the spiritual torment? A box on Cocles' ear, accompanied by an unexplained gift of 500 francs. These pedestrian facts, accentuated by Cocles' glass eye, suffice to turn even Damocles' death agony to ridicule.

Prometheus, moreover, drops his questioning; he is determined to avoid and even forget Damocles' fate. His funeral oration contains virtually no reference to the victim. Nor is it another effort at philosophical explanation and persuasion. He merely tells an amusing anecdote to a gaily laughing audience. Here is a sample of his "Histoire de Tityre":

> Et peu de temps après, ayant bien éprouvé que, somme toute, les occupations, responsabilités et divers scrupules, non plus que le chêne, ne le tenaient, Tityre sourit, prit le vent, partit, enlevant la caisse et Angèle et vers la fin du jour descendit avec elle le boulevard qui mène de la Madeleine à l'Opéra (pp. 337-338).

The echoes of our initial quotation make it clear enough that Prometheus' story is a reinterpretation, a narrative transposition of his experience. The differences, therefore, are significant. The tools of imprisonment no longer present a juxtaposition of heterogeneous spheres: they are all outgrowths of respectable living in a civilized modern society. Modernization has already taken place, Tityrus already lives in the kind of world into which Prometheus was being transplanted. His liberation is the familiar Gidean "départ" from a restrictive civilization. However, his is hardly a genuine liberation, since he goes to a place which is very much like the one he left. In fact he leaves "enlevant la caisse et Angèle," two objects that will prove useful between the Madeleine and the Opéra: his very "departure" seems to fall under the eminently social and pragmatic categories of larceny and elopement. Nothing can shock us in such a transition between homogeneous loci. Contrary to the previous incident, we are even told the protagonist's means of locomotion. To be sure, it is non-realistic (Tityrus "prit le vent"), yet it does not create an effect of violent incongruity. Suggesting the sphere of the romantic fairy-tale, it combines with the imprecise localization of Tityrus' point of origin and with the autumnal vagueness of his hour of arrival to suffuse the passage with a gently poetic atmosphere that tends to smoothen rather than to jolt. The gentleness of the process is underscored by the phrase "Tityre sourit."

Smoothness, poetic unreality and social pragmatism: the passage contains in a nutshell all the characteristics of the "story of Tityrus." The clash of irreconcilable elements is there replaced by a painless fusion of cultural spheres, where the paraphernalia of modern society (such as lending libraries) blend as easily with the domain of ancient literature as with echoes from the Gospel of St. John ("au commencement était Tityre," p. 335). Prometheus' biography as told in his previous speech, the heroic aquiline history of civilization, has become a smooth process of gradual development. This is underlined by the botanical symbolism into which the speaker now translates his experience. Under Tityrus' tender care, a seed sown in the swamp grows into an oak tree in whose shade a society emerges. The carnivorous eagle has turned into a seed, the inventor of fire into a patient gardener; the violent story of human self-transcendence is presented as a gentle process of vegetable maturation.

The effect is far from *saugrenu;* it is rather a feeling of wistful irony before such an impossibly idyllic picture of man's progress. The word "idyllic" should be taken literally, for Prometheus the Titan has changed into the shepherd Tityrus: the dark universe of Aeschylean tragedy has been replaced by the bright and poetically unreal world of Virgilian eclogue. The point of departure of the "story within the story," therefore, refers to a completely different tradition within ancient literature—one that is plainly non-tragic, already the nostalgic and artificial ideal of a late and complex civilization. No wonder that Tityrus painlessly makes the transition from antiquity to modernity which Prometheus has been unable to effect! We are told that an idea was put in Tityrus' mind when the seed was planted in the earth—"et cette idée était la graine, et cette graine était l'Idée" (p. 335): clearly a statement of the identity of subject and object, the unity of man and nature, which is the very essence of the bucolic dream.[3] Angèle succumbs to that dream right after her arrival in Paris. Between the Madeleine and the Opéra she meets the naked Moelibaeus, a pristine and integral type of man—and where indeed could this seductive pastoral image more properly emerge than in the very center of modern Alexandrinism? She heeds the sheperd's silent invitation, which is really her own urge to return to nature, and follows him to Rome (the Rome of Virgil).

When Angèle thus forsakes her companion Tityrus, he remains alone and completely surrounded by swamps, exactly as he was before he undertook his civilizing enterprise. The end rejoins the beginning, and his effort was absurd. Yet we do not experience this as distressing. Together with the public we gaily laugh at poor Tityrus who is left empty-handed. We have forsaken the Promethean view of linear progress. For the idyllic ideal, committed to nature with its alternation of the seasons, eternal recurrence is rather a positive value. In fact, for the ancients such circularity is not a symbol of absurdity but rather the very image of perfection. This ideal has survived in the aesthetic sphere, which aims for formal integration and self-sufficiency. Prometheus has become an artist, a teller of stories, and the circularity of his tale also denotes the closed perfection of the work of art.[4] Even more crucially, it stands for the structure of the creative process. The eagle, born of Prometheus, is fattened on his liver and finally eaten. The artist cultivates his experiences as raw material for the work of art. What counts is the work's beauty, the eagle's delicious taste— and of course the public's applause. The applause is forthcoming and the bird is consumed ("assimilated") at a mass banquet. What a change since Prometheus' lecture in favor of tragedy, which had been forsaken by the multitude! Here we touch upon the harmony between the poet's enterprise and social pragmatism. The artist has a useful social function. His task is to divert the public, even at a funeral oration. Precisely at a funeral oration, for he should make us forget tragedy and death. The main body of the *Prométhée* is still characterized by the violent (albeit comical) discord of the *saugrenu;* the story of Tityrus resolves everything into ease and harmony. Tragedy, after having been humorously degraded, is assimilated by the realm of the non-tragic. It is transformed into harmonious beauty, as symbolized by the eagle's feathers. And "c'est avec l'une d'elles que j'écris ce petit livre" (p. 341): the "je" who thus bursts the story's framework in the best tradition of romantic irony now reveals the presence of the true author of the tale—André Gide himself.

We see that the book plays on two levels. Its implications are individual as well as cultural. The integration of tragedy into the domain of boulevards and pleasant poetic dreams not only tells us something about modern civilization but also about the authenticity of the artist, specifically of the artist André Gide. Its statement about all these, ironically implicit, is hardly complimentary. A little creator aping the uncouth amorality of Zeus the big Creator, Prometheus demonstratively turns his back on Damocles' grave. But we cannot forget this grave, and we are struck by the deep inauthenticity of the protagonist's procedures. The closed vegetable world of the Tityrus story is clearly a parody of the work of art. Its author has become acclimatized in the modern world only by catering to its blatantly displayed superficiality. And Gide himself, fascinated by tragedy yet afraid of it, obliquely admits that he is (in Nietzsche's words) "nur Narr, nur Dichter."

Therefore, although distorted and finally consumed by the non-tragic spirit, tragedy finally gets its revenge by ridiculing its victor in its turn. Paradoxically, both the tragic and the anti-tragic impulse get their due: each affirms itself indirectly by negating the other. This structure of affirmation by reciprocal negation is ironic—and indeed what other means than irony is there to bridge an irreconcilable contradiction? Tragedy and its denial are fused in an *ironic synthesis.*

II

The Abortive Synthesis: Oedipe (1931)

Où va la reine? — Se cacher, parbleu! — Où est Œdipe? — Il se cache aussi. Il a honte. — Coucher avec sa mère pour lui faire à son tour des enfants... — Tout ça, c'est des histoires de famille; cela ne nous regarde pas. — Ça regarde les dieux qui s'en irritent. — Et puis il y a le meurtre de Laïus, qu'Œdipe, son fils, a commis. — Qu'Œdipe lui-même a promis de venger. — On peut dire qu'il s'est mis là dans de mauvais draps. — Le justicier doit s'en prendre à soi, et s'est désigné pour victime. — Sans doute, afin d'apaiser les dieux, ne fallait-il pas moins d'un roi, tant notre misère était grande. — Du reste, n'est-il pas naturel qu'un roi, pour son peuple, se sacrifie? — Oui, si ce sacrifice doit nous délivrer de nos maux (pp. 297-298).

After learning their fatal secret, Oedipus and Iocasta have just left the stage; soon we will hear about their self-immolation. Is the agitated dialogue of the "double chorus," here cited, in keeping with the pathos of the moment? Nobody could possibly claim it is. The best the speakers can do at first is to suppose that the rulers have gone into hiding out of "shame", thus reducing a tragic predicament to the puny dimensions of a moral scandal. Unlike the chorus of Sophocles' *Oedipus Rex*, that of Gide is hopelessly pedestrian. It seems bent on sabotaging the tragic atmosphere. Oedipus' behavior is a family matter which need not concern us: the universal realm of man's fate shrinks ot the narrow domain of domestic drama. And when the speakers (by a process of dialectics) finally realize that the affair does have wider implications, they still remain blind to its awesome horror. In their eyes, the king's self-punishment for guiltless guilt will be nothing but a means to relieve their own misery. As Cocles in the *Prométhée*, they subject tragedy to egoistically defined moral and pragmatic standards whose spirit is well expressed by the pious platitude: "N'est-il pas naturel qu'un roi, pour son peuple, se sacrifie?"

Their language betrays even more clearly the incorrigible commonness of their minds. An expression like "coucher avec," a construction like "tout ça, c'est des histoires," an ambiguous joke such as "il s'est mis dans de mauvais draps"—such forms of speech, colloquial to the point of vulgarity, hardly rise to the solemnity of the occasion. Moreover, they are deliberately anachronistic. Yet this language is typical of the entire play, and it is not only the chorus (the mouthpiece of public opinion) which speaks in such a manner. The dissolute princes Eteocles and Polynices are liberal with such vulgarisms as "coucher avec" and "je m'en fous" (pp. 279, 280). No wonder: does not their father, the tragic hero Oedipus himself, refer to Laius' still unknown murderer as a "cochon" (p. 258)? The play is filled with modern slang, and with exclamations such as "Ah! par exemple!" "Dieu! qu'il est embêtant, celui-là," says Oedipus, speaking of Tiresias, and he assures us that he is no "froussard" (p. 259). "Tu nous a fichus dedans," the chorus accuses him a little later (p. 260). Glaring anachronisms supplement these offenses against tragic dignity. We are jolted by the emergence of psychological and even psychoanalytic terms.

Ismene is "nerveuse" and her brother Eteocles "refoulé" because he has not yet slept with her (pp. 270, 281). Tiresias likes "les bien-pensants" and Antigone tops it all by planning to "entrer dans les ordres" (pp. 279, 266). Nor does anachronism stop before geography and the history of ideas: Eteocles is writing on the "mal du siècle" and his father does not care whether he is "Grec ou Lorrain" (pp. 270, 281, 272).

The basic procedure is that of the *saugrenu*, which here makes its last appearance in Gide's work. What a flat conclusion for this Gidean form of humor, which had arisen in the *Voyage d'Urien* of 1893 and attained such brilliance in the *soties!* Notably in the *Prométhée* is was light, versatile and truly funny; now it is one-dimensional and heavy-handed to the point of grossness. The earlier work's inextricable complexity is replaced by a simplistic and almost mechanical combination of two strains: vulgarization and modernization, colloquialism and anachronism. Is this perchance necessary because a play needs more obvious effects than the *sotie* of 1899? Hardly: the effects of the *Prométhée* are eminently theatrical. Technically they are typical instances of romantic irony, and the work resembles nothing as much as a play by Ludwig Tieck. The matter requires closer scrutiny. How and in what context does Gide now apply his old techniques, and just what is he trying to do?

Modernization is one of the elements of this latter-day *saugrenu*. The modernization of tragedy is a major concern of the 20th-century theatre. The attempt takes two contrasting forms. Many plays rework the subjects of ancient tragedy in a modern sense (examples are Anouilh's *Antigone* and *Les Mouches* by Sartre). Conversely, a much smaller group of dramas tries to infuse tragic archetypes into modern life (such as O'Neill's *Mourning Becomes Electra* and to some degree Camus' *Malentendu*). Both trends reflect the Gidean problem of the assimilation of tragedy. They seek to merge the ancient and the modern, present-day reality and the universality of myth—to weld together realism and the timeless patterns of man's fate. What Gide presents, of course, is the comical breakdown of such a synthesis. However, in this negative form *Oedipe* obviously represents the first group, whereas the *Prométhée* is an instance of the latter one. Camus believed that the problem had to be tackled by projecting tragic patterns into a modern setting. He was right: the setting is a datum and should coincide with what is really given; the dynamic assimilative effort should bear on the tragic spirit, which is crucial and cannot simply be taken for granted. If we ignore this and choose an ancient setting, concentrating our efforts on the modern content, we invert the natural order and the hierarchy of importance. We then risk getting a mere modern variation on an ancient subject that is nothing more than a static form.[5]

These considerations are also valid for Gide's negative treatment of the problem and go far towards explaining the difference between the humor of *Oedipe* and that of the *Prométhée*. In *Oedipe*, a static ancient setting "clashes" with a pedestrian modern spirit. In such a juxtaposition between the empty and the obvious, the latter easily prevails. Its triumph is immediate and cheap, it costs no effort and requires no real dynamism. Now dynamism is essential to the *saugrenu*, which (in all the *soties*) represents the very principle of movement. Thus the *Prométhée* depicts the hero's *movement* from his domain into ours, the *efforts* of the tragic spirit to get acclimatized and its *ultimate* subjection by the obvious. That subjection is the end result of an eventful process, a genuine though comical struggle between opposing forces. The relationship between the Caucasus and Paris is not static but ambulatory. Not so Oedipus' geographical manipulations when he declares that he does not care if he is "Grec ou Lorrain." The beloved province of Gide's nationalist adversary suddenly exposes Thebes as a mere backdrop; the mythical universality of Greece is abruptly contracted into the temporal and spatial narrowness of Gide's polemic with Maurice Barrès.

It is interesting to speculate why Gide turns to the formula of *Oedipe* despite its disadvantages instead of writing something in the manner of the *Prométhée*. Obviously he wants to stick quite closely to the *Oedipus Rex*. Is he drawn towards tragedy even while he sabotages the tragic spirit? This supposition is borne out by the deliberate *vulgarization*, the second element of the simplified *saugrenu*. Instead of an inextricable confusion of all spheres, Gide seeks a linear contrast between the poetic and the prosaic, the sublime and the grotesque. Tragedy is no longer dissolved in the universal levity of a romantic fantasmagoria; its high style is pointedly opposed by the low style of comedy. Vulgarization is the polar opposite of tragic pathos and thus a distorted way of maintaining it, for the thesis is always implied in the antithesis. The very heavy-handedness of the "low style" is still a negative reflection, a kind of mirror image of tragic gravity. But a truly dialectical contrast presupposes a relative equivalence of the opposing terms. Thus Shakespearean "comic relief" antithetically underscores the tragic essence. In *Oedipe*, however, the tragic term is purely formal, so that it is literally swamped by its antithesis and we are left with pedestrian grossness.

Language is not Gide's only means of undermining the tragic spirit. In Sophocles' play, the incestuous mixup of family relations reflects a basic metaphysical rottenness; in Gide's, it merely permits Creon to worry if Oedipus is his brother-in-law or his nephew (p. 294). Such contraction of tragedy into domestic drama, which is characteristic of the whole play, had already been criticized by Nietzsche as being a tendency of Euripides. Nietzsche had also blamed the strong dialectical, philosophical component in the work of that "destroyer of ancient tragedy."[6] Here again, Gide acts as if he were trying to outdo Euripides. Starting with Oedipus the self-made man and Creon the traditionalist, all his characters are vocal, anachronistic representatives of the ideas that play a role in Gide's intellectual universe. They argue incessantly and even when faced with catastrophe are still engaged in making points. The double chorus is very much in character when it requires a prolonged dialectical exchange to grasp the meaning of Oedipus' act! Together with the profusion of characters, this bent for ratiocination serves to weaken the dramatic buildup. The play has none of Sophocles' extreme economy, of his masterly concentration on Oedipus' inescapable entrapment by his guilt. The king's progressive discovery of the truth is relegated to the margin. The principal subject thus recedes into the background and the play acquires a static quality because argumentation pre-empts the stage. Act II is an orgy of discussions between everyone and everyone else, while the whole pathos of the final scene is dissolved by the blind Oedipus' argumentative exchanges with the priest.

The displacement of action by intellection is a typically Gidean preoccupation and one which is evident throughout his work. In *Oedipe* as well, it not only appears indirectly in the structure but actually moves into the play as an explicit theme. The king's predicament is interpreted in terms of this late romantic anti-intellectualism. Oedipus starts out as a proud and self-contained man of action, a kind of enlightened despot who relies only on his own strength. His activism is based upon the rejection of reasoning, the deliberate acceptance of ignorance. He never asked any questions, he merely answered those put by the Sphinx—not intellectually but by his living example. Action is blind, it is incompatible with thought. The ruler's downfall comes when he begins questioning and doubting, when he wants to elucidate the truth.

What is the inherent logic of this conception? Clearly the hero's degeneration into an anti-hero, the disintegration of a character paralyzed by his inner complexity. It should be the kind of thing Gide had done in *Saül*, but with a less pathetic and more intellectual protagonist, perhaps resembling Damocles in the *Prométhée*. But the conception is not followed through. It is clearly stated, to be sure. Oedipus starts by declaring that he is happy, "tout présent, complet en cet instant de la durée éternelle," and by rejecting all complexities (p. 253). Later Tiresias conspires with Creon to open up a breach in his armor by which "inquiétude" may slip in. And at the end of Act II the king in fact says that the time of quietude is over. But these are mere verbal declarations, unaccompanied by any true development. We sense no spreading of disquietude, the hero's "disintegrating" quest is relegated to the margin, and he really remains in control throughout.

The culminating point is the act of blinding, where the king symbolically destroys his "completeness". And here we clearly see that Gide's basic conception is not only undeveloped but actually crossed and pre-empted by one that is diametrically opposed. For Oedipus' deed is not, as it should be, an almost viceral outburst of impotence (such as Saul's killing of his wife or even Hamlet's murder of Polonius). It is a *deliberate* act of revolt and self-glorification, in pointed contrast to the whole theme of self-questioning and doubt. And it is far from being an atonement. The crime of incest had been conspicuously argued away by Eteocles' and Polynices' slippery remarks on their sisters, and Oedipus had tried to dissuade them from their designs by mere arguments of pride ("pour se grandir, il faut porter loin de soi ses regards," p. 282). Pride is the only thing that bothers Oedipus when he learns about his "sin". He might as well have calmly waited for the kingship he had "conquered", and his actions turn out to have been predetermined. "...Je ne me reconnais plus dans mes actes" (p. 296): like Lafcadio in the *Caves du Vatican*, Oedipus disgustedly watches the expropriation of his deed. And so he blinds himself because he wants to commit a truly autonomous act, and because he has reached a point of elevation that only gratuitous heroism can still surpass. He is not a successor of Saul and Damocles, he is in the line of Philoctetes and Alissa. The conclusion of *Oedipe* is not the final stage of a loss of self; it becomes the apotheosis of a man who possesses himself completely and concentrates all his forces into a supreme act of self-sacrifice.

The play, then, contains the two old Gidean themes of disintegration and active self-transcendence. Separately both have tragic potentialities for do they not point in the respective directions of Racinian and Cornelian tragedy? In his previous works, Gide did not fully utilize these potentialities; now, in *Oedipe*, he over-utilizes them by trying to merge the two opposite themes in the one character of Oedipus. The natural result is that they interfere with (and therefore cancel) one another. Is this what Gide wanted? Probably not, at least not consciously—but his procedure reflects a deep ambivalence that runs through the entire play. The author behaves as if he wanted tragedy (as much of it as possible) without really wanting it. Could this be the meaning of the self-defeating cumulation of tragic strains? In other ways as well, this is the work of impossible syntheses. Let us consider how surprising it is that the Sophoclean conclusion has been seriously retained at all. *Oedipe*, for all its linguistic, rationalistic and structural sabotage of the tragic spirit, reverts to an unmitigatedly tragic ending. In the *sotie* of 1899, we turn our backs on Damocles' grave. In the play of 1931, it is after all the image of the blind Oedipus with which we are left when the curtain goes down. Gide sticks to his model, and this is significant in itself. Is has already been suggested how this faithfulness to the Sophoclean subject, coupled with a kind of inverted adherence to the tragic spirit, spoils the humor of the work. Tragedy and anti-tragedy: Gide is obviously torn in two directions. The two contrary impulsions exist in the *Prométhée* as well, but they are ironically accorded. What *Oedipe* lacks is precisely this sovereign ironic detachment and control. Written at a time when Gide was trying to weld his discordant tendencies into a coherent whole, the play appears unable to avoid the impossible quest for a *positive* fusion of the tragic and the non-tragic spirit. These opposite poles no longer assert themselves by means of a delicately elaborated and carefully balanced indirection, but rather with a blunt and mutually hampering directness. Tragedy, divided in itself by an overloading of motifs, is weakened but not entirely abolished by anti-tragic elements, and especially by a grossly obvious version of the *saugrenu* which is in its turn weighed down by remnants of the tragic impulsion. The effect is not reciprocal negation but rather a paradoxical simultaneous affirmation. The resulting hesitation and ambivalence make *Oedipe* a mediocre play. The ironic synthesis of the earlier work has been replaced by an *abortive synthesis*.

III

The Confrontation: Thésée (1946)

C'était quelqu'un de très bien, Egée, mon père; de tout à fait comme il fallait. En vérité, je soupçonne que je ne suis que son fils putatif. On me l'a dit, et que le grand Poséidon m'engendra. Dans ce cas c'est de ce dieu que je tiens mon humeur volage. En fait de femmes, je n'ai jamais su me fixer. Egée parfois m'empêchait un peu. Mais je lui sais gré de sa tutelle et d'avoir, dans l'Attique, remis le culte d'Aphrodite en honneur. J'ai regret d'avoir causé sa mort par un fatal oubli: celui de remplacer par des voiles blanches les voiles noires du bateau qui me ramenait de Crète, ainsi qu'il était convenu si je revenais victorieux de mon entreprise hasardeuse. On ne saurait penser à tout. Mais à vrai dire et si je m'interroge, ce que je ne fais jamais volontiers, je ne puis jurer que ce fut vraiment un oubli. Egée m'empêchait, vous dis-je, et surtout lorsque, par les philtres de la magicienne, de Médée, qui le trouvait, ainsi qu'il se trouvait lui-même, un peu vieux en tant que mari, il s'avisa, fâcheuse idée, de repiquer une seconde jeunesse, obstruant ainsi ma carrière, alors que c'est à chacun son tour. Toujours est-il qu'à la vue des voiles noires... j'appris, en rentrant dans Athènes, qu'il s'était jeté dans la mer (pp. 1416-17).

There seems to be nothing problematical in this passage. Limpid, made up of clearly constructed affirmations, without detours though with some obvious innuendo, it shows the speaker exactly as he is: a man of action, straightforward yet a little wily, proud and somewhat cynical—devoid of any complexities that could threaten his intactness. We feel that this man truly forms a unity. The unity extends to the work, for it is Theseus' voice that we hear throughout most of this late revival of the Gidean *récit*. We immediately recognize some of Gide's constant preoccupations. There is the bastard theme, and also the familiar contrast between action and introspection. In fact when Theseus reluctantly questions the motives for his fatal forgetfulness, stylistic clarity momentarily gives way to an involved syntax that is almost parodistically reminiscent of certain coquetries of the young Gide.

The very use of the bastard theme, however, shows that a change has taken place. It is no longer Gidean but Goethean. Theseus echoes the author of *Dichtung und Wahrheit* who complacently reports the rumors about his supposed descendence from a noble lord. His remark, like Goethe's, is not meant to be taken seriously. In any case, the stress does not lie on the absence of family relations but on the fact that his family might be even more distinguished than one thinks. Illegitimacy as such is not at all a value. On the contrary, Theseus is deeply conscious of his royal legitimacy, which was precisely what had afflicted the Oedipus of 1931. "Que tu le veuilles ou non, tu es, comme j'étais moi-même, fils de roi," he tells his son Hippolytus. "Rien à faire à cela: c'est un fait; il oblige" (p. 1415). One should start out by understanding who one is, but then take over the legacy in order to bequeath it to one's children. Even his Machiavellian displacement of his father betrays more than an egoistic will to power, for it defends a law of family continuity and natural succession which is threatened by Medea's magic. "Continuity" is the key term here. The hero of *Oedipe*, solely concerned with self-realization, is entirely committed to the present. But Theseus, seeking continuity in time, cannot ignore any of its three dimensions. He is an Oedipus who has united with Creon, the representative of tradition, and who has instilled a sense of responsibility in his sons.

This makes him a superior statesman. Even his bantering remarks about women lead up to a statement on public affairs: despite his scepticism about the gods, he is grateful that Aegeus has reinstituted the cult of

Aphrodite. Decidedly, Theseus is a political animal! The "enlightened despot" side, incipiently present in Iocasta's husband, is fully developed in the widower of Phaedra. As the former he has subdued many monsters, thus narrowing the domain of the inexplicable and diminishing the power of superstition. His reforms in Athens are the very model of an 18th century "revolution from above": rational, idealistic, and somewhat facile. He introduces a touch of democracy by divesting himself of his royal powers, but this is merely an empty gesture. In reality he continues to rule very much in the way the *philosophes* had imagined. The people need illusions and beliefs, they need religious institutions; let them think that they govern themselves while they are actually being guided—for their own good. And so Theseus leads them, deifying the very Ariadne he had abandoned, rendering goodwill effective by the machinations of *raison d'état*.

His Machiavellism, exemplified by the failure to change the sails, often takes the form of a foxiness worthy of Odysseus. In Crete, when he is subjected to the ordeal of water to test the divine origin he had bragged about, he succeeds by distributing precious stones which he had brought from Greece but pretended to have picked up from the bottom of the sea. This act also prosaically devalues an ancient superstition. We find a similar banalization of the divine in Pasiphae's comical story about the bull and in Theseus' reaction to the news that Ariadne has married Dionysius: to him it means that she has taken to drinking. This common-sense interpretation of religious traditions is again in the manner of the Enlightenment, and in tune with the increasing rationalism of the later Gide. Theseus' language reflects both his cynicism and his prosaic frame of mind. "C'était *quelqu'un de très bien*, Egée, mon père; de tout à fait *comme il fallait*": the loosely conversational syntax, coupled with the use of modern colloquialisms, creates a slightly sarcastic negligence of tone. The same effect arises from the cliché "on ne saurait penser à tout." These are not really terms one would expect from an ancient hero. Other such instances are not hard to find. Theseus expresses himself anachronistically when he refers to Pasiphae and her daughters as "ces dames de la cour" (p. 1421). When he brands the dress of Cretan women as "impudique" (p. 1422), he exhibits too modern a sense of propriety—modern also in its hypocrisy, for who is Theseus to insist on modesty! He is the same man, after all, who floats from boudoir to boudoir and who tells us a little later about Ariadne: "son quant-à-soi me parut d'accès si facile que je ne puis croire que j'en fusse le pionnier" (p. 1429).

Modernization and even a touch of vulgarity; are we back in the world of *Oedipe?* Not at all, for strangely enough these realistic elements here do not clash with the setting and with the dignity of the subject. They simply underline that Theseus thinks and speaks as other mortals, even of today. He has his weaknesses and peculiarities. Thus he likes to brag, even to the point of ascribing to himself the feats of others (cf. p. 1419). Never mind: to speak well of oneself is Greek, and the king's all-too-human traits do not keep him from being a genuine hero. They merely infuse a human and individual content into an archetypal story, by which they are in their turn elevated and dignified. The humanization of myth joins with a mythification of reality, creating a unity of the topical and the timeless—of the particular and the exemplary—in which mythical universality still predominates.

Thésée, then, is related to *Oedipe* as the story of Tityrus to that of Prometheus: a smooth fusion between the ancient and the modern has been effected here. This is partly due to the sparing use of modernizing realism, which suffices to enliven but not to counteract the dominant atmosphere. However, the synthesis would not be feasible if that atmosphere were hostile to it—i.e., if it were even purportedly tragic. But Theseus is in his own way as untragic as Tityrus. He is predestined for success and not for sacrifice, the Theseus of Sophocles' *Oedipus at Colonus* much more than the one of Euripides' *Hippolytus* or Racine's *Phèdre*. Yet tragedy always threatens man, and the events of *Hippolytus* cannot be ignored. Our initial passage shows how the hero handles potentially tragic situations. He is as guilty of parricide as Oedipus. How does he react? He does not see the matter in the glaring light of tragic absolutes but (expressing "regrets", and after some muddling) in the medium colors of domestic wisdom which are suited to his dynastic preoccupations: Aegeus was too old for his young wife. This situation recurs several times. Minos is an elderly husband with an unmanageable wife, and there is poetic justice in the fact that the king of Athens himself will not escape this kind of ordeal with Phaedra. How does he speak about the destruction of his family? It leaves him inconsolable, no doubt, but he does not experience it in a tragic way. It furnishes him with a series of humble moral lessons, proper to the sphere of domestic drama: spouses should not differ too much in age; one should neither rely on women nor on the gods (cf. pp. 1449-50). Besides, he looks back on his life from a transfiguring distance. A lonely old man, he still affirms his ultimate triumph in the last words of his memoirs.

> J'ai fait ma ville. Après moi, saura l'habiter immortellement ma pensée. C'est consentant que j'approche la mort solitaire. J'ai goûté des biens de cette terre. Il m'est doux de penser qu'après moi, grâce à moi, les hommes se reconnaîtront plus heureux, meilleurs et plus libres. Pour le bien de l'humanité future, j'ai fait mon œuvre. J'ai vécu (p. 1453).

Who can fail to perceive echoes of the dying Faust's words («Es kann die Spur von meinen Erdetagen / Nicht in Äonen untergehn»), or even of the exclamation of Lynceus ("Es sei wie es wolle, / Es war doch so schön!")? Just as Tityrus, Goethe's Faust had been draining swamps; just as Theseus, he had been useful to mankind. Now that the turmoil has subsided, he can feel that all is good. It is a conspicuously non-tragic culmination of the drama, an "avoidance of tragedy" in the words of a recent Goethe critic.[7] Goethe, however, deflects tragedy into lyricism. So does Gide in the "Histoire de Tityre," at least by ironic implication. Not so in *Thésée*, whose dominant atmosphere is not poetic but oratorical. Gide's work does not hark back to the Virgilian countryside but to a place equally far removed from the Caucasus: the Athens of the rhetor Isocrates. Tragedy has not been replaced by the eclogue but by the encomion.

The encomion, the idealized "autobiography" of ancient Greece, the rhetorical praise of self: that is the real precursor of Gide's last *récit*. True, the hero is not free from faults; idealization has been tempered and humanized, inflected in the direction of modern realism. Yet it remains dominant as the principle of stylization for the synthesis of Gidean traits. In the last analysis, the fusion of myth and reality has an autobiographical significance. It is a mythification of self, an elevation of a particular existence into an exemplary destiny, a transformation of an individual into a *persona*. A synthesis of Gidean traits: we are far from the Gide who refused to suppress any of his tendencies and wrote that only the rich human fauna of a huge decentralized novel could accommodate all his inner contradictions. Theseus is Gide as he was and would have liked to be, subjected to a severe process of selection, stylized and shaped into one of those heroes whose lives (as Daedalus says in *Thésée*) have become timeless symbols (p. 1436); he is Gide reduced to the essential, modeled into a harmonious Goethean mask.

The protagonists of Gide's *récits*, to be sure, had usually presented a selectively coherent pattern of Gidean characteristics. However, the accent had always been critical, never positive and idealizing. Those "heroes" had been dominated by flaws which led to their ultimate ruin. Only a bare trace of this is left in Theseus' weaknesses, with their strictly subordinate function. Yet he has one limitation which seems to go beyond the function of humanizing an otherwise too perfect being: his anti-intellectual activism. "...Je me laisse toujours guider par un instinct que, pour plus de simplicité, je crois sûr" (p. 1444): we cannot help remembering the self-deceiving minister in *La Symphonie pastorale* who (albeit in a different context) is guided by an instinct "as sure as conscience." The situation is underlined by the hero's sharply pointed confrontation with Daedalus the intellectual, the first man (as he admits) who did not bow down before him. The old artificer tells Theseus, indirectly but unmistakably, that he is really rather stupid![8] Here is a remnant after all of Gidean contradictoriness and dispersion. For a moment the author is Daedalus more than Theseus, and we see Gide the real intellectual laughing at Gide the would-be activist. But then Daedalus states almost immediately that thinking is not the man of action's business. He even illustrates its dangers by presenting the shade of his son Icarus, consumed by issueless questioning, a vivid image of the Damoclean form of tragedy. Besides, it is after all Theseus who kills the Minotaur, although with his interlocutor's help. The irony of the thinker cannot belittle the triumph of the doer. Reflection, however necessary, is but the servant of action which does the job, and the king is not unjustified in concluding: "Au surplus, même Dédale me fut soumis" (p. 1450).

More important than the meeting with Daedalus is Theseus' final confrontation with the aged Oedipus, the majestic hero of Sophocles' last play. This time the king feels that he faces not only his equal but one who may be on an even higher plane. True, he takes care to ascribe that superiority exclusively to the victory over the Sphinx, Man's triumph over the divine enigma; in Oedipus' downfall he sees nothing but defeat. But with this judgment he merely displays his limits. Devoid of any sense for tragic grandeur, he faces Oedipus' physical blindness with a deeper (a spiritual) cecity of his own. Yet there is something in that "defeat" which bothers him. Why has the Theban hero, by blinding himself, contributed to his undoing? And thus Theseus presses Oedipus with questions, trying to reduce the tragic phenomenon to categories which he can comprehend— and supersede.

It does look as if he succeeds, for his interlocutor's answers are confused. But Theseus' superiority in argument is suspect. He forces discussion on his own level, that of common sense, while tragedy is irrationally self-evident and cannot be explained. Two chief trends emerge from the old hero's groping explanations. On the one hand he speaks like the Tiresias of *Oedipe:* the world is sullied by original sin, and with the eyes of the soul he sees a spiritual world behind appearances, truer and closer to God. On the other hand he admits that his act of self-sacrifice may have been due to "je ne sais quel secret besoin de pousser à bout ma fortune, de rengréner sur ma douleur et d'accomplir une héroïque destinée" (pp. 1452- 53). Humility and pride, renunciation and self-transcendence, Christian "other-worldliness" and tragic heroism: although Oedipus makes a feeble attempt to accord them, these do not agree too well.[9] It looks as if the Theban is retrospectively trying to "christianize" his story. Why does Gide introduce the Christian overtone? No doubt for the sake of autobiographical completeness, for it once did play a major role in his life. Perhaps he is also, in a final upsurge of ambivalence, trying to muddle the image of tragic heroism which his Oedipus embodies. His groping Theban hero is all too different from the monumental, imperious and passionate protagonist of *Oedipus at Colonus!* Gide thus introduces a serious aesthetic flaw, for the end effect of *Thésée* is obviously based upon the contrast between the tragic and the non-tragic. Fortunately the effect is only weakened, not abolished; the tragic image, though muddled, still exists.

The jarring introduction of Christian spiritualism (and this may be its ultimate purpose) permits Theseus to establish a questionable superiority. Quite in the spirit of the old Gide, he rejects mysticism and affirms that man is a child of this earth. "Sans doute as-tu su faire bon usage de ton infortune même et tirer parti d'elle pour en obtenir un contact plus intime avec ce que tu nommes le divin" (p. 1453): is it really Oedipus whom he dares pay this left-handed compliment, patronizing and full of scepticism? "Faire bon usage," "tirer parti," "obtenir": the great Theban's experience is being reduced to criteria of a puny pragmatism. But Theseus the statesman naturally thinks this way. Does he not also want Oedipus to stay in Athens because happiness is promised to the earth where the old hero's bones will rest? "...Je me félicitai," he informs us, "que les dieux aient su faire aboutir Thèbes à moi" (p. 1453). Thebes has been swallowed by Athens just as Tityrus' seed by the surrounding swamp, or the Caucasus by the Parisian boulevard. Tragedy has been assimilated by the realm of the non-tragic and the useful, which it will usefully serve to fertilize. Oedipus apparently ends up by being as "soumis" to Theseus as Daedalus.

And thus, in his last words, Theseus can proclaim his final triumph, specifically in comparison with Oedipus. But is he justified? Surely his "victory" is built upon a sleight-of-hand. What he has pounced upon and "subordinated" is only Oedipus' Christian mysticism; the tragic heroism he has chosen to ignore. And thus it is not tragedy at all what is being "assimilated" by the soil of Athens. The Theban's bones may rest in it, but his tragic image remains irreducible. Theseus' pragmatism has no hold on it, and the ruler of Athens may in fact be lowered more than exalted by his questionable triumph. On the other hand, the last word is his, the work bears his name and tells his story. Who really prevails in this final encounter between Goethean equilibrium and Nietzschean grandeur—that opposition which also runs through Gide's two late essays on Goethe?[10] Here as there, the answer is impossible to give.

The harmonious integration of Gide's tendencies remains incomplete, for duality reappears in the last pages of his "dernier écrit." In the face of worldly success and serenity there emerges the tragic ideal, unsuppressed, unassimilated and unassimilable. Exposing what had always been implicit, this final *confrontation* is the key to the preceding works as well. It is the same contrast which is veiled yet revealed by the ironic synthesis of the *Prométhée*, and which wrecks the attempted synthesis of *Oedipe*. The clear exposure of duality replaces the comical collision of the *saugrenu*. With the *saugrenu*, *Thésée* also loses the specifically cultural dimension of the previous writings. The problem of tragedy no longer presents itself as an assimilation of the ancient and the modern; everything appears on the level of antiquity. This does not mean, however, that only individual significance remains. True, *Thésée* stylizes Gide's lifelong oscillation between two contrary impulsions—his toying with the temptation of tragedy, always avoided yet somehow sought in the very process of avoidance. But raised to the plane of a hieratic confrontation between two mythical *personae*, Gide's all-too-human oscillation has been frozen into the timeless contrast between two paradigmatic forms of the human mind.

Cornell University

Notes

[1] André Gide, *Romans, récits et soties, œuvres lyriques*, Bibliothèque de la Pléiade (Paris, 1958), p. 304. Future page references to both the *Prométhée mal enchaîné* and *Thésée* will appear in the text and refer to that edition. References to *Oedipe* will also appear in the text, but will refer to Gide's *Théâtre*, published by Gallimard in one volume in 1942.

[2] Prometheus can be "bound" or "unbound," but he cannot be "sloppily bound" and still remain tragic. Tragedy deals with absolutes, not with the medium realm of the half and half. The dual meaning of the title is implicit in this consideration. On the face of it, the title says that tragedy gets loose and re-emerges in our world. Evaluated stylistically, it suggests that what is freed is no longer really tragic. This duality is of course the very essence of the book.

[3] We have a play here on the word "idea". At the beginning it recalls intellectuality, self-consciousness, questioning—i.e., the dynamic principle of development in Prometheus' public lecture and in Damocles' tragic experience. At the end (underscored by the capital letter) it denotes idealism, the ideality of the work of art. In the second acceptation, it does not suggest dynamic linear development but rather the circular perfection, the compositional closedness of the artistic work, which is also indicated by the circularity of the entire statement. That idealistic view is succinctly expressed by the young Gide's statement: "L'idée de l'œuvre, c'est sa composition" (in the "Feuillets" of 1893, *Journal 1889-1939*, Paris 1948, Edition de la Pléiade, p. 49).

[4] Cf. the preceding footnote. Of course the "Promethean view of linear progress," which makes Prometheus the conscious advocate of historicity, is a specifically modern extension of the aquiline experience. The ancient conception of time is circular rather than linear. It is therefore in this case the exaltation of circularity which constitutes a return to antiquity—but to a non-tragic aspect of antiquity which, moreover, had never ceased to be crucial in the aesthetic sphere.

[5] But what about French 17th-century tragedy? It goes back to ancient subjects because it seeks universality through removal. True, it also represents a reinterpretation, but the modern content (the 17th-century ways of speaking, feeling and experiencing) is anti-realistic and highly stylized. Classical stylization readily merges with removal in time and space. What is new in the 20th-century theater is precisely that it seeks downright realism along with universality. Incidentally, Käte Hamburger points out that the Oedipus subject leaves very little room for extension and variation and that also Corneille's and Voltaire's versions were not very successful (*Von Sophokles zu Sartre*, Stuttgart 1962, p. 175ff).

[6] Cf. Friedrich Nietzsche. *Die Geburt der Tragödie*, in *Werke in drei Bänden* (München, 1954), Erster Band, esp. pp. 72-73 and 80-81. In Gide's play, Oedipus appears on the scene at the very beginning and tells us who he is and how matters stand at the moment. This also is a Euripidean procedure, blamed by Nietzsche as rationalistic.

[7] Cf. Erich Heller, "Goethe and the Avoidance of Tragedy," in *The Disinherited Mind* (New York, 1957), esp. pp. 55, 57-58.

[8] Cf. pp. 1430-31: Daedalus says that Hercules was stupid and then praises Theseus for virtues he has in common with Hercules, without explicitly exempting him from the latter's stupidity. A discreet innuendo, but it is there.

It is amusing to see how Theseus tries to evade the domains where Daedalus is superior to him. His father had taught him that weapons are less important than the arm which carries them, but that the arm is less important than the intelligent will which guides it (p. 1416). Daedalus insists that machines are more important than strength and that Theseus could never have performed his warlike feats without his weapons (p. 1431). Thereupon Theseus enters the labyrinth without weapons, in order to prove to Daedalus that he can triumph without those tools (p. 1483). But whose is the intelligence that guides him on his mission?

[9] "Peut-être ai-je pressenti vaguement ce qu'avait d'auguste et de rédempteur la souffrance; aussi bien répugne à s'y refuser le héros. Je crois que c'est là que s'affirme surtout sa grandeur et qu'il n'est nulle part plus valeureux que lorsqu'il tombe en victime, forçant ainsi la reconnaissance céleste et désarmant la vengeance des dieux" (p. 1453). We see that Oedipus is continually vacillating between a tragico-heroic and a non-tragic Christian point of view.

[10] "Goethe" (1932, in *Feuillets d'automne*, Paris 1949) and "Introduction au théâtre de Goethe" (1942, in *Attendu que...*, Paris 1943).

As we have seen, there are some French writers (represented in the early 20th century by Péguy) who saw many admirable things in Greece, particularly on a human level, but whose literary works bear virtually no specific marks of a Greek influence. Then, there are others—like Gide—who used Greek themes and myths as the materials from which to create a very personal contemporary artistic statement. However there is another Hellenist tradition—little represented in earlier centuries of French literature—which one might call a current of spiritual kinship.

In some respects, this kinship is evident in certain works of Montherlant, Valéry, and Ramuz, but it is most striking in the literary creations of several 19th century writers like Mistral and the little-known Paul Arène, and in contemporary times in those of Vercors, Henri Bosco, and—most importantly—Jean Giono. In discussing the literature of southern France, Henri Peyre has pointed out that "la survivance de Rome et de la Grèce est l'un des traits les plus saillants de la physionomie littéraire de ce midi provençal."[1] In a sense, the very real kinship that an author from Provence like Giono felt for Greece is not at all surprising because this part of France had historically once been a part of that great empire of antiquity.

It is well known that Giono was actually awakened to his vocation as a writer by reading translations of Homer and Sophocles—doubtless he found in them a profound echo of his own spirit—and one can see a conscious use of Greek materials in certain of his writings, particularly the early volumes.[2] However, as Professor Konrad Bieber points out in his essay, the very special relationship that exists between Giono and the Greek heritage that he drew from the soil of his native Provence is what marks his work in so very distinctive a way. One might say that Giono was aware—in essentially *Greek* terms—that man was an integral and intimate part of a natural Cosmos. In the final analysis, it is this Greek-like sense of union between the human and the natural world that is the most striking and original element in Giono's Hellenism, and the one that makes him virtually unique among French writers of today.

Notes

[1] Henri M. Peyre, *L'Influence des littératures antiques sur la littérature française moderne* (New Haven-Oxford, 1941), p. 70.

[2] Peyre, *op. cit.*, pp. 74 and 79, and "What Greece Means to Modern France," in *Historical and Critical Essays* (University of Nebraska Press, 1968), p. 103.

JEAN GIONO'S GREECE: A KINSHIP BETWEEN DISTANT AGES

By Konrad Bieber

Stripped of Greek influences and sources, much of Western tragedy would either collapse or be missing altogether. The same may not be true to the same extent in poetry, or in the field of the novel. To be sure, our time is witnessing an emancipation from tradition which, more often than not, takes the form of an outright rebellion against the past. It is not yet clear whether such revolts will lead to valid art or are merely the passing phenomena that accompany every revolution.

With varying degrees of faithfulness in understanding and interpretation, poets, playwrights, and even novelists have striven over the ages to revive the world of the Greeks. In so doing, writers have taken great liberties not only with style and expression, but also with the history and character of the people of ancient Greece. Each succeeding age has put Greek names on men and women of its own time and culture. Troilus has known medieval and Renaissance twins; for us, Timon of Athens bears Shakespeare's indelible seal. Eyebrows were raised and heads shaken when Jacques Offenbach brazenly undertook his charming travesty of Gods and heroes. A watercolor by Maurice Sand, the son of the famous novelist, painted around 1860, shows a Jupiter already pathetically close to the ungodly schemer portrayed by Sartre in his *Flies* (*Les Mouches*). Electra has suffered innumerable alterations of her personality to suit shifting moods and moral or philosophical contexts, and one may wonder which of her most recent recreations—by Giraudoux, Cocteau, O'Neill, or Sartre, to name only a few—has least betrayed her Greek image.

Perhaps our time has grown so callous or so blasé that such violences done to ancient Greece rarely perturb the modern reader or viewer. However, perhaps the ancient models may sometimes regain a part of their lost beauty and stature through the talent of the modern imitator, his skill, or his style, or in a word through his ability to truly recapture the spirit of Antiquity by a mixture of irony and poetry. Irony does not necessarily betray a lack of heart in a writer. If ancient characters come to life, and if the classical scenery does not remain a mere empty shell, anachronisms and other deficiencies in the modern reworking of classical materials will not detract from our enjoyment. True, it takes more than an accumulation of classical names, *décor*, and plots to produce a modern "classical" work; we must feel a breath of congeniality throughout the bold recreation, the glow of the Aegean sun and the majesty of pure lines, be it in marble or in verse. At various times in the literary history of the West, many writers have attempted to renovate the treatment of ancient subject matter. To the twentieth century, Pope's Homer may smack of anything but the real thing, yet Pope felt genuine kinship with the bard. The German adaptor, Voss, created a Rococo Homer; but even he was able to convey an idea of homeric greatness and beauty that remained valid for generations after him.

Naturally, each of those who sought to paraphrase classical inspiration brought his own standards of beauty, of taste, of style to his recreation. Psychologically, this endeavor created a logical dilemma that had to be resolved by a literary convention. As William Arrowsmith pointed out, "Hektor the Trojan speaks Greek, and we accept it; and then, in translation we also accept Hektor the Greek-speaking Trojan who speaks English."[1] Leconte de Lisle's scrupulously "Greek" spelling of names does not make his *Herakles* or *Hypatie* any more authentic than uncounted less faithful variations on the old theme. To be sure, his translations of Greek tragedies are congenial and often felicitous; the atmosphere in his poems is an aesthetically fine approximation of the original and, of course, has a poetic color of its own.

However, in general, presentation of minutely accurate historical incidents, or psychological portraits conforming to what scholars have gleaned from ancient artifacts or art works are not enough to make a modern literary endeavor a true resurrection of a Greek type or model. Jules Lemaître even more frankly produced a disarmingly hybrid world of ancient types in the garb of his own period. Pierre Mille carefully sought out anecdotes placed in classical Greece. His psychology is a skillful blend of ancient and modern, even though his sensuality is less unbridled than Pierre Louÿs' truculent fantasies. The ancients recreated by Anatole France are often gracious phantoms permeated with nostalgic recollections and learned subtleties interspersed with semi-jocular words of wisdom. For Gide, as for many writers in many lands, Greece is the *prétexte* for philosophical and aesthetic developments unconcerned with authenticity, but even in our day, the spell cast by the Greece of Euripides and Aeschylus continues to capture readers and theater audiences everywhere.[2]

Most recently, during the summer of 1967, the new adaptation of Sophocles' Oedipus, by Vercors, presented in open air theatres at La Rochelle and Sète won great acclaim both because it was faithful to the essential message of the Greek original, and because the modern version's language was powerful in its beauty. However, Vercors took a few careful liberties with the ancient drama. Thus the *choéphore* is represented much like a peasant of our time; his language is direct and uninhibited, even though the lines he speaks are based on the text of Sophocles' chorus. In this way, the modern adaptor gained a new vitality and truth for the ancient play, elements not necessarily present in more traditional translations. Vercors' Greek peasant is one of us, a fellow human being whom we immediately understand; these are men and women of our time, akin to Greek people of all times through their concern for the forces of nature.

Although Vercors does not understand Greek, he has been uncannily successful in recapturing the spirit of ancient Greece; his adaptation of Sophocles—fusing both *Oedipus Rex* and *Oedipus at Colonus*—is highly satisfying artistically and aesthetically. This success is all the more amazing when compared with Leconte de Lisle's scrupulous but rather synthetic versions of Greek plays. These latter lack immediacy and thus have had a far less powerful impact on men in modern times. Leconte de Lisle, with his careful spelling of Greek names in the most scholarly fashion, was certainly eager to convey the depth of feeling he sensed in the Greek originals; unfortunately, he failed to create anything but a miniature of external circumstances. His lines rendering the Greek text into French remain beautiful, poetic, but strangely lifeless, whereas Vercors succeeded not only in retelling the old tale in one breath, but at the same time, he made credible the unbelievable horror of fate's dictum for mortals. He recaptured the Greeks' sense of human awe before the unknown, before the Gods and destiny.

Many were the seekers for the Greek truth, and many there have been who—in the search for that truth—have created works of beauty in their own right. It is not surprising that there is often little close resemblance between viable works of our era and classical models. In art as well as in literature, conditions have made it impossible to erase the gap between the ages, even though there is admittedly a great deal more general knowledge today about classical Greece and her arts and letters than ever before. What we may measure, however, is the depth of understanding that a modern creation may show if the artist happens—by temperament or formation—to feel truly close to the world that was Greece. This may occur in almost any medium. For example, a drawing by Jean Lurçat, entitled "Héraclès," portrays a man of a strength and cunning rarely seen in one and the same individual, thus evoking a few traits of the hero that had gone unnoticed by generations of story-tellers.

Critics have often wondered how and why Jean Giono came to achieve so forceful and rounded a renewal of antiquity in his work. There is no need to recount here the story of Giono's initiation to Greek literature, a subject thoroughly dealt with by both Christian Michelfelder and Maxwell Smith.[3] Suffice it to say that the young bank clerk in Manosque bought his copy of Homer through the mail; as he later admitted with rare candor, one of the reasons he preferred Homer to Anatole France was that the Greek poet's books were cheaper! As Henri Peyre has pointed out, this poor cobbler's son did not know Greek, "but he grew up in a land where peasants to this day winnow their grain, pluck their olives, and milk their goats much as their Mediterranean forefathers did in the time of Ulysses or Theocritus."[4] Thus when Giono was exposed to the classics, he responded to them spontaneously and vigorously. As he later recounted in his autobiographical novel, *Jean le bleu*, a farm laborer loaned him a copy of a translation of the *Iliad*, which he read during the rest periods of harvest time. It moved him deeply: "Into me was Antilochus throwing the spear. Into me was Achilles ramming the soil of his tent, trampling in the wrath of his heavy feet. In me was Patroclus shedding his blood."[5]

This revelation of Greece not only struck a responsive chord in Giono, but it opened the wellsprings of his imagination. As Peyre put it, "dès lors, sa vocation était trouvée; il ressuscitera Pan dans les clairières et les labours des Basses-Alpes et, avec plus de démesure et parfois plus d'intempérance prophétique ou rhétorique, il refera en prose la tragédie, l'épopée et l'idylle antiques."[6] In 1937, Giono himself gave an interview[7] in which he specifically underlined his desire to revive—or rather to make actual—the heroes of Homer and Sophocles whom he found about him in his native province, and thus to renew the Greek tragedies.

Although a writer must not always be held strictly responsible for declarations of this sort made in a moment of confidence and reminiscence, this statement is valuable because it clarifies Giono's literary aims in a general way. He has never shunned his responsibilities, and this rather proud claim should not arouse scepticism as to his sincerity. But did he succeed in his purpose? Has he indeed given us a kind of modern sequel to Homer or Sophocles? If such has really been his intention, it must be said that he has fallen short of the mark. To be sure, in setting out to tell the story of *Haute Provence*, his homeland, he did create a world often close to the Greek scene, and his characters bear a distinct resemblance to the Greeks of antiquity. This is all the more noteworthy since he was not actually reworking Greek materials. If the *Pan* novels have a flavor so definitely evocative and sometimes congenial to Greek models, it is primarily as a by-product of the author's art. These peasants, by being themselves—earthy, simple, suffering and loving people—at times vividly recall traits of epic dimensions. As Peyre points out, there are accents of a primitive bard in Giono's early work, and his protagonists are epic heroes in the most venerable Greek tradition, "not because they accumulate feats in violent battle but because they are the very forces of nature embodied in simple, strong creatures."[8] Although Giono's Provençaux speak in a manner unlike that of any living peasants, his art and vigor in portraying them has an authenticity that defies narrow-minded "realist" measurements.

It has been said that in those of his works in which Giono purposely sought to attain an atmosphere of Greek epic or dramatic proportions, he has been less successful, but this does not mean that these deliberate attempts were all futile. *Naissance de l'Odyssée* (first published 1930) has a charm of its own; it is a good literary sketch of life in ancient Greece, not unlike those of many other modern writers. Of course, there is an overabundance of local color; Giono tries to make up what he may lack in systematic learning by supplying correctly selected details of daily life in antiquity. Nevertheless, his Ulysses appears as a worried, ruined landowner rather than a man of royal gait and temper. The other characters, too, give an impression of bawdy small town life, immersed in petty scheming and quite unemotional sensuality. At times, there are real moments of grandeur, of epic dimensions, such as during the recital of Ulysses' deeds by the blind minstrel.

The quarrels and insults lavishly scattered throughout the pages of *Naissance de l'Odyssée*, a novel that was initially refused by the publisher, are distinctly non-homeric; yet they are endowed with a grace and fragrance of Giono's own mixing or making. Even the guitar player is not as anachronistic as we might have assumed. The author is very skillful in presenting the mule driver's account of Penelope's misbehavior, as well as the minstrel's song on Ulysses' "death". Sometimes the trials of Ulysses in Giono's book recall certain of Jules Lemaître's all-too-clever fantasies. The latter's "Mariage de Télémaque" uses devices not unlike Giono's nimble irony. However, in Lemaître affection for his hero is missing, or at best veiled, while Giono showers love on a Ulysses so human that we may at times be shocked to see him act like a coward. (Ulysses the coward becomes, ironically, the avenger of his honor when, through a chain of events possibly borrowed from burlesque shows or the grotesque cinema, he conquers a brawny, conceited Antinous.) Lemaître's "Nausicaa", admittedly inconsistent with his Télémaque, offers more of a parallel with Giono, because in it the deft humor of the modern writer includes a warm sympathy for the much-tried hero.

The psychology used in *Naissance de l'Odyssée* is a happy medium between what we know of the Homeric Penelope, Telemachus, and the legendary Ulysses, and what a fanciful modern could add to these characters. Penelope's hesitations, Telemachus' scorn for the prudent returning father, the pronouncements of a few minor figures are certainly in keeping with what an admirer of antiquity is allowed to embroider around the given tradition. It may even be advanced that it would be a hard test to ascribe authorship of the book; a graduate student would have to concentrate on the few typical Gionesque images to identify the author who was still discreet in this early work and did not allow his verve to entirely overcome the respectful elaboration of an old theme.

However, Ulysses—the central character of the book—is drawn with great precision and with an obvious effort to be faithful to known facts about Greek religion and superstitions. His flight through the thick brush after being awed by the presence of a vengeful god, is, I believe, one of the highlights of this charming, though uneven novel. Giono knew how to make Ulysses' anxiety believable because the hero was no longer sure of his erstwhile pact with Pallas Athena. Pursued by hostile gods whom he persists in defying, he takes flight through inhospitable countrysides, while the blind guitarist has hitched a mule ride and arrives in comfort at the same destination—an ironic sidelight to the dramatic buildup felicitously achieved by Giono.

Perhaps a little too much has been made of atavistic fears in this part of the story; Ulysses appears too urbane a man to yield to such utter despair and terror. Giono's solid paganism stood up well in the novels of the *Pan* cycle, where it was limited to such perennial human problems as struggles with the elements, but his *Naissance de l'Odyssée* at times sins by an over-eager reconstruction of the ancient Greek mentality; no wonder the manuscript had to await Giono's fame before a publisher would accept it.

Yet in this book there are many graceful moments, and pictures of great beauty and truth. Kalidassa the maid servant goes to the market, and Giono furnishes us a magnificent still-life of sea food, a verbal masterpiece of no mean proportions. His humor, too, proves both original and sound in more than one circumstance in this novel. Kalidassa's speech is rhythmic and musical, much in the vein of Homeric chants.

This feature and others like it prove a considerable advance over Giono's earliest published pieces, *Accompagnés de la Flûte* (1924) where the poet had already shown a happy disposition toward grace and style. These texts, full of bucolic descriptions, were often sketched out right in the middle of the fields where Giono was working and on any scrap of paper he happened to have handy. He used epigraphs drawn from the *Aeneid* or from Plato's *Banquet*. As one critic points out, "the slightly obsolete scent of these poems evokes a bucolic hellenism; its artifice recalls some pages in Anatole France or even Catulle Mendès... [these] Sunday poems, composed on returning from a walk in the country, are just a bit too well planned, are typically mediterranean; mythology here offers less a theme than a prétexte."[9] Yet their images already suggest the power of the best Giono.

A revealing sample of this material from *Accompagnés de la Flûte* is the following passage: "Ma femme a fait une séquelle d'enfants aux larges bouches. Le blé, cette année, est léger; il n'a pas assez plu pour gonfler les fèves; mes oliviers n'ont pas grainé et, il est juste enfin et rare que, un métal ouvré pour la guerre entre, paisible et bienfaisant, dans la vie d'un homme."[10] The choice of subject and image denotes a faithful interpretation of Latin bucolic poetry; the epithets are Homeric, and yet this is a variation on a theme bringing antiquity right back to our daily life. Here, as in much of the later Giono, whenever he strove earnestly to "revive" ancient themes, an impression of "a Yankee at King Arthur's court" is inescapable. Again, it must be said that the very effort to "be authentic" was damaging to poetic inspiration, for, with the exception of certain chapters in *Naissance de l'Odyssée*, the best classical features in Giono occur when the author's mind is bent elsewhere, when his imagination is unbridled, and when he creates beauty without the minute concern for accuracy in things Greek.

Giono seems closest to Homer when, as in the novels of the *Pan* trilogy, he sets out to tell the story of simple village people, for such a tale is also inextricably involved in the story of nature and its boundless forces. It is in these early stories that he seems most fully congenial to his Mediterranean heritage. He knew how to create an atmosphere of suspense, not so much about the people and their lives, as about the ominous presence of occult power in the elements that surrounded them on every side and constantly intruded into their existence. In the second novel of the *Pan* trilogy, *Un de Baumugnes*, there are only a few clear indications of an outright debt to the Greeks. Clarius in his anger is a far cry from Ajax, and the little Durance, described with loving care and personified to a point, is too unimportant, here, to rival such river gods as the Simois. However, some images may distinctly recall the Greek model. Consciously or not, the image of the bee in the flower may have come to Giono through Sophocles' *Antigone*, where love is also likened to a bee.

Regain, the third part of the trilogy, is even less rewarding in reminiscences of things Greek. Yet, here too, we find images and expressions worthy of notice in this context of Greek influence. Even though we may be far removed from Greek elemental gods such as Zephyr or Aeolus, Giono still manages to convey a distant echo of those more powerful winds: "...le beau vent, large d'épaules... (...) celui-là, c'est un monsieur."[11] Panturle's portrait is Pan-like as his name seems to suggest: "Le Panturle est un homme énorme. On dirait un morceau de bois qui marche. Au gros de l'été, quand il se fait un couvre-nuque avec des feuilles de figuier, qu'il a les mains pleines d'herbe et qu'il se redresse, les bras écartés, pour regarder la terre, c'est un arbre." Panturle is no Cyclops, since he is slowly awaking to love. The end of the novel, less than subtle in its symbolism, shows Panturle "...solidement enfoncé dans la terre comme une colonne..."[12], reemphasizing the "return-to-the-soil" message typical of Giono in the thirties.

A faintly Greek note may be perceived when we are told of Mamèche's husband who had come from Italy to be a well-digger: "Ce qui l'avait tiré de là-bas (i.e. from Italy) ici, allez le chercher: le destin!"[13] If such an explanation is not fully satisfactory, it is because readers are more sophisticated than the primitive people of Giono's novels in whose life fate, not unlike its Greek counterpart, comes to be so prominent a force. Stylistically, *Regain* would make a worthwhile study, for there are a number of strikingly beautiful lines of prose poetry, akin to anapaestic verse and indirectly reminiscent of Greek poetry as filtered through Hugo, such as the lines: "Vers leur pas la nuit s'avance; elle pousse devant elle les débris de la Trinité."[14]

However it is in *Colline*, the first and perhaps most successful volume of this trilogy, that the Greek atmosphere is most evident. The people in this alternately poetic and harshly frugal story are dominated entirely by the forces of Nature. The central mystery consists in the struggle between man and that Nature which he believed to be his good neighbor, but which occasionally seemed to assert its independence, its wickedness. The crude and crafty farmers who had learned how to cling to this wild piece of land live under the terror of the unnamable, of an only too well-known unknown. Their attempt to conjure up a spell of protection against the elements is moving but unsuccessful. Their fight against the forest fire is obviously doomed to failure beforehand. In order to stress the deep meaning of such a conflict, Giono has arranged his themes by order of importance. The earth, the wind, the water, the fire—all the elements participate one by one. The use of images, metaphors, symbols (sometimes inspired by classical models) all seem to suggest that the book has a quasi-musical structure. To support this hypothesis, one may note the extraordinary frequency of classical images at the very beginning of the text. However, this device is gradually abandoned, and such images are only sporadically employed in the latter part of the novel. Some pagan mysticism might be read into the character of old Janet. He seems to embody the mysterious forces of evil, but his death, a natural event, solves the apparent mystery. As Pierre de Boisdeffre has pointed out, water is the main feature of the book, because the drying up of the spring is the key event; all the other catastrophes are linked to this initial omen of bad things to come.

It would be erroneous to accuse the author of conscious or unconscious naïveté. The great simplicity of his plot is beautifully suited to a dramatic and psychologically satisfying working out of the story. The characters act from what they believe to be the dictates of their free wills, but the reader cannot rid himself of the impression that they are only tools in the hands of a higher power. Thus the naïveté is only on the surface; the people in *Colline* live right at the heart of Nature, but they cannot view her as their enemy.

A few stylistic devices enhance the impression of classical inspiration. A not unhomeric redundance is found a few times, as in this description, at the beginning of the text, of the wild boar wallowing in the cool marshy water: "La fraîcheur le traverse d'outre en outre, de son ventre à son échine."[15] Other pleonastic pictures are found in this novel as elsewhere; they are certainly always consciously employed. A more typically Homeric sequence may have come to Giono via the poetry of Hugo or Vigny: "Il boit; il s'essuie l'oseraie de ses moustaches."[16] There are a number of such similes, and they have a definitely Greek ring, even if we remember that the novelist had to consult translations, or rather precisely for that very reason.

As to the fundamental question of influence, of course one would have to examine the book as a whole. And on this point it is striking to see that its structure owes a good deal to models from antiquity. When we ask in just what ways Giono's characters are intrinsically like the Greeks, we are obliged to admit that they are not really comparable to the heroes of the *Iliad*. Old Janet does not have the scope of an Achilles in his wrath, not even that of a Diomedes. And yet, Giono's men do have a stature of their own: nourished with healthy, fresh sap they hold on to the earth with the fierce courage and love of wrestlers determined not to let go. Their chtonic strength ultimately succeeds in opposing the superior power of the elements and in conquering it. It is here that their Homeric dimension is to be found, and also in the rough and yet graceful voice with which they speak.

In general, the women in Giono's early novels are not women of classic grandeur, but they speak and laugh, love and jest in a natural way, very much akin to Greek women of old. Their problems are also often similar. Joséphine (*Que Ma Joie demeure*) may be no Helen of Troy, but she too is torn between her children and her family tasks on one hand, and her furious desire for the mysterious Bobi on the other. In the same novel, Madame Hélène's wild outbursts of mourning and moaning are not unlike the cries we hear in Aeschylus' play *The Persians*. Old men vent their anger or their joy much in the vein of Homeric Greeks, while men in the prime of life express their thoughts in action or through gesture more often than in words. Giono's silences, the loneliness pervading his characters, are different from the classical mentality as he could have learned about it from books on antiquity. But as soon as we are confronted with elemental forces at work, there is a striking similarity in imagery, in thought and expression:

the modern author came quite close to his model in these respects, often without even trying to do so.

The sea is largely absent from Giono's work. When in one of the rare allusions, in *Que Ma Joie demeure*, the alpine site is compared to the sea, the picture is consistently drawn. Winds, rain, the earth—all are endowed with supernatural powers, much in the way of ancient divinities. Giono's streams may be only a trickle compared to the gushing fluvial gods of Homer. And yet, little Durance inspires genuine awe when she is swelled by torrential rains—a scene strongly reminiscent of one of Zola's early stories. (This coincidence is not surprising when we remember the friendship between Giono's and Zola's fathers, both of Italian extraction, both long time residents of the country on the banks of the Durance). All the elements exert a strange power over the human characters. Even though we know much of the dramatic storm is exaggerated, we may find the impact of Nature on humans to be quite believable: Giono's man lives according to Nature's dictates, he never really rebels against Nature but rather seeks to integrate himself in her framework. Pan-like creatures animate Giono's wilderness. Their strength is derived from their unique nearness to the sources of life; their chtonic, or if you will telluric force is renewed through contact with the ground.

In almost all of the other examples of Giono's work up to 1945, the imprint of classical Greece is undeniable; its presence often adds a refreshing note to the original modern work and underlines the nearness of man and the earth. Numerous examples of traces of classical inspiration could be pointed out in this portion of Giono's writings, but a few particularly compelling illustrations will suffice to show how closely the writer followed a model from the classical world.

In the volume of short stories entitled *Solitude de la Pitié*, there are several strong indications of Giono's affinity for the ancients. "Prélude à Pan" is a powerful bacchanale, overflowing with life and joy, suggestive of Giono's deep understanding of man and beast, of the beast in man, of what constitutes the majesty of sensuous rapture. The story is also alive with humor, illuminated by a sound and superior irony, especially when it comes to the fruits of the strange intermingling of man and beast.

In his outline of *Le Chant du Monde*, announcing the beautiful novel to come, (1934) the author noted: "Un fleuve est un personnage."[17] What more Greek concept could be enunciated? In fact, the ultimately finished novel well demonstrates that precept; in the book, we find a microcosm of pagans, living and loving or hating in ways that suggest the author's careful reading in Greek epics.

Even in a volume of polemic prose, *Les Vraies Richesses*, we may encounter occasional glances at beauty; buried in the floods of invective against the evils of culture, there are a few quiet words of admiration for Greek ideas, to offer respite from the heat of the battle. I am not thinking of the none too convincing invocation of Demeter, but rather of a quite simple and moving passage that is worth quoting: "La vie m'ensevelissait si profondément au milieu d'elle sans mort ni pitié que parfois, pareil au dieu, je sentais ma tête, mes cheveux, mes yeux remplis d'oiseaux, mes bras lourds de branches, ma poitrine gonflée de chèvres, de chevaux, de taureaux, mes pieds traînant des racines, et la terreur des premiers hommes me hérissait comme un soleil."[18]

In *Triomphe de la Vie*, the sequel to *Les Vraies Richesses*—an equally violent book but not quite so edifying to read—after "un mississippi de jurons magnifiques et tendres"[19] we encounter Médé who has "une voix de cuivre,"[20] like Menelaus. After that, should we be offended if Giono, in a slight betrayal of Homer's spirit, declares: "Tenons-nous-en à la vieille définition si on préfère: 'Ce n'est pas de raconter les choses réellement arrivées qui est l'œuvre propre du poète, mais de bien raconter ce qui pourrait arriver'."[21]

Giono's Hellenic vein lies in simplicity. It has frequently been said that his simplicity smacks of over-elaboration. That may well be. It is not, however, an argument against the power or the attractiveness of his style. Just as Homer was bound by convention—a metric law, prosody, and tradition—so Giono submits to certain laws, even if they are of his own making.

At times, Giono comes close to an image not seldom found in Homer, as in *Que Ma Joie demeure:* "Maintenant, du haut de son cheval, il voyait ses larges prés écumeux..."[22] At other moments a description is truly Homeric in its breadth; we may frown on weaving looms when the painting of their portrait is done after Achilles' shield. But that is precisely Giono's strength—to transfer images from the extraordinary to the ordinary.

One final illustration of Giono's fine sense of language in its relation to the Greek model may be helpful in pointing up the poetic gifts of the author of *Que Ma Joie demeure*. We are apprised of young Aurore's suffering. Her heart is afflicted, and her mother is confronted with the boundless pain of the young girl: "Aurore ne parle plus. Aurore se colle le nez à la fenêtre. Aurore regarde la pluie et ne bouge plus. Aurore ne mange guère."[23] Of course, honesty requires us to add the last sentence of the paragraph which somehow explodes the poetry by its desperate prosaic tone: "J'ai l'impression que cette petite ne dort pas." But even if the poetic spell is broken, we have had enough of a chance to face the flow of Giono's prose in its natural ease. After all, Homer's heroes, too, had moments of everyday concern in their speech, and his Gods had frightful but all to human tempers.

Only one other writer in France today approaches this mysterious gift of Giono's. Henri Bosco, like Giono a son of the Mediterranean land, knows how to evoke the beauties of nature in a manner not too dissimilar from that of our author. Bosco's characters, too, have the gift of silence, of blending into the landscape, of knowing how to conjure nature's spells. His description of near-magic has a charm comparable to some of Giono's scenes. He is also fond of herbs, of simple pleasures close to the joys of ancient Greece. The basic difference is in the respective formation of both writers. Giono's knowledge of the ancient world was self-taught, while Bosco's was acquired through a life-time of study of the classics. If Giono's peasants often voice a bacchic *joie de vivre*, Bosco's are pure and somewhat ethereal, at least as far as their sensuality is concerned.

The fact that he discovered Greek beauty through translations, rather than via the original texts, has not impeded Giono's feeling of kinship with the ancient world. On the contrary, he has a freshness of touch that is rarely equalled, and it is tinged with an enthusiasm devoid of nostalgia. By contrast, consider for a moment a poet who, two centuries earlier, wrote many poems on "the Gods of Greece," i.e., Friedrich Schiller. The German classical poet bitterly regretted that he was so far removed from Greece's eternally blue skies, and in a youthful poem, "Resignation", he exclaimed: "Auch ich war in Arkadien geboren." Thus he symbolized the modern era's stifling lack of freedom through his antithetical exaltation of Greece's realm of joyous liberty.

Peyre succinctly characterized Giono's forceful early work and underlined his special stature as a writer when he said that the author of the *Pan* cycle "Antaeus-like, seems to draw unto him the strength of the earth and Atlas-like carries the weight of the skies on his shoulders."[24] As such he has obvious affinities with a Homer. His early novels in particular open up before our eyes a garden filled with living beings, with flowers and their scents, but also overshadowed by dark clouds and often beaten by strong winds. His is not an idyllic world, but a rough and beautiful one—a world of love and struggle quite like Homer's. Any specifically Hellenistic elements are largely incidental. When he consciously attempts to emulate the ancients, Giono is usually less successful. The strong impression left on us by his best novels stems from the unique combination of a strong and simple plot, fundamental characters, and an array of descriptions so suggestive in their totality that we can visualize the site, hear the ring of the bells, smell the acrid smoke rising from wet wood. If Giono is versatile— and his more recent novels prove that he is—he is also solidly steadfast; a modern, building on the platform of the best of antiquity with materials that will endure. But most interesting of all, critics would generally agree that he is most truly Greek when he least tries to be so. In that sense, he is profoundly a 20th century Hellene.

State University of New York
at Stony Brook

Notes

[1] "The lively Convention of Translation," in *The Craft and Context of Translation* ed. by William Arrowsmith and Roger Shattuck, New York, 1964.

[2] If more important names are missing in such an enumeration of Hellenistic themes, it is mostly out of respect for Henri Peyre's exhaustive and very suggestive work on this question, *L'Influence des littératures antiques sur la littérature française moderne*, New Haven, 1941.

[3] Christian Michelfelder, *Jean Giono et les religions de la terre*, Paris, 1938, and Maxwell A. Smith, *Jean Giono*, New York, 1966.

[4] *The Contemporary French Novel*, New York, 1955, p. 129. (The text is identical in the 1967 ed. entitled *Contemporary French Novelists*.)

[5] Quoted by Peyre, *op. cit.*, p. 130 from a passage in *Jean le bleu*.

[6] Peyre, *L'Influence...*, p. 79.

[7] *Les Nouvelles Littéraires*, March 13, 1937.

[8] Peyre, *Cont. French Novel*, p. 138.

[9] Pierre de Boisdeffre, *Giono*, Paris, 1965, p. 109.

[10] *Accompagnés de la Flûte*, Paris, 1924, (1951 ed. p. 32).

[11] *Regain*, Paris, 1930, p. 98.

[12] Ibid., p. 236.

[13] Ibid., p. 17.

[14] Ibid., p. 80.

[15] *Colline*, Paris, 1928, p. 11.

[16] Ibid., p. 22.

[17] *Solitude de la Pitié*, Paris, 1932, p. 215.

[18] *Les Vraies Richesses*, Paris, 1937, p. 17.

[19] *Triomphe de la Vie*, Paris, 1942, p. 135.

[20] Ibid. Let us remember Homer called Menelaus " $\beta o \dot{\eta} \nu \ \dot{\alpha} \gamma a \theta \acute{o} \varsigma$ ".

[21] Ibid., p. 43.

[22] *Que Ma Joie demeure*, Paris, 1935, p. 355.

[23] Ibid., p. 328.

[24] Peyre, *Cont. French Novel*, p. 136.

The preceding essays have indicated the special ways in which three representative authors of the early 20th century—Péguy, Gide, and Giono—have utilized classical materials in their works. Yet it is important to note that among contemporary writers, it is the playwrights who have most consistently—and successfully—turned to the Greek world for the raw materials of their literary creations. Jean Giraudoux, that "virtuose de l'intelligence"[1] has made a particularly varied and meaningful use of elements from antiquity in his plays. To be sure, as Professor Peyre has pointed out, in several instances Giraudoux employed legendary materials simply as a "prétexte à ses fantaisies ailées," those light, precious bits of brilliant fluff which graced the French stage during the "Entre-Deux-Guerres" period.[2] But however fanciful and "escapist" he may have been at such moments, one should not forget that as a professional diplomat he was also deeply involved in the historical happenings of his time and very much of a political realist.

Giraudoux was well aware that the Greeks were men as we are, and he felt that the vicissitudes of the legendary beings who lived in the early ages of mankind bore witness to the continuing validity of certain profound truths about human life. In this sense, he considered the Greek heroes to be timeless, and in bringing them to life again on the modern stage he evidently intended to make the universal value of their adventures obvious to his contemporaries. Thus the stories of Amphitryon, Electra, and the Trojan war were not only an occasion for him to exercise his verbal virtuosity; they also inspired him to present some of his most dramatic and striking confrontations between man and Destiny.

Professor Lamont's provocative analysis makes it clear that beneath the glitter and preciosity of a work like *La Guerre de Troie n'aura pas lieu* there lies a profound message for today. Giraudoux's updated portraits of the Homeric figures—particularly Hector—are remarkable because while they remain faithful to the general spirit and thrust of the classical legend, they make a very meaningful statement of certain elements in the human predicament with which modern man is particularly concerned. In a very real sense, Giraudoux the humanist was drawn to the Golden Age of Greece because he saw in it certain possibilities, certain timeless elements that would be understood by human beings of all times—simply because they were men.

Notes

[1] Henri M. Peyre, *L'Influence des littératures antiques sur la littérature française moderne* (New Haven-Oxford, 1941), p. 80.
[2] Peyre, loc. cit.

GIRAUDOUX'S HECTOR:
A HERO'S STAND AGAINST HEROISM

By Rosette C. Lamont

The defeat of victory, of every victory issuing from a bloody war, haunts that memory of the future which constitutes the particular gift of poets and prophets. Such is the painful awareness of Giraudoux's Hector, unheedful of Cassandra's warning of the dangers of imminent destruction. In *La Guerre de Troie n'aura pas lieu* Homer's doomed but unquestioning hero becomes the anti-hero *par excellence*, the protagonist whose passive resistance to the idea of heroism and active struggle against the collective folly of war makes him the living conscience of that period known in France as "L'Entre-deux-guerres." Ushered in by Céline in his violent modern epic, *Voyage au bout de la nuit*, the twentieth century anti-hero of fiction or drama, be his name Bardamu or Hector, shares a similar revelation: "La vérité c'est une agonie qui n'en finit pas. La vérité de ce monde, c'est la mort."[1]

With Céline's novel, the reader finds himself at the very core of that Hegelian truth which includes the negative. If the nineteenth century could have believed in the Kantian myth of fundamental order, the twentieth seems to illustrate Hegel's fear of the forces of war and slavery, forces shaped by the failure to grasp man's basic quality, his freedom. The life process itself, conceived as a concrete, dynamic power, constitutes the ultimate reality for Hegel. Embedded in a cultural unity the hero/anti-hero dialectic serves as one of the principal levers of the contemporary ideological drama of history. Within this drama, seen as a scale in which our epoch weighs Malraux's *conquérants* and martyrs against Beckett's passive heroes of lucid endurance, Giraudoux's *La Guerre de Troie* occupies a place at the very center. Its protagonist does not refuse to act as much as he voices his opposition to a certain kind of action. He is in fact embarked upon a one-man struggle against the heroic code by which his society wants to live and die. He knows this code to be antiquated, a key piece in the puzzle of grand illusions. Hector espouses the negative: non-action will become the right kind of action.

The problem of national identity puzzled Giraudoux from the time he began preparing an *agrégation* in German. Nor did it stop preoccupying the mind of the sergeant of World War I, twice wounded, decorated for bravery, but whose own brother suffered amnesia as a result of battle

fatigue in that same war. Giraudoux, the career diplomat, no longer
regarded war as an opportunity to live on an epic scale, but he continued to
consider the Franco-German conflict as one of the truly serious questions
of Western Europe. When Philippe Berthelot's protégé at the Ministry of
Foreign Affairs was sent to Germany on a special mission, he observed a
defeated country. Later, as Head of the Services of Press and Information,
and as Inspector General of Diplomatic and Consular Posts, Giraudoux
continued to feel the pulse of that sick land. Thus, the pure poet known for
his antirealism in literature, became intent, by his own admission, on a
polemical study of the way in which the forces of reaction that precipitated
World War I arose again after the victory of the Allies.

The protagonist of his novel, *Siegfried et le Limousin*, and of the two
plays he drew from this novel, is a German statesman, unaware of his
French origin because of amnesia. This duality makes him especially
receptive to the influences of the very forces he despises. His idealism is
vitiated from the start. In her book, *Jean Giraudoux, The Theatre of
Victory*, Mrs. Agnes Raymond stresses the fact that Giraudoux's thinking
"was so realistic and so topical that his literary antirealism was often a
convenient mask."[2] Thus, Siegfried "is a symbol of the German Republic,
born, as the name suggests, of the Allied victory and peace."[3] *Siegfried von
Kleist*, and the version entitled *Siegfried*, adapted for the Jouvet Company
from that first play, reveal Giraudoux's concern with those *hommes-tigres*,
the sad progeny of *Le Tigre* (Clémenceau) who, as Prospectors, Presidents,
and Brokers stand ready to devour this earth, sacrificing all human values
for the sake of financial gain. It is they who turn Germany and France
against each other, for, as the dramatist states in *La Guerre de Troie*,
summing up one his fundamental beliefs, the two countries on each side of
the Rhine are not natural enemies. More often than not, as Ulysses
explains to Hector, war is a fratricidal combat:

> Pourquoi toujours revenir à ce mot ennemi! Faut-il vous le redire? Ce ne sont pas les
> ennemis naturels qui se battent. Il est des peuples que tout désigne pour une guerre, leur
> peau, leur langue et leur odeur, ils se jalousent, ils se haïssent, ils ne peuvent se sentir...
> Ceux-là ne se battent jamais. Ceux qui se battent, ce sont ceux que le sort a lustrés et
> préparés pour une même guerre: ce sont les adversaires (Act II, scene 13).[4]

In his brilliantly destructive essay, "M. Jean Giraudoux et la philosophie
d'Aristote," Jean-Paul Sartre posits the rhetorical question: "M. Giraudoux se divertirait-il à faire le schizophrène?"[5] Obviously, the high priest
of French Existentialism who describes life as "cette pâte molle parcourue
d'ondulations qui ont leur cause et leur fin hors d'elles-mêmes, ce monde
sans avenir, où tout est rencontre, où le présent vient comme un voleur, où
l'évènement résiste par nature à la pensée et au language, où les individus
sont des accidents, des cailloux dans la pâte, pour lesquels l'esprit forge,
après coup, des rubriques générales,»[6] is the man most unlikely to understand the poetic universe of a Giraudoux, the novelist and dramatist intent
on presenting a slice of eternity.

For Sartre, the world of Giraudoux is "un monde sans indicatif présent,"[7] one in which the only form of freedom is the realization of the promises extended to the individual by his essence. Nor will Sartre dignify this archetypal world by calling it Platonistic. He sees it as falsely original, indeed, upon close examination, as obsolete in what he defines as its Aristotelian determination to observe, classify and generalize. From a scientific point of view it is outdated, absurd, being the world of Linné rather than Lamarck, Cuvier rather than Geoffroy de Saint Hilaire. It appears above all as a world "tout fait et que ne se fait point."[8] The philosopher who is best known for his statement that existence precedes essence cannot forgive Giraudoux for creating characters strangely free of Becoming, characters who find that change is a series of states linked by inevitable, oriented alterations, each bringing one closer to one's essence. It is a universe free of determinism, causality, contingency. "Le monde de M. Giraudoux est celui des virginités reconquises,"[9] says Sartre, alluding no doubt to Giraudoux' *Judith*.

What Sartre is temperamentally incapable of perceiving is that Giraudoux's "rationalisme de politesse"[10] disguises a profound awareness of tragic inevitability. Underneath the "préciosité" of a twentieth century Musset one detects the anguish of a man just as *engagé* in the politics of his era as Sartre himself. But whereas the Existentialist philosopher still adheres to a Cartesian definition of rational behavior tempered by a Germanic longing for the triumph of the Will, Giraudoux, not unlike Homer, is haunted by a sense of destiny. Perhaps Homer's Gods whom the Greek poet did not fail to treat with a certain ironic familiarity have become History in Giraudoux, yet this transformation does not in any way weaken the tragic movement of his plays. As Christian Marker notes: "Le coup de force de Giraudoux est d'avoir enraciné l'au-delà dans l'imma-nent."[11]

The very title of his play, *La Guerre de Troie n'aura pas lieu*, betrays the ironic point of view of a man who was always ready to battle against destiny. Hector's dilemma is that of Giraudoux himself, indeed that of modern man. We have become aware that what we call peace is only a respite between wars. During this false lull, "cet entr'acte de la vie du pays, ... ce congé du médiocre,"[12] the mediocrity of war seeping into the mediocre well-being of peace corrupts it further. The germs of war come alive again in the weakened body of the nation. A mortal disease, that of conquest, is diagnosed by the dramatist in his Prelude to *Sodome et Gomorrhe*. This Plague, to use Camus' term, is sensed by the poet long before it becomes obvious to everyone else. His duty is to find the language most suitable for expressing his awareness. Since it is the nature of the intellectual to be divided, that part of him which is human rises with indignation at the senselessness of future destruction, while the seer envisions the Trojan war immobilized in an eternal present of wrath and death. Christian Marker writes with rare intelligence: "C'est peut-être la première fois depuis le monde de la Tragédie, que l'œuvre théâtrale renonce à la surprise et aux tiroirs, pour consister essentiellement en une continuelle *mise au point* de sa vérité sur un être choisi, ou un groupe."[13] Cassandre could tell Hector what Anubis reveals to the Sphinx in the second act of Cocteau's *La Machine infernale:* "Le temps des hommes est de l'éternité pliée."

The tragedy of Homer's Hector is that of Troy. According to several outstanding scholars (notably Richmond Lattimore), Hector is not a natural warrior. He "fights from a sense of duty and a respect for the opinion of others."[14] Robert Graves goes so far as to suggest that an inveterate hatred of war appears throughout the poem. Although Homer's Hector despises his brother Paris for being frivolous, irresponsible, light-hearted, ironic even in the midst of battle, and more interested in love-making than in his honor, Hector himself is not a pure hero either, at least not in the sense that Diomedes and Patroclus are. He is after all the man who upon coming face to face with Achilles runs thrice round the walls of the city pursued by his opponent. Lattimore alludes to a hidden weakness, and this may be an injustice. Yet Homer evidently intended to present Hector as the most human of his heroes. He does not have the stupid pride, the arrogance, the stubbornness of Achilles whose greed, sensuality and self-indulgence make him, according to Graves, the villain of the song. Nor is he a weak, lying, boastful, irresolute meddler like Agamemnon who vacillates in his thinking, confuses his allies, makes enemies of former friends, and who, despite a kingly bravery, manages to almost always do the wrong thing and for the wrong reason. Without being a *sophron* like Odysseus, Hector is wise. He does not seek out danger, yet he does not avoid it. He is of course all the more courageous because he knows fear. Before triumphing over other men he must first triumph over himself. As son, husband, and father he is the incarnation of the man of good will. A champion, fighting for a cause he knows to be both hopeless and unjust, he appears as the great victim of Homer's poem. Through his sacrifice we participate in the age-old ritual of death, disintegration and dismemberment.

If, as Joseph Campbell states, "tragedy is the shattering of the forms and of our attachment to the forms,"[15] then Hector's desecrated body, dragged head down in the dust behind the chariot of his proud victor, symbolizes the approaching annihilation of the city and the passing of all that seemed most alive and significant. Hector's death is one of the elements which transmute chronicle into drama. The death of Achilles, being foreseen, looms as a reminder that all victory is relative, that the humiliation of death must follow upon the glory of a bloody triumph. In that sense Achilles is as much a victim of destiny as is Hector whom he kills. A death-ridden hero returns the corpse of the king's son to Priam. In the scene in which the old, defeated ruler, and the doomed hero weep together, a sense of a transcendent force, anonymous, pitiless, all-pervasive begins to haunt the mind. "The burning of Troy is final because it is brought about by the fierce sport of human hatreds and the wanton, mysterious choice of destiny," writes George Steiner.[16] Like Dante's *Purgatorio*, the *Iliad* is centered on the human realm and deals with what Fergusson calls "the endless forms of moral change," thus appealing to "our direct sense of the changing life of the psyche."[17]

Giraudoux's *La Guerre de Troie* may be tragic in the sense that human sacrifice is still the subject of the play, and that "the audience is learning what it has always known,"[18] but it is perhaps too Racinian, and too French to focus on the irrational or supra-rational aspects of the psychic life. Thus it does not attempt to translate "the movement or focus of the soul" as it "actualizes its essence moment by moment,"[19] but prefers to suggest as does *Bérénice* or *Phèdre*, the tragic incommensurability which exists between the actual world of the senses and the logical realm of thought as it shines through the refractions of verbal expression.

Claude-Edmonde Magny states in her classical study, *Précieux Giraudoux*, that the particular universe of the author of *Intermezzo* is created by language.[20] No one realized more keenly than Racine's admirer that language is the instrument through which myths crystallize into signs as familiar to the poet imbued with an unfailing cosmic sense as traffic signals which guide the motorist. Combined with a profound tenderness for the modest realities of flesh, that sense of the transcendent allows the dramatist to comprehend the provisional and perishable character of nature, and yet to make of it what Rilke called, in many of his private letters, his property and his particular friendship.

Moving away from a Christian view, Giraudoux envisions Man as the transformer of a universe so utterly free of the presence of a God that the Hero is able to usurp that place. But the desire to effect this substitution proves to be a lethal temptation. Andromaque questions her husband: "Ah? Tu te sens un dieu, à l'instant du combat?" He answers, thoughtfully, that being less than a man, he is nevertheless at such moments godlike, being both pitiless and full of love: "Certains matins, on se relève du sol allégé, étonné, mué. Le corps, les armes ont un autre poids, sont d'un autre alliage. On est invulnérable. Une tendresse vous envahit, vous submerge, la variété de tendresse des batailles: on est tendre parce qu'on est impitoyable; ce doit être en effet la tendresse des dieux" (Act I, scene 3). Having lost one's human attributes and become vested with those of a divinity, one is ready to impart death. The human being is now one's adversary, touchingly naked and vulnerable, slightly grotesque in his common humanity: "Puis l'adversaire arrive, écumant, terrible. On a pitié de lui, on voit en lui, derrière sa bave et ses yeux blancs, toute l'impuissance et tout le dévouement du pauvre fonctionnaire humain qu'il est, du pauvre mari et gendre, du pauvre cousin germain, du pauvre amateur de raki et d'olives qu'il est. On a de l'amour pour lui. On aime sa verrue sur sa joue, sa taie dans son œil. On l'aime... Mais il insiste... Alors on le tue" (ibid). Giraudoux's Judith explains that killing can be an act of supreme charity and love, a caress of such finality that it saves the one who receives it from the mediocrities of daily compromise. Andromaque echoes this revelation when she exclaims: "On ne tue bien que ce qu'on aime" (ibid).

After such knowledge, the true hero, the man who, in the words of Joseph Campbell makes it "possible for men and women to come to full maturity through the conditions of contemporary life,"[21] must become, paradoxically, the enemy of the concept of heroism. Having lost his unequivocal inner unity, Giraudoux's Hector perceives that the symphony of war is played off tune. He can no longer believe in the exceptional ethos which allowed him the right of life and death over other living creatures. No longer single-hearted and single-minded, born to be reborn in his final destruction, Hector finds himself excluded from the illusory harmony which connects the rest of the world. The guilty fact that he discovers is a form of suicide. "Auparavant ceux que j'allais tuer me semblaient le contraire de moi-même. Cette fois, j'étais agenouillé sur un miroir" (ibid). In *La Guerre de Troie*, Homer's reluctant but dutiful warrior has become the sworn enemy of that self-destructive principle, violence.

"Cela devient impossible de discuter d'honneur avec ces anciens combattants. Ils abusent vraiment du fait qu'on ne peut les traiter de lâches." (Act II, scene 5). The point is well taken by Demokos, the Trojan court poet who harbors a banal, all-pervasive love for war. It is important to establish the fact that Hector's courage cannot be doubted since we will see him endure all manner of humiliation to avoid new conflict. He winces and clenches his fists as the gross Oiax slaps his face, and when that same drunken lout reappears towards the end of the play, intent on making love to Andromaque, Hector, instead of leaping to his wife's defense, bides his time, unwilling to compromise the shaky agreement he has reached with Ulysses. However ironic Sartre's judgment of Giraudoux may be, he would recognize in this behavior one of his most passionate affirmations: not to act is also an action.

The contemporary anti-hero has learned the value of passive endurance. Having abandoned the dangerous fallacies of the antiquated heroic code, he is no longer concerned with saving face. This is demonstrated in the scene in which Paris and Helen are persuaded to part. Though they agree quite readily since——this is Giraudoux's wonderful invention——they do not really love each other deeply, the Greeks will not accept the wife of Menelaus unless they can be persuaded that she is unsullied. Judith's miracle cannot be applied easily to Leda's daughter. Half amused by such a preposterous notion, Paris, the faithful follower of Aphrodite, accepts this slur on his virility. But his men, the sailors on the ship used for Helen's abduction, will not endure the destruction of their symbol of *machismo*. The eye witness account they offer of Paris' amatory prowess—a truly epic performance—clears their prince of the suspicion of impotence, but brings Troy to that brink of war Hector seeks to avoid. In this highly erotic passage of prose poetry, the dramatist who wanted to promulgate VÉRITÉ, SENSUALITÉ, ÉGALITÉ as the motto of the French Republic, suggests that the freedom of desire is perverted by the little people's simple-minded admiration for the acrobatics of seduction, and by their dangerous notions of what constitutes national honor and pride. Giraudoux uncovers the corrosive connection which exists in people's minds between a false idea of virility and a bellicose attitude. To Demokos' assertion that the true hero must prove himself on both battlefields: «Tuer un homme, c'est mériter une femme» (Act I, scene 6), Hecuba provides a slightly vulgar but most revealing answer: "Ils veulent faire la guerre pour une femme, c'est la façon d'aimer des impuissants" (ibid).

Giraudoux's Hector is wise enough to see through the false glitter of words such as courage, honor, and pride, and to reach for the ultimate truth buried under the shimmering surface; life is the only irreplaceable gift. In order to rescue it from those who seem so eager to sacrifice it, the poet, whose universe is shaped by words, must be ready for the supreme sacrifice, that of his vocabulary. This is illustrated in a conversation between Hector and Demokos, a caricature of the academic poet whose perusal of abstractions has encouraged him to isolate himself from the realities of existence.

> Demokos.— Hector, je suis poète et juge en poète. Suppose que notre vocabulaire ne soit pas quelquefois touché par la beauté! Suppose que le mot délice n'existe pas!
> Hector.— Nous nous en passerions. Je m'en passe déjà. Je ne prononce le mot délice qu'absolument forcé.
> Demokos.— Oui, et tu te passerais du mot volupté, sans doute?
> Hector.— Si c'était au prix de la guerre qu'il fallait acheter le mot volupté, je m'en passerais.
> Demokos.— C'est au prix de la guerre que tu as trouvé le plus beau, le mot courage.
> Hector.— C'était bien payé.
>
> (Act I, scene 6)

Hector's bitterly realistic answer makes him the true son of Hecuba who appears, in Giraudoux's play, as a woman singularly devoid of sentimentality. In the course of the same scene she applies her wry humor and her unfailing common sense to the destruction of the hero image when she says: "Nous connaissons le vocabulaire. L'homme en temps de guerre s'appelle le héros. Il peut ne pas en être plus brave, et fuir à toutes jambes. Mais c'est du moins un héros qui détale."

Hector knows that if war equalizes all men in their common condition of mortality, the true victors are those who manage to survive. For the famous French saying *qui vivra verra* he would no doubt substitute *qui survivra verra*. In his moving address to the Dead, delivered at the ceremony of the closing of the Gates of War—a ritual he insists upon though it proves in the end pitifully brief—he apologizes for being among the "déserteurs que sont les survivants," stating that there is only one true decoration for valor on the battle field, the palms of life. There are no dead heroes for this modern Hector who asserts: "Les vivants, vainqueurs ou non, ont la vraie cocarde, la double cocarde" (Act II, scene 5). Did Sartre recall this scene when he showed Electra dancing in celebration of life at the Festival for the Dead, Aegisthus' great show of public repentance? It is also in praise of life that Hector speaks when he wonders whether those who no longer see or touch, who do not hear or feel, the absent, inexistent, forgotten ones, those without occupation, rest or being will ever forgive him, and others like him who are still above ground, for stealing from them the supreme good: warmth and light.

War is given a particularly modern treatment by Giraudoux when he reveals its absurd character. The Trojan War is to be fought because an

ostensibly happy couple of lovers has become the center of an international
conflict. To stress the absurdity of this war, and by implication of all wars,
Giraudoux depicts a frigid Helen and a promiscuous Paris. A kind of
Hollywood starlet endowed with a technicolor vision of the future, this
Helen claims that she enjoys rubbing men against her like large cakes of
soap. Paris, a womanizer, is convinced that parting is the high point of a
relationship. These two may "adore"one another but they do not know the
meaning of love. Since they have become the symbol of it, they could do
without the reality. Yet they are not happy at the idea of parting, Helen
because she prefers this kind of *amour-goût* to passion love ("L'aimanta-
tion, c'est aussi un amour, autant que la promiscuité," she explains to
Andromaque—Act II, scene 8) and Paris because he enjoys the aloofness of
Helen ("... avec elle, j'ai l'impression d'avoir rompu avec toutes les autres
femmes, et j'ai mille libertés et mille noblesses au lieu d'une."—Act I, scene
4). Despite their harmonious, uncomplicated life together they agree to
separate for the sake of peace.

Helen, however, does not believe in the possibility of that peace.
Seemingly malleable, yet unchanging, Giraudoux's Helen is a dumb as fate.
Nor does her acquiescence reassure Hector who cries out, addressing the
prophetess of the family: "Ecoute-la Cassandre! Ecoute ce bloc de néga-
tion qui dit oui! Tous m'ont cédé. Paris m'a cédé, Priam m'a cédé, Hélène
me cède. Et je sens qu'au contraire dans chacune de ces victoires appa-
rentes, j'ai perdu" (Act I, scene 9). Helen, Hector, and Ulysses know that
war is unavoidable, but whereas the two men will attempt to change the
tide in the affairs of men, Helen, a woman, and a divinity, Helen, daughter
of Leda and the Swan, allows herself to be the instrument of destruction. If
she seems hard it is because she belongs to that race of people issued from
Baudelaire's Dandy who having no self-pity cannot feel for others. Baudelaire would consider her a non-woman according to his definition of the
female: "La femme est naturelle, c'est à dire abominable."[22] To Andromaque who is above all a woman, and a wife, Helen explains that the world
is divided between two groups of people: "Ceux qui sont, si vous voulez, la
chair de la vie humaine. Et ceux qui en sont l'ordonnance, l'allure. Les
premiers ont le rire, les pleurs, et tout ce que vous voudrez en sécrétions.
Les autres ont le geste, la tenue, le regard" (Act II, scene 8). The stupid,
beautiful starlet of Act I reveals herself in Act II as Nemesis, a classical
divinity who could, like Baudelaire's "La Beauté", declare:

Je trône dans l'azur comme un sphinx incompris;
J'unis un cœur de neige à la blancheur des cygnes;
Je hais le mouvement qui déplace les lignes,
Et jamais je ne pleure et jamais je ne ris.

Ulysses will call her later "one of the hostages of destiny."

Hector's only hope against this subtle trap lies in man's rational mind.
Lucidity, a willingness to talk, to listen, these are the only instruments with
which one could sever the slender, invisible threads of the web. Like
Homer's Hector who scorns superstitions when he tells Polydamas: "A

divine message? The best divine message is: ' Defend your country!'" (*The Illiad*, Book 12), the hero of *La Guerre de Troie n'aura pas lieu* will attempt to solve the dilemma in which his country is embroiled by accepting fully the challenge of being a man of this world. Greece may be ridden with divinities: "Paris dit que le ciel en grouille, que des jambes de déesses en pendent" (Act I, scene 8), Hector will not raise his head to look at them. The human level is his norm.

A confrontation with two men plays a central role in Hector's struggle. The first is Busiris, a jurist and an expert in international military law. The second is the Greek ambassador, Ulysses, a rational man of good will. Under the threat of imprisonment, Hector forces Busiris, a narrow pedant in love with his vocabulary of aggression, to reinterpret the facts, making every negative into a positive. In a comical about-face which reveals the ambiguous character of all legal philosophy, the Greeks' advance, seen at first as a provocation to war in its insulting placement of the pennants, and its aggressive fleet formation, are subsequently interpreted as suggesting a friendly visit. Busiris is able to fashion a new truth, the truth needed by Hector who, for his part, never doubted the jurist's ability to alter his original thesis since "le droit est la plus puissante des écoles de l'imagination" (Act II, scene 5).

Having won the first round, Hector summons Ulysses to what one would call today a summit meeting. Giraudoux, the career diplomat, demonstrates the futility of such encounters—a political fact which haunted the generation involved in the impotent struggles of the League of Nations. However, it is the gratuitousness of the meeting between the two leaders which lends a strange kind of dignity to their thwarted attempt at reaching an understanding. In Kierkegaardian terms one could say that they renounce their role as heroes in order to assume a superior one as Knights of Faith. In the course of their brief conversation they stand in absolute relation to the Absolute. Though they stand defeated by the destiny they wanted to trick, they are free of the despair which characterizes the prisoners of determinism. Their mission proved futile, but they triumph in having hoped against all hope.

Being the older of the two, Ulysses is the more sceptical, yet, the confrontation between the Greek ambassador, and the Trojan prince—a brilliant invention on the part of the modern dramatist—serves to bring into sharp focus the anti-heroic aspect of their convictions. If Hector is more outspoken in his rejection of the heroic code than Homer's dutiful warrior, Giraudoux's Ulysses could be an early portrait of Homer's *sophron*. By showing that Hector and Ulysses share a common desire, the playwright brings to light Homer's own distaste for war, a feeling made apparent in his delineation of the character of the King of Ithaca.

Both royal and cunning, Homer's "polytropic hero"[23] is not satisfied with being a warrior. He is a farmer who loves growing things, an intellectual whose curiosity leads him round the Greek world, an actor-clown able to assume the disguise of a tramp in order to spy or play the fool. Full of the paradoxes of human existence he is a draft-dodger forced to fight, a wanderer longing to go home, a philanderer loyal to his wife.

Human creation is his homeland. If he is a hero, he is that hero of comedy who is reborn without dying.

Civilized, intelligent, self-possessed, Athena's accomplice is convinced of the futility of ambition. Nor does he require Napoleon's painful apprenticeship to reach the conclusion that any army marches on its stomach. A passionate realist as portrayed by Homer, this first anti-hero of Western literature is not ashamed to refer to his "cursed belly" when he is brought half-starved to the court of Alcinoos.[24] It is the belly, he states, that forces man to remember it, commands him to drink and eat even when sorrowful. It is that same belly which is responsible for all wars of conquest because it forces men to "fit out fleets of ships and scour the barren sea, to bring misery on their enemies" (ibid, Book XVII). Though Lucian alleges that Odysseus died of gout, and Plato was shocked by his praise of banquets, this short-legged, broad-shouldered man of all-odds, with hair fleecy as a ram, and the mien of a "skipper of a trading crew, plying in a broad hocker, thinking of cargo, keeping an eye on the goods and grabbing what profits one can" (ibid.. Book VIII), possesses in fact the quality most admired by the ancient Greeks: *philia*. the attachment to one's natural social environment. A trickster well-versed in the Autolycan arts of slithering out of tight holes, he believes that prudence is superior to bravery. This inherent ethical ambiguity, the essence of intelligence, is profoundly disturbing to a conventional hero such as Achilles, but it is responsible for Odysseus' superb skill in handling the affairs of men. Giraudoux understood perfectly Homer's message, that only through moderation, modesty, and a realistic understanding of the human condition can man hope to achieve victory in life. As Stanford points out in his excellent book, "passionate heroism, glorious as it is, disrupts society and causes senseless destruction."[25] Thus, the civilized gentleness of Hector and emergent humanism of Odysseus are the qualities needed by a world which rejects the archaic notions of heroic violence. And so when Jean-Paul Sartre speaks with ironic scorn of Giraudoux's "eudémonisme païen," of his "morale de l'équilibre, du bonheur, du juste milieu,"[26] he forgets that the cult of happiness is not solely a bourgeois characteristic, that it is in fact part and parcel of a Hellenic sense of respect for the human. Happiness is not only the final reward of "la créature de M. Giraudoux;" it is also the fruit which the Homeric Odysseus will savor at the end of a life of wandering when he finds "ein reines, verhaltenes, smales /Menschliches, einen unseren Strefen Fruchtlands /zwischen Strom und Gestein."[27]

As we see him in Giraudoux, he is not yet the Odysseus who will discover that brawn without brain is of little use. However he already has the outward calm of a statesman. His extraordinary objectivity perplexes and shocks Hector until he comes to realize that the Greek ambassador does not want to *win*, because he does not believe in victory. His is a civilized mind in a world ruled by the dark forces of the irrational. Giraudoux's Ulysse is Odysseus, but he is also Philippe Berthelot and Aristide Briand. He is that man who could free man from man, and make of humanity a race superior to humanity. To Hector, the future undeserving victim, he offers the possibility of reconciliation. By choosing to dramatize a meeting between Hector and Ulysses, Giraudoux reveals both his deep understanding of Homer's message, and his own humanistic conception of the eternal problem of pain and death.

The real combat then is a dispute between the two envoys of their nation. They proceed to weigh upon the invisible scale of cosmic justice the right of one people to destroy another. Neither wants war, but Ulysses has little hope of averting it. With profound bitterness he states that their meeting is "le duo des récitants avant la guerre" (Act II, scene 13). As he leaves, the Greek ambassador expresses his fear that the road which leads from the quiet platform of their agreement to the port where the ships are waiting is "long comme le parcours officiel des rois en visite quand l'attentat menace" (ibid). It is not he, however, who will be killed. Ironically, the war will take place because Hector, no longer able to control himself, stabs the poet Demokos for beginning his song of war. Demokos accuses Oiax before dying. Thus, an absurd incident precipitates the catastrophe which could have been averted.

Giraudoux's Hector is a brilliant sketch. As a modern reinterpretation of the Homeric hero it manages to transform the character only by making him evolve in the direction pointed out by the Greek bard himself. Fatalistic and energetic, realistic and imaginative, tolerant, honest, Hector represents the disciplined mind that would stem the tide of folly which threatens the city. It takes great intellectual courage to go against all the clichés of one's epoch, to fight a single battle against heroism. Giraudoux's anti-hero is a hero, a man who knows that bravery is as complex a human emotion as any other. He cannot win, but his nobility resides in refusing to give up the absurdity of his hope, the rationality of his respect for life.

Queens College
City University of New York

Notes

[1] Céline, *Voyage au bout de la nuit*, Gallimard, 1952, p. 202.

[2] This book was published by the University of Massachusetts Press, 1966. Cf. p. 33.

[3] Ibid., p. 44.

[4] Giraudoux's text was first published by Grasset, late in 1935. It has been reissued in a number of editions since. Further references to the play will be given in the text.

[5] Jean-Paul Sartre, *Situations I*, Gallimard, 1947, p. 82.

[6] Ibid., p. 83.

[7] Ibid., p. 88.

[8] Ibid., p. 92.

[9] Ibid., p. 90.

[10] Ibid., p. 98.

[11] Cf. *Giraudoux par lui-même*, Seuil, 1952, p. 23.

[12] Quoted from Giraudoux's *Sans Pouvoirs*, in *Giraudoux par lui-même*, p. 160.

[13] *Giraudoux par lui-même*, p. 15.

[14] Cf. the "Introduction" to Richmond Lattimore's translation of *The Iliad*.

[15] Joseph Campbell, *The Hero with a Thousand Faces*, Meridian, 1956, p. 28.

[16] George Steiner, *The Death of Tragedy*, Hill and Wang, 1963, p. 5.

[17] Francis Fergusson, *The Idea of a Theater*, Doubleday, 1953, p. 18.

[18] Wallace Fowlie, *Dionysius in Paris*, Meridian, 1960, p. 67.

[19] Fergusson, p. 61.

[20] This work was published by Editions du Seuil, Paris, in 1945.

[21] Campbell, p. 388.

[22] *Mon Cœur mis à nu*, V.

[23] W. B. Stanford, *The Ulysses Theme*, Barnes and Noble, 1964, p. 80.

[24] *The Odyssey*, translated by W. H. D. Rouse, Book VII.

[25] Stanford, p. 40.

[26] Sartre, p. 96.

[27] Rainer Maria Rilke, "The Second Duino Elegy."

In a provocative article entitled "What Greece Means to Modern France," Professor Peyre continues the inquiry he had undertaken in his book a decade earlier.[1] Among other things, he suggests that a large proportion of the major French literary artists of the middle years of the 20th century are basically what one might call moralists. Their central preoccupation is man, and they are particularly concerned with exploring the ethical, philosophical, and political dimensions of his situation in the modern world. Indeed, as Peyre notes, many contemporary writers look back on Greece as being exemplary because it was "the land in which literature and art did not have to be divorced from morality"—or indeed from politics. In those days, the artist "could feel at one with his audience."[2] Such a desire for the writer to be united with and committed to a larger human collectivity is an aspect of several modern literary schools, but it is a particularly noteworthy element in what may be called, broadly, the "existentialist" current.

On another level, our modern world is permeated with a wide-spread spirit of revolt against the Divine, and this also establishes a particular kinship with many of the classical Greeks. For at certain periods in the long cultural evolution that is reflected in their literature and mythology they too revolted against the gods and wrestled with the same fundamental problems of human freedom and responsibility that perplex contemporary man. As Peyre puts it succinctly, figures like Prometheus, Oedipus, and Sisyphus are "elder brothers of the Existentialist heroes."[3] Camus is perhaps the contemporary author whose affinities with Greece are most profound (and most studied), but Professor Alex Szogyi's probing essay makes clear the ways in which—somewhat unexpectedly—a major figure like Jean-Paul Sartre has made an effort to rework Greek elements within an existentialist framework in two of his plays. Dr. Szogyi's detailed analysis of *Les Mouches* and *Les Troyennes* (amplified by a number of revealing comments by Sartre himself) points up both the values and the shortcomings of such a use of original Greek materials. In the final analysis, what emerges most clearly from this study—and what is most important—is the fact that these timeless myths still have force and value as restatements of the truths that succeeding generations of men have wrested from the universe in which they have been condemned to live.

Notes

[1] This article, originally published in the December, 1950, issue of *Yale French Studies* has been reprinted in Peyre's *Historical and Critical Essays* (University of Nebraska Press, 1968), pp. 100-112.

[2] Peyre, *op. cit.*, p. 109.

[3] Peyre, *op. cit.*, p. 111.

SARTRE AND THE GREEKS:
A VICIOUS MAGIC CIRCLE

By Alex Szogyi

> Oreste: Tu me donneras la main et nous irons...
> Electre: Où?
> Oreste: Je ne sais pas, vers nous-mêmes.
>   (*Les Mouches*, III-3)

It is ironic that Sartre should have chosen to invade the domain of the Greeks only twice, i.e. in his first and in his most recent dramatic works. Twenty-two years elapsed between Charles Dullin's performance of Sartre's first audacious theatrical adventure, *Les Mouches*, in June of 1943 and Georges Wilson's production of the Sartrean adaptation of Euripides' *Trojan Women* at the Théâtre National Populaire, March 10, 1965. *Les Troyennes* was his first theatrical venture in six years (since the Algerian parable, *Les Séquestrés d'Altona*). He had written nine other plays in the intervening twenty-two years but only one of them had been an adaptation: *Kean*, based on a play by Alexandre Dumas. Although Sartre has written more plays than novels and philosophical works, his contribution to the theatre is less generally known and applauded than his philosophy, his perspicacious criticism, and his novels and tales. To be sure, *Huis Clos* is often considered to be a very important play of the century, and *Les Mains Sales* and *Le Diable Et Le Bon Dieu* have attracted attention and respect, but nevertheless, Sartre's theatre is usually considered to be handmaiden to his politics and philosophy, more polemical and propagandistic than purely theatrical. To put it bluntly, his dramaturgy is not quite as revolutionary as his thought, and the characters in his plays are often not quite as compelling as his intellectual convictions. Since his is basically a theatre of ideas and ideals, it is not surprising that Greek theatre attracted him, for he realized that great assimilated myths may be very effective means of influencing and moving the modern sophisticated mind. Since the late 1930's, Giraudoux and Anouilh as well as Sartre have used Greek myths as the vehicle for their basic message, and Argos was often France.

Les Mouches and Les Troyennes are both plays of crisis, symbolic of a moment in which an old order is dying and a new one must somehow be born out of despair. Today Les Mouches appears to be a particularly cogent demonstration of the principles of literary existentialism. Oreste, its existentialist hero, denies the power of the gods, embodied in a quixotic, quizzical godhead, Jupiter and, realizing his terrible new-found freedom, accomplishes his ritualistic act of murder only to enter a state of total responsibility. Freedom and the humanism that freedom requires is a desperately lonely state. Whereas the *Oresteia* of Aeschylus presented a state of disorder which divine justice and retribution turn again into order, a chaotic universe restored, Sartre's play insists on the necessity of chaos. In *Les Mouches* Jupiter (who does not appear in the Greek plays but is represented by the vengeful Athena and the messenger Apollo) is an ambiguous God who realizes full well the limit of his powers. Orestes' confrontation of Jupiter and his affirmation of self reveal the basic thrust of Sartre's message. The Greeks affirmed that out of disorder must come divine order. The Sartrean postulate is that out of disorder a new inner order must arise, based on the positing of the self in a world which must make its own way. Sartre's catharsis, if one may speak of it as such, is human.

Any strict comparison with the Greek trilogy is pointless because Sartre wrote the play for a French audience which was disillusioned by war, but which was close to the moment when victory and a newly found freedom would come. In short, his was a world which would soon have to find new meanings for its acts.[1] Thus, in a very real sense, Sartre's play was an event: the first theatrical work of a new intellectual force on the French theatrical scene, produced by one of the great directors of the century, Charles Dullin, at one of the most humiliating moments of French history, the end of the Pétain régime. One should never forget that although theatre remains as literature, it begins as an event. *Le Cid*, *Phèdre* and *Hernani* were all events. While the first two will undoubtedly always remain (because they embodied deep literary values as well), the third is now only a moment of theatrical history. It is perhaps too soon to know whether *Les Mouches*, Sartre's first play, will survive and become a literary classic.

Les Troyennes is, in a sense, not a surprise in the canon of Sartre's work, for he had tried an adaptation before. Euripides' *The Trojan Women*, the great anti-war play of all time, seemed a fine vehicle to him for a number of reasons. It is first and foremost a play of one major idea. It has a set number of sequences which make for a slow and majestic linear development. One of Sartre's major difficulties with stagecraft has been the integration of melodramatic plot and philosophical or ideological content. He has often attempted to combine conventional nineteenth century dramaturgy with radical ideas, but as in the plays of Arthur Miller (though Miller is less adept than Sartre, if more spectacular and stagy), the psychological materials are never quite as subtly developed as the philosophy. *The Trojan Women* is an ideal propaganda play. It never makes its central point within the text: its totality is somehow greater than the sum of its parts. The suffering it depicts is futile. It shows beautifully the utter futility of war. Unlike Shaw (whose Undershafts stood to benefit from the finances of war), Sartre wanted to make it quite clear that not even the gods could survive the holocaust. He gave this message to Poseidon in a final scene which he added to his original version in order to clarify his intention: "A présent vous allez payer. / Faites la guerre, mortels imbéciles, / ravagez les champs et les villes, / violez les temples, les tombes, / et torturez les vaincus. / Vous en crèverez. / Tous. "[2] These words end the play, and their meaning is unmistakable. Although the work did not make its appearance at a moment that was quite as dramatic as that of *Les Mouches*, its message war more simple and universal. The Jupiter of *Les Mouches* needed the people's remorse, the status quo. The gods of *Les Troyennes* were totally humanized: as petty, vengeful and fallible as men.[3]

Sartre has not written prefaces for his other plays, but the published version of *Les Troyennes* contains an introduction which is most illuminating. Critics may have been tempted to avoid discussing the Greek models when assessing the merits of the Sartrean dramatic conception, yet Sartre himself insists that his translation for the stage is motivated by certain very specific considerations. The first question one might be tempted to ask is why Sartre chose to write a play in verse when none of his previous works were in such a poetic form. *Les Mouches* does occasionally use a prose poetry of a kind, but there was nothing substantial to indicate that Sartre might attempt free verse in a theatre piece.[4] His "poetry" is, to be sure, a very special prosy creation—pithy, monosyllabic, almost arid, but with an unmistakable power and, strangely, surprisingly theatrical. At first glance, prose poetry of this sort would seem to be almost a mimic of poetry. Yet in reality it was just one in a series of refined considerations that suggest how carefully Sartre conceived his adaptation of the play and how meaningful each of his decisions was. As Bernard Pingaud explained it:

Pourquoi *Les Troyennes*? La tragédie grecque est un beau monument en ruine qu'on visite avec respect, sous la conduite d'exégètes scrupuleux, mais que personne n'aurait l'idée d'habiter. Périodiquement, les dévots du théâtre antique tentent de ressusciter les drames d'Eschyle, Sophocle ou Euripide, tels que pouvaient les voir les Athéniens. Mais il est difficile de croire à des parodies, si pieuses soient-elles. Ce théâtre est loin de nous, parce qu'il s'inspire d'une conception religieuse du monde qui nous est devenue complètement étrangère. Son langage peut séduire: il ne convainc plus.[5]

These are loaded remarks, for they point to a careful justification of Sartre's purpose in adapting the original Greek text. Sartre's universe is irreligious, his language anti-poetic. However, with much the same given dramatic material, he wishes to capture the conscience of a mass audience, just as the Greek playwrights did, and to impose his own sense of ritual. It is more difficult for modern play-wrights to capture an audience. No single religion or way of life seems to unite any group of spectators these days. But that may hardly be necessary; Greek religion, as such, was the handmaiden of politics, and because the sense of politics is so strong in Sartre, it may take the place of religion for him. *Les Mouches*, for instance, substituted the affirmation of the self for a religious value so effectively that there is no sense of void in this adaptation of a play in which religion originally was a major element.

Greek polytheism presupposed a primitivism and a religious freedom which a highly developed and decadent society with its fixed dogmatic religions could not possibly emulate. Sartre saw polytheism as a symptom of primitive freedom. However since *Les Mouches* required a god, he substituted Zeus for Pallas Athena and Apollo, realizing that he was writing for a society which could easily reject the notion even of a single god. *Les Troyennes* reinstated (or kept) the gods as they were, perhaps precisely because existentialist atheism is not a major consideration in the later play. For in *Les Troyennes* gods and men are equated, and they suffer the same fate. In that sense alone, *Les Troyennes* is a subtle answer to *Les Mouches*. Man's acts, as well as those of the gods, are equally doomed: freedom to make war is freedom to destroy *all* forms of existence.

Religion was a form of politics in ancient Greece. Professor Kitto makes this point most adroitly in his discussion of the *Oresteia*, and as he points out,[6] Orestes' murder has many meanings for the Greek society which it could never have in a modern context. The resolving and the pardoning of the crime is most intricate and complicated, as well as necessary,[7] but Aeschylus' plays are imitations of a process well known to the public. They illustrate the best way to maintain law and order:

> To Aeschylus the mature polis became the means by which the Law is satisfied without producing chaos, since public justice supersedes private vengeance: and the claims of authority are reconciled with the instincts of humanity... The trilogy ends with an impressive piece of pageantry. The awful Furies exchange their black robes for red ones, no longer Furies but 'Kindly Ones' (Eumenides): no longer enemies of Zeus, but his willing and honoured agents, defenders of his now perfected social order against intestine violence. Before the eyes of the Athenian citizens assembled in the theatre just under the Acropolis and indeed guided by citizen-marshals, they pass out of the theatre to their new home on the other side of the Acropolis. Some of the most acute of man's moral and social problems have been solved, and the means of the reconciliation is the polis.[8]

Thus one might be tempted to say that Greek theatre was a subtle form of political propaganda. It was the very mirror of its time, as theatre so rarely ever dares to be.[9] The important fact is that the *Oresteia* was a play which presented religion not as dogma, but as a way of life and a form of politics. Religion and politics were fused into a modus vivendi, and the result was a liveable, viable society. In *Les Mouches*, Sartre showed that the polis was rotten, that man must make his own individual way, an individual among individuals, for the good of all, but individually. Zeus didn't wish Egisthus to be killed. He hoped that remorse and collective guilt would result in a repentance that would keep the polis intact. He championed the police state and the status quo. As we can readily see, Sartre's play uses the given elements of the Greek play to go in a direction which is diametrically opposed to the Greek original. The cartharsis of order chez Sartre, if there be any, is man-made resistance to the maintenance of the status quo.

In the introduction of *Les Troyennes*, one of the most valuable commentaries on the continuing validity of literary language, Sartre maintains that Euripides' audience was a far cry from that of Aeschylus (just as the Pétain régime was worlds apart from the de Gaulle state, though this could hardly be safely articulated at the time). He first makes the point that Greek theatre was highly sophisticated, a ceremony for the spectator to behold. But he qualifies this by maintaining that the whole dramatic undertaking was very different in the time of Euripides than it was in Aeschylus' age. Euripides' work represents a transition from tragedy to the comedy of Menander, because the value of the basic myths had changed. As Sartre put it, the reason for this was that

> Au moment où Euripide compose *Les Troyennes*, les croyances sont devenues des mythes plus ou moins suspects. Incapable encore de renverser les vieilles idoles, l'esprit critique des Athéniens est déjà capable de les contester. La représentation a gardé sa valeur rituelle. Mais le public s'intéresse davantage à la façon de dire qu'à ce qui est dit; et les morceaux de bravoure traditionnels, qu'il apprécie en connaisseur, prennent à ses yeux un nouveau sens.[10]

Thus Sartre makes the compelling point that the proper appreciation of such a work of theatre depends primarily on its use of language and consequently on the nuance of a language at a given period. This statement is intensely revealing: the subtleties of language are the heart of the work, and yet paradoxically the meaning of any given line is its least decipherable factor.[11] As Sartre cleverly points out, since the value of a given word or sentence changes with the period in which it is enunciated, there is no such thing as a fixed totality of meaning; the overtones are always changing. "La tragédie devient ainsi une conversation à demi-mot sur des poncifs."[12] One may say the same for Sartre's milieux. Argos was once Pétain's régime, but it could be de Gaulle's. *Les Troyennes* might be about Algeria or Vietnam. or next year's war. In the final analysis, a play is a blueprint, whose full meaning varies with each audience.[13]

Thus, Sartre's conception of *Les Troyennes* is obviously based on what one might call a certain esthetic distance. He cannot possibly translate the original imagery as such. Moreover he must avoid the traditional Greek epithets, for they are typical of the eighteenth century in France, and the audience would take them too literally. (In four or five centuries, will it be possible to interpret Beckett or Ionesco, and how?) Sartre knew that he must adapt or "recreate" the play to make it truly meaningful to a contemporary audience. As he put it:

> Entre la tragédie d'Euripide et la société athénienne du Vᵉ siècle existe un rapport implicite que nous ne pouvons plus voir aujourd'hui que du dehors. Si je veux rendre ce rapport sensible, je ne peux donc pas me contenter de traduire, il faut que je l'adapte.[14]

Basically, such an adaptation is not so much a linguistic problem as it is a cultural one. Euripides' text contains numerous allusions which the Athenian public would comprehend immediately but which are meaningless to an audience which doesn't know the underlying legends. For instance, the Greeks were well aware of how Hecuba's life ended, and so Cassandra did not need to go into details. At the end of the play, her predictions are verified, but an untutored modern audience might imagine that Hecuba was going off to a better life rather than to an imminent death.

This fully justifies Sartre's addition of Poseidon's final monologue to the original Greek text. (Of course this scene also gives the playwright an opportunity to make a final sermon against war.) He makes the same point about Menelaus' bending to Helen's inexorable will. The original play, as it stood, could lead us to think she would be punished. But Helen won out, and that point also had to be stressed for a modern audience.

Other modifications Sartre made had to do with the form of the play itself. As he sees it, the Greek work is an oratorio and not a tragedy per se. Therefore, he wished to accentuate and dramatize certain conflicts between characters which are only implicit in the original text, most importantly Hecuba's struggles with Andromache. Sartre sees Andromache as nothing more than a "petite bourgeoise." It is true that Sartre tends to emphasize the bourgeois element in all his plays. To be sure, this is not out of keeping with the general tradition of the French stage.[15] As Diderot saw clearly in the 18th century, tragedy had to be democratized and made bourgeois in order to be comprehensible to contemporary audiences. Molière's Tartuffe was perhaps the first bourgeois drama. Playwrights like Giraudoux and Anouilh have tried hard to rescue tragedy from its bourgeois bondage, but to little avail. Their Greek characters are just as bourgeois as those of Sartre. This is perhaps because heroic literature in France is invariably psychological in orientation. La Chanson de Roland was perhaps France's last non-bourgeois tragedy. Even Musset's Lorenzaccio, although it is probably the major heroic French play of modern times, does not neglect bourgeois values. In any case, Euripides' plays lend themselves to the bourgeois treatment even more than do those of his predecessors.

Although the philosopher in Sartre often tends to stifle the poet, nevertheless in Les Mouches he did manage a kind of ironic and intellectual poetry. As he himself has pointed out, his theatre is a drama of the word itself: "Oui, pour moi, le problème principal est là: il s'agit de trouver une organisation de la parole et de l'acte, où la parole ne paraisse pas superfétatoire, où elle garde un pouvoir au-delà de toute éloquence. C'est même la première condition d'un théâtre vraiment efficient."[16] This curious affirmation smacks of Verlaine's dictum in his "Art Poétique": "Prends l'éloquence et tords-lui son cou." The word and the act must go hand in hand, neither one dominating the other. The eloquence or lyricism of a Racine is not for Sartre. Nor is the well-made play à la Scribe, Sardou or even Becque. The language of the play and its action must somehow interact in order to be truly effective. Although language is at the heart of his theatrical problem, this does not mean that language is more important or takes precedence over the theatrical action. For the Sartre of Les Mouches, the essence of theatre is the revelation of personality through the efficacy of a definitive act. As he put it in his 1960 speech at the Sorbonne,

On croit toujours que l'action dramatique veut dire grands mouvements, remue-ménage, non, ça n'est pas de l'action, c'est du bruit, c'est du tumulte: l'action proprement dite, c'est celle du personnage; il n'y a pas d'autres images au théâtre que l'image de l'acte, et si l'on veut savoir ce que c'est que le théâtre, il faut se demander ce que c'est qu'un acte, parce que le théâtre représente l'acte et ne peut rien représenter d'autre. La sculpture représente la forme du corps, le théâtre représente l'acte de ce corps. Par conséquent, ce que nous voulons récupérer quand nous allons au théâtre, c'est évidemment nous-mêmes, mais nous-mêmes, non pas en tant que nous sommes plus ou moins pauvres, plus ou moins fiers de notre jeunesse ou de notre beauté, mais c'est nous récupérer en tant que nous agissons, que nous travaillons, que nous rencontrons des difficultés et que nous sommes des hommes qui ont des règles et qui établissent des règles pour ces actions.[17]

Thus, for Sartre, the failure of the modern theatre is the failure of the modern bourgeois to wish to see himself lucidly, to take full cognizance of his acts.

Conscientious as he always is, Sartre feels that his use of Euripides's play, *The Trojan Women*, may not warrant his borrowing of its contents. He was attracted to it because of its implicit analogies with the contemporary situation in Algeria. The play had always been a political one, even in Euripides' time, and it contained within it an implicit condemnation of colonial expeditions. But in the last analysis Sartre sees the play as a perfect image of our present society, menaced as it is with complete destruction. The war against Troy seems very much like all of our petty crusades. And the expression "sale guerre" is also to be found in Euripides, and with the same intonation. As for the gods, Sartre feels he has modernized them fairly and has created a certain religious esthetic distance:

Les Dieux qui apparaissent dans *Les Troyennes* sont à la fois puissants et ridicules. D'un côté, ils dominent le monde: la guerre de Troie a été leur œuvre. Mais, vus de près, on s'aperçoit qu'ils ne se conduisent pas autrement que les hommes et que, comme eux, ils sont menés par de petites vanités, de petites rancunes.[18]

He also suggests that the polytheism of Euripides' times was an untenable religion, for the various beliefs often cancelled one another out. (At this point, he indulges in some slight anti-religious propaganda: "Comme il n'utilise les poncifs que pour mieux les détruire, Euripide se sert ainsi de la légende pour faire apparaître, toujours sans appuyer, en opposant seulement les mythes les uns aux autres, les difficultés d'un polythéisme auquel son public ne croit déjà plus." And as a wry clincher, he adds: "Le monothéisme échappe-t-il à cette condamnation?"[19]) Finally, Sartre sees Hecuba's prayer to Zeus as a form of religiosity à la Renan, the obeisance that history gives to a supreme reasoning power. But the strange paradox of the play's ending is that the discord among the gods is the true revenge of the Trojans. The plays ends for Sartre in pure nihilism. The Greeks sensed this nihilism, he claims, but it is even more poignant now. In the end, all such struggles end in total despair, and Sartre's final comment on the play underlines his insistence on the futility of the situation. "J'ai voulu marquer ce retournement: le désespoir final d'Hécube, sur lequel j'ai mis l'accent, répond au mot terrible de Poséidon. Les Dieux crèveront avec les hommes, et cette mort commune est la leçon de la tragédie."[20]

In his reworking of the Greek original, Sartre shifted the emphasis of the play. The murder of Astyanax, the center of Euripides' play, is subordinated to the Sartrean checkmate scene in the duel between Helen and Menelaus.[21] Thus he has made a most important contribution to our understanding of the overtones of the work: it is not the senseless murder of

Astyanax which is the ultimate horror of the story, but rather the ludicrous triumph of Helen. Much may be made of this Sartrean insight: Helen's triumph and Menelaus' forgiveness are truly absurd elements, for they render all the actions during the ten-year war meaningless. As an Ionesco might have done, Sartre has put his finger on a ludicrousness inherent in the original Euripides conception. Menelaus *is* a "cocu magnifique," and the whole war had been fought for nought. In the *Oresteia*, order is restored; in *The Trojan Women*, order is ludicrous. In *Les Mouches*, Oreste revenges his father's murder and declares his own freedom, although it is rendered less than valid by Electra's recantation. In *Les Troyennes*, the war was fought for no valid reason and remains the ultimate affirmation of man's death instinct. By means of these two explorations of Greek drama, separated by a distance of twenty-two years, Sartre has come to the theatrical conclusion that individual aggression is meaningless. Orestes' act had real meaning in 1943, but in a world that has since gone mad with war, Athena's fickle attitudes and Hecuba's prayers are both equally useless. The dissolution which one senses in the change of attitude from Aechylus to Euripides may be felt just as poignantly in Sartre's work. Turning more and more to polemics rather than to literature, he seems to have lost faith in the viability of the work of art as such. No longer interested in the novel and rarely attempting theatre, he seems now to be more successful when he writes about Tintoretto or the Jewish question, and he is at his very best when he deciphers his own early life in a work like *Les Mots*. One might say that like Camus and Malraux before him, his real gifts are those of a political or esthetic critic, rather than of a writer of fiction.

But a writer must be judged for what he did, and not for what he couldn't or wouldn't do. Did Sartre create an authentic twentieth-century tragedy from his Greek sources? Are *Les Mouches* and *Les Troyennes* revivifications of a glorious genre? One would tend to think not. Sartre remains a prose writer even when he is most lyric. He has not managed to create a new epic verse.[22] However, he does unquestionably have a strong sense of theatre, and since his plays are never devoid of intelligence they stimulate the kind of interest which is aroused by an exciting mind at work. In a real sense, one might call these plays *critiques* of tragedy, for they are ultimately a shade too intellectual, too critical of themselves to be really tragic.

And, after all, this ancient theatre could not in any sense of the word be revived today. Greek drama was a re-enactment of episodes from Greek mythology. A myth may be defined as a symbolic expression of a collective unconscious. It is equally meaningful for the individuals who live in a society, and for the social collectivity as a whole. Myths are not only expressive of the essence of a society, but also of its contradictions and tensions. In this sense, myths depict the inner man and his projections into the outer environment. As Kenneth Cavander has put it:

> As is often pointed out, myths project 'inner' psychic processes. Perhaps more important they embody in the images of gods, heroes, monsters, as well as in the traditional stories and forms, the outlines of what people regard as 'superior' powers, values that supersede

accepted man-made morality, forces that transcend the individual while still including him. In short, myths are the maps of an inner cosmos or (to use an older word) the soul.[23]

Can it then be said that Sartre created modern myths by which we do or may live? Can the existentialist act take on the power and value of a myth any more vividly than the "gratuitous" act which Gide sought to establish as the hallmark of authenticity? Orestes, the existentialist hero, defined by his own act, realizes at the end of *Les Mouches* that only in collectivity, in a collective acceptance of his act, can there be any true salvation. This act is rendered meaningless by Electra's repentance and the vengeance of the Furies. In *Les Troyennes*, Poseidon speaks for all humanity when he states that war will kill us all. The use of myth in this work is far less individual than in the earlier play. In this sense, *Les Mouches* may be viewed as an effort to codify the existentialist act in the form of a re-evaluated myth. *Les Troyennes* depends on no such limited philosophical stance.

To many, it may be surprising to learn that Sartre does not wish his theatre to be philosophical. Of course he is the first to recognize that philosophy as such is a genre apart and must be used sparingly in the realm of theatre.[24] But even so, in order to convey such ideas in his dramatic works, he prefers myth to philosophical statement. As he has pointed out, the play must be an accurate vision of the myth and reveal it theatrically, and the myth itself must insinuate rather than pontificate:

La pièce théâtrale doit présenter un mythe aux spectateurs... Il me semble que le théâtre ne doit pas dépendre de la philosophie qu'il exprime. Il doit exprimer une philosophie, mais il ne faut pas qu'on puisse à l'intérieur de la pièce poser le problème de la valeur de la philosophie qui s'y exprime. Il faut que la pièce donne une vision totale d'un moment ou d'une chose, mais il faut en même temps que ce qui s'y révèle, se révèle d'une manière entièrement théâtrale... Le mythe ainsi, à mon avis, doit être beaucoup plus insinuant, c'est-à-dire, doit être tel qu'on ne s'aperçoive même pas que c'est une philosophie.[25]

In other words, a play is a magnet to capture the conscience of an audience without their being aware of it.[26] Theatre must be magic, with the secret power of a charm, or of a karmic experience. All great theatre, from the Oresteia to a musical epic such as *West Side Story*, contains this essential magic. What Sartre is saying (and it has been said in various ways by many other writers[27]) is that a work of art must suggest and insinuate, never state. As Gide once put it, the problem must be stated well, not necessarily solved.

Thus theatre needs myth, a magic force to mesmerize the audience with its ideational content expressed in an entirely theatrical way. It has the power to mesmerize, to transform and work upon the conscience of an audience through the medium of words and, more important, above and beyond them. But, as one perceptive critic put it, "when an actor stands at the center of a magic circle (which is what a Greek theatre, if you include the audience, was) at the focal point of all the nervous energy activated by a community of several thousands, he exposes himself in a way that is virtually unheard of today."[28] There lies the crux of the matter. Theatre on an epic level worked for the Greeks, but it doesn't seem to work for us any more, precisely because it must involve people in a special kind of mystification and irony. Genet in *Les Nègres* and *Les Paravents* has caught the polemical essence of modern tragedy with more panache than the intellectual Sartre. For a Sartrean play is a magic circle which tends to be vicious. The hero destroys his own value by means of his act. The whole scaffolding comes tumbling down. Instead of achieving the catharsis of meaningful resolution which the Greek plays produced in their audience, Sartre's dramas leave us with little more than the bitter ashes of unhappy absurdity. Lacking even the exaltation of Camus' perhaps spurious lyricism, his works serve primarily to make the world conscious of its own futility.

But perhaps in the final analysis, the failure of Sartre to create modern tragedy is due much more to his choice of language than to his use of myth, symbols and action. Tragic lyricism is not his forte. Stylistically, *Les Mouches* is a mixture of many verbal mannerisms, from the colloquial to an often bitterly ecstatic (and sometimes unsucessful) lyricism of prose poetry. The language of *Les Troyennes* is more uniform, intellectually hard and probing and especially more theatrically effective in its manipulation of the isolated word and of the monosyllabic term. Neither play is totally successful in creating a stage language which might compare in eloquence with the Greek texts, or even with writers such as Giraudoux and Claudel, both of whom forged a theatrical speech of some brilliance and individuality. Sartre's language cannot claim to have scaled such heights; nevertheless, it is inimitable, with an intellectual force and vigor unmatched by any other of his contemporaries. He is a most eloquent persuader, whether he is speaking in the guise of Orestes, of Jupiter, or of Poseidon. His Hélène de Troie may not be as beguiling as Giraudoux' heroine in *La Guerre de Troie n'aura pas lieu*, but Sartre makes her a much more convincing speaker.

The poetry of *Les Troyennes* is a kind of free verse. It has its own bitter, prosy, hammering tone, and it is most forceful in isolated, often monosyllabic words. Sartre is more of a master of verbal effects here than he was in the vacillating style of *Les Mouches*. Twenty-two years have passed. Moveover his more universal theme is simpler to handle. He does not have to prove a hypothesis, nor define a philosophy in terms of a stage action. No single act is paramount in this adaptation of the Greek original. His play is a collection of acts, all inevitably futile, and he does not aim for verbal grandeur as he often did in *Les Mouches*.[29] The tone is hard and lucid, bronze rather than brass, calm instead of clarion voiced. The verse is free, unfettered by the demands of rhyme or rhythm, and thus more unified than the prose of the earlier play. Still, it has neither a true poetic exaltation à la Claudel, nor a gentle prosiness à la Prévert. Its stylistic sins make it sound more like verse than poetry. It succeeds best in the monosyllable or the single word, stark, alone, surrounded only by its own created overtones, as in Poseidon's final speech: "Les Troyens sont morts. Tous."[30]

Thus in Sartre's Greek-inspired plays, there is no true catharsis, either through action or language. Orestes' act has given him freedom, but not happiness. It has confirmed his exile. Hélène has reconquered Menelaus and the Troyennes go off to their destinies. War will decimate us all. As a total experience for an audience, these plays are prophets of doom. They do not re-establish joy or order or any desirable state, as in the Oresteia, but testify to the terrible price of freedom, the plight of man in a world without God and constantly shadowed by the awful spectre of war. In a real sense, theatre such as this is ultimately more tragic than tragedy itself. It is a ceremony of defeat, a legacy of mankind's inability to attain peace and harmony, a warning to us all. Sartre's magic circle is a vicious one. Would that it weren't.

Hunter College of the
City of New York

Notes

[1] It would perhaps be more interesting to speculate whether *Les Mouches* could be performed in a major theatre again today. The play could not be very popular during a Gaullist regime, certainly; like Anouilh's *Antigone*, it is appropriate when a new regime must rise phoenix-like from the ashes of the old. No play can ever hope to be reborn in the same context: the durability of any work for the theatre is proportional to the degree to which it successfully absorbs new intonations and implications in a time very different from the time it was written. The Dullin production of 1943 utilized masks and made an enormous impression on its audience, as the following account suggests:

> Représentée en juin 1943, sa première pièce: *Les Mouches*, ne s'inspire de l'Orestie que pour camoufler aux yeux de l'occupant le problème de la liberté de l'homme et de la mort nécessaire des tyrans. Parlant de la vengeance d'Oreste, J.-P. Sartre disait alors: "Libre en conscience, l'homme qui s'est haussé à ce point au-dessus de lui-même ne deviendra libre en situation que s'il rétablit la liberté pour autrui, si son acte a pour conséquence la disparition d'un état de choses existant et le rétablissement de ce qui devrait être."

(*Comoedia*, 23 avril 1943). On ne pouvait parler plus net. D'ailleurs, il aurait été difficile de se méprendre en entendant Egisthe parler comme Pétain, en voyant le peuple d'Argos se repentir de fautes imaginaires, en entendant et en voyant enfin bourdonner les mouches attirées par les charniers, dernier avatar des Erynnies.

...*Les Mouches* furent pour Dullin l'occasion d'une mise en scène très extraordinaire, où les décors, tout en plans inclinés, et les costumes du peintre et sculpteur Adam, où l'incessant bourdonnement des "mouches", plus la présence de quelques esclaves hydrocéphales et d'une statue informe et grimaçante de Jupiter composaient le tableau le plus sombre qu'on puisse imaginer. Charles Dullin, lui-même, perruque de porc-épic et maquillage assyrien, était un Jupiter menaçant et caricatural (qui avoue cependant à Oreste son impuissance en face de la liberté de l'homme) dont je n'oublierai jamais l'étonnant aspect."
Encyclopédie du Théâtre Contemporain, ed. by Olivier Perrin (Paris, 1959), vol. II, p. 177.

[2] *Les Troyennes* (Paris, 1965), p. 130. Future references will be to this edition of the play.
[3] The Palais de Chaillot production, benefiting from the counsel of Greece's ambassador of tragic theatre, Cacoyannis, made for a wildly emotional experience which detracted from the value of the play:
The evening I spent watching all those white robed actresses doing symbolic dances and crypto-ethnic gestures of mourning on the great dark stage of the Palais de Chaillot was not terribly memorable... No doubt he (Mr. Cacoyannis) was trying to instil a sense of majesty and awe in me through his use of old-fashioned breast-beating and stage-thumping, but the contortions he put his cast through only succeeded in reminding me of Zero Mostel miming the poses of Hysterium's erotic pottery in *A Funny Thing Happened on the Way to the Forum*. As a director, Mr. Cacoyannis has an astonishing naïveté: he has his Andromache walk firmly across the stage holding Astyanax by the arms, his legs frantically pumping to stay upright as he moves backwards, and yet the audience laughter at this ludicrous moment does not move him to change the blocking, though a very powerful scene in the text is thereby totally subverted...."
"Sartre's War—and Our Own," by David Copelin, in *Yale/Theatre*, No. 1 (Spring, 1968), p. 116.
Although the commentary here quoted may seem arbitrary and somewhat flippant, it indicates clearly that playing a Greek play in a Greek fashion for a non-Greek audience can skirt parody, and perhaps destroy the fundamental of the tragic élan. It further suggests that present Greek methods of staging Greek plays may be as antiquated as the Moscow Art Theatre's conception of Chekhov, or worse heresy, the Comédie Française's view of Molière. To match Sartre's eclectically modern Euripides, a production would have to have been ersatz Greek and totally contemporary in spirit.
[4] This consideration brought me back to a moment during the rehearsals of *Les Séquestrés d'Altona* in the late summer of 1959. I had had the singular good fortune to be permitted by Sartre to attend rehearsals of the play. One afternoon, during a break, the actor, Fernand Ledoux asked Sartre whether he had ever thought of writing a play in verse. Sartre's immediate rejoinder was an emphatic no, and it seemed to me that Ledoux' kind question was one of those purely academic queries which plague an author unfairly and show a total misconception of his work. But Ledoux was seemingly more clairvoyant than one would have thought, for Sartre did just that for his next play.
[5] "Propos recueillis par Bernard Pingaud dans *BREF, Journal mensuel du Théâtre National Populaire*, février 1965," cited in the preface to the Gallimard edition of the play, p. 2.
[6] Kitto, H. D. F. *The Greeks*, Penguin (Baltimore, 1964), p. 76:
How intimately religious and "political" thinking were connected we can best see from the *Oresteia* of Aeschylus. This trilogy is built around the idea of Justice. It moves from chaos to order, from conflict to reconciliation: and it moves on two planes at once, the human and the divine. In the *Agamemnon* we see one of the moral Laws of the universe, that punishment must follow crime, fulfilled in the crudest possible way: one crime evokes another crime to avenge it, in apparently endless succession but always with the sanction of Zeus. In the *Coephori* this series of crimes reaches its climax when Orestes avenges his father by killing his mother. He does this with repugnance, but he is commanded to do it by Apollo, the son and the mouthpiece of Zeus—why? Because in murdering Agamemnon the King and her husband, Clytemnestra has committed a crime, which, unpunished, would shatter the very fabric of society. It is the concern of the Olympian gods to defend

Order: they are particularly the gods of the Polis. But Orestes' matricide outrages the deepest human instincts; he is therefore implacably pursued by other deities, the Furies.... The Furies have no interest in social order, but they cannot permit this outrage on the sacredness of the blood tie, which it is their office to protect.

[7] Kitto, *op. cit.*, pp. 76-77, notes:

In the *Eumenides* there is a terrific conflict between the ancient Furies and the younger Olympians over the unhappy Orestes. The solution is that Athena comes with a new dispensation from Zeus. A jury of Athenian citizens is empanneled to try Orestes on the Acropolis where he has fled for protection, this being the first meeting of the Council of the Areopagus. The votes on either side are equal: therefore, as an act of mercy, Orestes is acquitted. The Furies, cheated by their legitimate prey, threaten Attica with destruction, but Athena persuades them to make their home in Athens, with their ancient office not abrogated (as at first they think) but enhanced, since henceforth they will punish violence within the polis, not only within the family.

[8] Kitto, *op. cit.*, p. 77.

[9] Kitto, *op. cit.*, pp. 77-78:

A few minutes later, on that early spring day of 458 B.C. the citizens too would leave the theatre, and by the same exits as the Eumenides. In what mood? Surely no audience has had such an experience since. At the time, the Athenian polis was confidentially riding the crest of the wave. In this trilogy, there was exaltation, for they had seen their polis emerge as the Pattern of Justice, of Order, of what the Greek called Cosmos; the polis, they saw, was or would be the very crown or summit of things.... To such an extent was the religious thought of Aeschylus interwined with the idea of the polis: and not of Aeschylus alone, but of many other Greek thinkers too, notably of Socrates, Plato and Aristotle. Aristotle made a remark which we most inadequately translate: ' Man is a political animal.' What Aristotle really said is ' Man is a creature who lives in a polis ': and what he goes on to demonstrate, in his Politics, is that the polis is the only framework within which man can fully realize his spiritual, moral and intellectual capacities."

[10] Sartre, *Les Troyennes*, p. 3.

[11] Collaterally, we might be tempted to say that the Comédie Française's productions of Molière for instance, articulated in a fixed pattern, are no more faithful to the meaning of Molière than the modern, socially oriented re-explorations of Roger Planchon's Théâtre de la Cité. Planchon has investigated language to find new nuances, whereas the Comédie Française (at least until recently) has opted for a clarity of polished diction which is uniformly laquered.

[12] Sartre, *op. cit.*, p. 3.

[13] Sartre, *op. cit.*, pp. 3-4:

Les expressions qu'emploie Euripide sont les mêmes, en apparence, que celles de ses prédécesseurs. Mais parce que le public n'y croit plus ou y croit moins, elles résonnent autrement, elles disent autre chose. Pensez à Beckett ou à Ionesco, c'est le même phénomène: il consiste à utiliser le poncif pour le détruire de l'intérieur, et naturellement la démonstration sera d'autant plus forte que le poncif s'affichera avec plus d'évidence, avec plus d'éclat. Le public athénien "recevait" *Les Troyennes* comme le public bourgeois reçoit aujourd'hui Godot ou la Cantatrice chauve: ravi d'entendre des lieux communs, mais conscient aussi d'assister à leur décomposition.

[14] Sartre, *op. cit.*, p. 4.

[15] In all fairness, Sartre didn't invent this tendency: in the seventeenth century when they collaborated on their *Psyché* Molière and Corneille took the myth and made it more bourgeois: Zeus and his wife talk like irate parents with a recalcitrant daughter-in-law.

[16] Sartre, "Théâtre Populaire, no. 15," in *L'Art du Théâtre*, edited by Odette Aslan (Paris, 1963), p. 329.

[17] Sartre, "Conférence en Sorbonne, 29 mars 1960" cited in *L'Art du Théâtre*, p. 330.

[18] Sartre, *Les Troyennes*, p. 7.

[19] Sartre, *op. cit.*, pp. 7-8.

[20] Sartre, ibid.

[21] David Copelin, "Sartre's War—and Our Own," p. 118:

The play's center shifts in adaptation. The bestial murder of Astyanax is the point of concentration of the earlier play, for Euripides is very clear about how this particular cycle of revenge is broken: not by the forgiveness of the gods, but by the final extermination of a nation. The scene between Helen and Menelaus is black comedy, showing the rottenness of the society to which the Greeks are returning, for they have soured it themselves. The heroes are cowards. For Sartre, the baby's death is a commonplace, and the real interest in his mind shifts to the reconciliation. If Helen goes back to Menelaus, then the entire war was fought for nothing, and all actions during its ten years are rendered meaningless.

[22] Only Claudel of his contemporaries had such a command of the language, although Claudel's lush plays are too diffuse to make very moving tragedy. Montherlant's and Gide's postures are easier to understand but infinitely less lyric. Giraudoux succeeds in manufacturing an original preciosity of language, and Anouilh's natural theatricality excuses his earthbound language.

[23] Kenneth Cavander, "Magic Circles/Inner Space," in *Yale/Theatre*, no. 1 (Spring, 1968), p. 21.

[24] Sartre, "Perspectives du Théâtre, no. 4," in *L'Art du Théâtre*, pp. 330-31:
Je ne pense pas ou alors il faut préciser que le théâtre soit un "véhicule philosophique" pour reprendre votre expression. Je ne pense pas—pas plus d'ailleurs que dans le roman ou au cinéma—qu'une philosophie, dans sa totalité et en même temps dans ses détails, puisse s'exprimer sous une forme théâtrale. Car au fond, elle ne peut s'exprimer que par des ouvrages philosophiques.

[25] Sartre, *op. cit.*, p. 232.

[26] Kenneth Cavander, ibid., p. 23:
A myth has the power to magnetize, and I think it is this power that draws modern audiences to Greek plays, *not* the cleverness of their plots, *not* the subtlety of their characterization, *not* the brilliance of their dialogue, *not* the originality or profundity of the author's ideas, but a sense of participating in an experience, that pushes *out* the frontiers of the self. If this is so, then perhaps we should stop analyzing the plays in the old Aristotelian fashion, searching the characters for motives, examining the plots and speeches for signs of the authors' message about God, politics, or society. The meaning of the play would lie elsewhere, beyond the personal emotions and concerns which make up conventional modern drama and dramatic criticism. Their logic would be closer to the logic of the parables of the Zen Koan. What could this mean for the theatre in our time? The word "magic" has become shop-soiled by generations of handling in reviews of Broadway musicals—but it is not far off the mark. We should take more seriously the possibility that the Greek theatre was at least as much of a magical ceremony as, for instance, the performance of shamens, with their implications of self-transcendence and functions of healing.

[27] Henry James was said always to have been in search for perfect plots, the very nature of which would so totally express what the author sought to express that they would obviate all explanatory justification. Surely this is one of the major reasons for the success of Dostoievsky and de Maupassant, to name two divergent talents, i.e., their ability to find plot and character that will perfectly convey the essence of what they wished to say. An eloquent plot is universally comprehensible. Baudelaire maintened that all great art depended on this "poncif", i.e., some symbol so well understood that it would make a universal truth of a banality. Art became the search for such "poncifs." It was also said of Henry James that he had a mind so fine that no idea ever penetrated it. This facetious remark articulates what Sartre has suggested.

[28] Kenneth Cavander, ibid., p. 24.

[29] Sartrean lyricism is voluptuous, vaguely sensual: "...tu devais penser quelquefois que le monde était pas si mal fait et c'était un plaisir de s'y laisser aller comme dans un bon bain tiède, en soupirant d'aise" (*Les Mouches*, p. 59). There are lyric moments in the play when the plight of the characters becomes poignant through a sudden insight into their lives by a sudden compassion in the language. Oreste's solitude, his sense of not existing, not belonging, is beautifully evoked in Act II, scene 4 of Tableau I: "Que suis-je et qu'ai-je à donner, moi? J'existe à peine: de tous les fantômes qui rôdent aujourd'hui par la ville, aucun n'est plus fantôme que moi. J'ai connu des amours de fantôme, hésitants et clairsemés comme des vapeurs; mais j'ignore les denses passions des vivants" (pp. 60-61). The use of *denses* has genuine poetic weight, the subtlety and sensuousness of genuine taste. At moments like this one wonders why Sartre would have hesitated to make his entire play consistent. Had he the ability? Or perhaps he was afraid that the beautiful phrases would prevent us from absorbing the drama. After all, great lyric plays sacrifice some drama for poetry, except for Racine, say, or Musset.

[30] Sartre, *Les Troyennes*, p. 14.

Several of the preceding essays have emphasized the Timelessness of Greek myths by underlining the meaning that these ancient stories may still take on at the hands of certain twentieth-century authors, particularly some of the outstanding playwrights. However, modern man is acutely conscious of his place in historical time, and contemporary writers who re-use classical materials are in a sense caught on the horns of a dilemma. They may choose to view Greece as myth, but they also cannot help knowing Greece as part of history. Professor Eric Hicks' essay on anachronism brings a certain balance to our discussion of modern Hellenism by pointing out the aesthetic and philosophical role that such devices have in the mythologically based plays of Cocteau, Anouilh, Giraudoux, and Sartre. His careful analysis makes it clear not only that there are certain surprising patterns to the most commonly used anachronistic details, but that they seem to be employed primarily for the purpose of "degrading" the ancient Timeless myths, thus bringing them into historical time. To a large extent, this effort is itself a reflection of what he calls the modern, post-Hegelian view of the world.

Yet to be clearly aware of the passage of history in a very real sense enables the writer and his audience to dominate or transcend historical time. Viewed in this light, the deliberate use of anachronisms is a particularly revealing element of contemporary dramatic practice. The self-conscious playing-off of timely details—what Professor Hicks calls "chronisms"—against a contemporary reality has become in the hands of a Cocteau or a Giraudoux a very meaningful literary technique: it establishes on the stage the simultaneous presence of past and present history, thus creating a new timelessness for myth. As the following essay makes clear, the imaginative mingling of Greek and modern materials that is so characteristic of much of the contemporary French stage is itself symbolic of the two philosophical poles—Essentialism and Existentialism—between which modern man is torn. No less important however is the fact that such concrete manifestations of the basic alternatives to the problem of the human condition have become the source of a new aesthetic dimension—and pleasure—in the works of today's major mythological dramatists. Thus the legacy of ancient Greece has been renewed once more.

ANACHRONISM IN THE MODERN THEATER OF MYTH: A STUDY IN TIME AND PARADIGM

By Eric C. Hicks

> We are nevertheless forced to touch upon the problem of man as consciously and voluntarily historical, because the modern world is, at the present moment, not entirely converted to historicism: we are even witnessing a conflict between the two views: the archaic conception, which we should designate as archetypal and anhistorical: and the modern, post-Hegelian conception, which seeks to be historical.
>
> —Mircea Eliade, *The Myth of the Eternal Return*[1]

Myth is timeless, but Greece belongs to Time. From the vantage point of the ethnographer, an almost exclusive consideration of the irreversible aspects of Time seems to dominate the historical perspectives of the modern era. Eliade's post-Hegelian man sees History as a linear process generated by particularistic events: he values these events, not for any exemplary or paradigmatic mythical essence, but for that existential oneness which distinguishes them from all other happenings along the temporal continuum. This attitude is in direct contrast with the mentality of mythically oriented peoples, who seek Reality in events which can be superimposed upon others. Myth strives to isolate recurrent patterns and define them as types, and it is to these patterns, rather than to the continuum of History, that the mythical mentality accords ontological significance.

In its quest for archetypes, myth remains largely indifferent to the passage of linear Time, and such naive neglect for the singularity of a given Historical moment is anachronism in its broadest, etymological definition. This is the sincere anachronism of the medieval sculptor or the seventeenth-century stage. Yet however flagrant this violation of the principles of historical criticism may appear to the post-Hegelian intellect, it is not anachronism within its own temporal assumptions. For anachronism, like Beauty, is in the eye of the beholder: to play *Antigone* in modern dress, some two hundred years after the "realist" Voltairian reform of the stage, is something quite distinct from the broader anachronism of an earlier, anhistorical era. Modern anachronism, as the product of a cosmopolitan temporal outlook,[2] consciously flouts the order of Time; it alone is anachronism in any meaningful sense of the term.

There is a remarkable degree of consistency in the types of anachronism which appear in the modern mythological drama. The recurrence of similar motifs through so broad a range of subjects, and in authors of such diverse inspirations, can be attributed to a basic temporal conflict arising from the use of ancient settings in the treatment of contemporary themes.[3] Modern historical perspectives have been gained to a considerable extent at the expense of universalist reality, and the sense of temporal distance which is the basis of objective historiography is the tacit negation of the paradigmatic values expressed in myth.[4]

The overpowering reality of the temporal thus limits the kinds of Events which can be presented as meaningful before a modern audience: anachronism, as the intrusion of the contemporary in an alien historical context, is in a sense a condition of the modern relevance of classical myth. Yet if Greece must be betrayed for myth to become meaningful in the modern world, the choice of mythology as a vehicle of expression reveals a continuing commitment to universalist thinking. And if the simple appropriation of cyclical patterns remains impossible in the post-Hegelian era, the contradictions of Time itself are such as to provide escape from the overwhelming particularism of History.

THE DEGRADATION OF MYTH

The most striking anachronisms are those which can be objectively defined. Of these, allusions to military and police functions compose the most obviously homogenous category in the modern mythological theater of France. On the level of specifically modern objects we find the personal identity "papiers" of Cocteau's play *Orphée* (p. 87)[5] or the handcuffs in Anouilh's *Antigone* (p. 60). Like the soldiers of Cocteau's *Machine infernale*, Anouilh's guards stand at attention in the presence of superiors (*A*, p. 49; *MI*, p. 32); specifically modern references to "le service" (*MI*, p. 21), with its "voie hiérarchique" (*MI*, p. 22), "capitaines" (*MI*, p. 17), "première classe Boudousse" (*A*, p. 51; cf. "Bidasse"), its "deuxième classe" (*MI*, p. 17) or "gradé" (*A*, p. 50), all appear in conjunction with the traditional psychological stereotypes of the military (e.g., "gueuler après les chefs," *MI*, p. 29). Military honors are likewise expressed in modern terms: Anouilh's guard Jonas presents himself before Créon[6] as "volontaire, la médaille, deux citations" (*A*, p. 51). Soldiers and guards, almost invariably, think in terms of modern firearms: Cocteau's soldiers "s'immobilisent au port d'armes" (*MI*, p. 32), Anouilh's Créon, identifying men with weapons, refers to the number of his "fusils" (*A*, p. 54), and although Giraudoux has Hector boast of his skill in throwing the javelin, (*GDT*, p. 147), Andromaque proposes the amputation of trigger fingers ("l'index de la main droite," *GDT*, p. 19) as a plausible means of ending war. Amphitryon too speaks in matter-of-fact fashion of "les tranchées de la guerre" (*A38*, p. 22), as of "plans de bataille" more appropriate to the mass movements of modern firepower than the single combats of ancient epic (*A38*, p. 25). And while the military is of practically no importance in Sartre's *Mouches*, the soldiers serving as palace guards, with their passing reference to a "permission de vingt-quatre heures" (*LM*, p. 68), are clearly serving in a conscript army of the modern type.

A second set of concrete anachronisms relates to domestic matters. Many items in this category have to do with food or drink. The most obviously inappropriate is coffee, mentioned briefly in Giraudoux's *Electre* (p. 140), and the subject of some discussion in the breakfast scene of Anouilh's *Antigone* (p. 22). The latter evokes a single modern context intended anachronistically, for it is doubtful that the audience is actually expected to raise the question of the historicity of Greek "tartines". And although the ancients assuredly did have red wine, "le rouge" is so specifically a French expression as to exclude the past, even if, as in Anouilh, wine were not expressly measured in liters (*A*, p. 132). "La goutte" and "la soupe chaude" (*M*, p. 398) are further examples of the present's monopoly on certain spheres of reality: their association with the French peasantry reinforces the specifically modern nuances in the portrait of the old nurse as a "bonne femme." We note the same temporal displacement in Giraudoux's *Electre*, as the president's "tisane" (p. 160) appears in a broad context of comfortable repose. Any modern French audience would recognize as contemporary the ethos of the "gueuleton" as exposed in Anouilh's guards; one of the cafés mentioned is, in addition, called "Le Palais Arabe" (*A*, p. 62). One might finally include, as essential to this modern gustatory complex, tabacco in nearly all of its forms, from the cigars in Giraudoux (*E*, p. 30) to the plugs chewed by Anouilh's guards (*A*, p. 66; *M*, p. 398).

The anachronisms in this second category generally suggest calm and repose, as distinguished from the aggressive or potentially aggressive ones associated with the functions of the military. Anouilh's Eurydice (*A*, p. 11) has in fact no other role than to thus remain the embodiment of calm, knitting sweaters for the poor, until her turn to die has come. Helen's cakes of soap (*GDT*, p. 68) clearly have little to do with acts of war. Again, we note among the fringe benefits of serving in Créon's guard the vocabulary of a specifically French perspective on comfort: "logement, chauffage, allocations" (*A*, p. 116). Indeed the only significant exceptions to this general anachronistic polarization are those objects which are not in keeping with the characters to whom they are assigned. Cigarettes accompany aggression in the rebellious sons of Oedipe because they are their first cigarettes (*A*, p. 91); the peelings which Sartre's Electre dumps on Jupiter's statue are, for the princess in the kitchen, a ready means of aggressive revolt (*LM*, p. 27).

Most of the anachronisms discussed above can be directly linked to two topical roles of the modern mythological play: the soldier-policeman and the "bonne femme." These characters are as remarkable for the specifically modern tone of their speech as for the anachronisms associated with their functions. They emphasize the primary anachronism of any mythological theater—contemporary or not—as that of language. Neither the audience nor the actors speak Greek,[7] and the existence of the play itself is the tacit negation of speech as a historical fact.

The anhistorical theater of earlier eras, as typified by the French classical stage, circumvented the problem through the expedient of elevated diction; French-speaking Greeks enjoyed a conventional idiom which the public perceived as appropriate to ancient context. This traditional idiom was fundamentally abstract, and the exclusion of the contingent simply was equated with the abolition of Time. But few things are so circumscribed by Time as colloquial forms of language. This is true partly because popular speech tends to crystalize in concrete metaphors, and such expressions as "lécher les bottes" (*MI*, p. 33), "morts en série" (*A*, p. 77), or "une espèce d'absolution" (*GDT*, p. 45) are in fact objectively anachronistic. Yet syntactic forms themselves are often identified with class, as class with modern society. As a result, certain expressions completely devoid of objective content (e.g., "dis voir," *MI*, p. 26; "que je te dis," *LM*, p. 69) become as unmistakably modern as metaphors of the type: "abattre le Sphinx et gagner le gros lot" (*MI*, p. 16). "Allez, ouste! Videz la place!" (*MI*, p. 164) therefore cannot be transferred from Paris to Thebes. The generalized "popular" is preempted by the present, and the twentieth century enjoys a temporal monopoly on the speech of the masses. The "bonne femme" and the soldier belong to the present by virtue of the conventional idiom they speak, just as the stylized diction of seventeenth-century tragedy situated Racine's characters securely in the "past".

While arms and domestic matters are thus primarily associated with the episodic roles of essentially topical characters, a third and final category of anachronistic terms is more intimately linked to the protagonists of the modern mythological play. This is the category of the festive. For if celebrations are universal, the "jours fériés" of *Les Mouches* (p. 36) and the "vacances au bord de la mer" of the Oedipe household (*A*, p. 67) are specifically contemporary. Similarly, certain types of dancing would be appropriate to the context of ancient Greece, but the ball is a characteristically modern form, and one repeatedly found on the mythological stage: examples are Anouilh's *Antigone* (p. 43), Sartre's *Mouches* (p. 32), and the stage version of Cocteau's *Orphée* (p. 78). Often, as in *La Machine infernale* or *Médée*, references to night-clubs or cafés suggest the atmosphere of a "bal populaire." The festivities accompanying Jason's marriage in *Médée* are the most flagrantly anachronistic, however, as firecrackers and shotgun blasts add a modern chapter to the long tradition of the pastoral in literature.

Anachronistic festivities are consistently portrayed as vulgar. Polynice returns from an evening of modern dissipation, cigarette between his lips, to strike his father (*A*, p. 91); Hémon, on the other hand, is drawn to Antigone at a ball precisely because she seems so out of place (p. 43). Médée's scorn for Créuse's wedding feast needs little enough emphasis, as does the attraction of Thebes' "boîtes de nuit" for the aging Jocaste of Cocteau's *Machine infernale* (p. 57). A related theme, that of informal relationships between young people strolling in the street, appears in Anouilh (*A*, p. 31) and in Sartre's *Mouches* (p. 31): "les promenades de

Corinthe" recalled by Oreste, like the "voyous" who turn to stare at Antigone, suggest a kind of courtship dance common in modern Western society, yet quite incompatible with the traditions of patriarchal Greece.

There are other instances of anachronism in modern mythological plays which, strictly speaking, could not be subsumed in any of the categories outlined above. However a common view of reality links them to the military, the domestic, and the festive. All are facets of the vulgar, and hence of the real, for History is consistently identified with the banal. This is of course axiomatic in the topical roles of the soldier and the "bonne femme," while leisure and festivities are seen as elements of temptation for the exemplary destiny of the mythical protagonist. Amusement, particularly collective amusement, operates on the level of guards chewing plugs or playing at cards in Anouilh (*A*, p. 12): it is of a reality unworthy of the mythological hero. Thus audience and hero relate antipathetically to concrete anachronistic elements; the specifically modern is a contingency which steadfastly degrades. Modern units of measure are used to describe Agamemnon's obesity, as Sartre's guards portray an Argive champion "qui faisait, bon an, mal an, ses cent vingt-cinq kilos" (*LM*, p. 68). Hector throws the javelin seventy meters (*GDT*, p. 147), surely no mean feat, but the intent of this particular passage is to underscore the military inadequacy of the poet Demokos. Giraudoux's "géomètre" also uses modern standards ("Il n'y a plus de mètres, de grammes, de lieues," *GDT*, p. 44) in a scene revealing the base and cowardly character of the patriotism of the Trojan masses. The "watch-the-birdie" scene in which Demokos seeks inspiration for his "chant de guerre" (p. 93) serves a similar purpose, and the same camera motif is used by Hector to degrade Helen's very real sense of destiny, as he compares her second sight to an "album de chronos" (p. 72). Even the "carte postale" metaphor in Anouilh, which evokes the beauty of the waking world for Antigone, ultimately represents the temptation of the base and vulgar, for life itself will be the supreme obstacle to the fulfillment of the role of renunciation the heroine is to play.[8]

The climate of anachronism, of whatever quality or origin, is thus the climate of everyday experience. It is, moreover, an atmosphere whose intimate quality shrouds the persons of the drama in a heavy mantle of family secret. The modern dramatist seeks to penetrate the decorous façade of ancient myth; he sets his action behind the scenes, in the private lives of his public figures. This is in striking opposition to the practice of classical Greek drama, whose action was characteristically set in the public place: in fact, to enter one's house is, in Sophocles, synonymous with leaving the stage. In this sense, the simple act of closing the window, as in *La Machine infernale*, *Les Mouches*, or *Antigone*, is much more than an isolated anachronistic gesture: it is the symptomatic withdrawal from public life to the private domain, and the acceptation of a particularistic, Historical perspective.

Nowhere is this link between the anachronistic and the intimate more evident than in Anouilh's final confrontation scene between Antigone and Créon. A previous quarrel in the Oedipe family is recounted as the prelude to the dispute between the protagonists themselves; Antigone is initiated into a world of domestic secrets as she learns how an aging and respected *père de famille* was shamefully mistreated by his unworthy sons. Créon first describes Polynice and Etéocle, who smoke cigarettes, wear formal dress, slam doors when leaving the palace, drive their cars too fast, spend their nights in bars or clubs, and generally lead a life of modern debauchery. But the most striking lines of the king's apologia for expediency are found in a relatively short passage[9] relating the true circumstances of the burial of the "good" brother, Etéocle.[10] The flow of anachronisms here is impressively rapid: from the military sphere we encounter "s'engager", "les honneurs militaires," and the word "attentat" with its contemporary political overtones; modern institutions are mentioned ("les enfants des écoles... les sous de leur tirelire"), or simply supposed ("un saint"); cliché and colloquialism are frequent, and the banal and familiar tone in which the entire scene is set is in complete harmony with the intimate key of this, the most secret setting of the play (pp. 94-96).

Whenever possible, the modern mythological dramatist creates just such an intimate atmosphere within the familiar setting of an interior decor. Thus we are present in Jocaste's bridal chamber (*MI*, acte iii), and learn the most secret desires of the protagonists. The audience likewise eavesdrops on a conversation between the two palace guards in Agamemnon's throne room, to discover that the hero was uncommonly fat (*LM*, p. 68). We are present at Amphitryon's morning toilette, and privileged to observe the hero's humanity as he cuts himself shaving (*A38*, p. 33). As a quarrel between generations, *Antigone* is appropriately situated within the home, as is *La Guerre de Troie n'aura pas lieu*, for the matters of state of ancient Troy appear as family affairs. Nor is intimacy necessarily limited to strictly domestic contexts: the Sphinx and Anubis, outside the walls of Thebes, are in a sense "at home" to passers-by, and the young lady does indeed receive visitors—"la matrone" and her child—with polite and hospitable airs. Jocaste and Tirésias could scarcely speak a more familiar idiom in the privacy of the palace than on the lonely walls of the city. We find the same informal speech, set in a more savage tone, in Médée's conversations with Jason and Créon, as they meet with the magician before her "roulotte" on the outskirts of Corinth.

In domestic situations, the language used by central figures is often identical with the normal diction of episodic characters. It strikes the modern reader as anachronistic for essentially the same reasons. To the degree that his historicity may be taken seriously, Pâris surely did address Helen as "Hélène chérie," but cliché is preempted by the present. Ancient heroes who express themselves in such terms are in danger of losing both their antiquity and their heroism. Pâris speaks for all domestic antiquity when he observes that "cette tribu royale, dès qu'il est question d'Hélène, devient aussitôt un assemblage de belle-mère, de belles-sœurs, et de beau-frère digne de la meilleure bourgeoisie" (*GDT*, p. 56).

Pâris' remark implies a separation of genres traditional in Western literature and the importance of class structures in the formation of our temporal perspectives should not be underestimated. If the intimate climate need not necessarily be temporally defined (it is certainly not so in Racine),

a high level of abstraction and a disregard for concrete detail are precon-
ditions of any timeless intimacy. Matter belongs to becoming, and common
or vulgar sentiments are contemporaneous with the matter in which they
are grounded. Thus although one may dress Molière's "types" in modern
costume, some recalcitrant details usually remain to affirm the classical
provenance of the drama. On the modern stage, the intimate perspective,
while perhaps not inherently anachronistic, creates a climate favorable to
the expression of such objectively anachronistic detail as "tartines", dogs
wetting on carpets, cakes of soap, kilograms and miles, playing cards, or
even an Isadora Duncan scarf (*MI*, passim) and a methane gas theory for
the apparition of ghosts ("Peste! voilà un spectre des plus savants et qui ne
cache point sa science!" (*MI*, p. 24).

The intimate perspective is not only the climate of anachronism, it is a
critical perspective as well; it sacrifices the abstract in its affirmation of the
personal and refuses paradigm for History. This is the tradition of Offenbach
and ultimately of the burlesque, for the primary effect of both anachronism
and intimacy is the degradation of myth. For the modern dramatist, truth is
not identified with the great themes of classical antiquity; it is found in a
deceptively familiar normality.[11] The value thus placed upon the familiar
and transitory Event denounces myth as a lie, and anachronism and the
critical perspective become common functions of Historicism. The search
for secret truth behind the traditional façade of myth leads the modern
dramatist to banality, and the banal, in its concrete manifestations, is most
effectively and perhaps necessarily portrayed in anachronistic detail. The
grandiose and the abstract give way before the concrete and the familiar as
a world of becoming is substituted for mythical Being. Nothing then could
be further from the truth than to view anachronism as a device for
modernizing traditional themes; the values of myth do not belong to
History at all, for they are, precisely, atemporal.

The intimate perspective of the modern dramatist is thus an orientation
fundamentally at odds with the timeless, paradigmatic values of the
mythical mentality. The figures of mythology lead, by definition, a public
existence; they have no private lives, in the sense that they have no secrets
to reveal other than the express content of myth. The content of myth itself,
however intimate in guise, is manifest content, while the common assump-
tion of modern dramatists seems to be that traditional truth, as public
record, is somehow opposed to objective truth. Giraudoux exposes the
Homeric account of the Trojan war as fraud: Helen was no more than a
public symbol, and the true cause of the conflict was the murder of a
hitherto unknown poet within the confines of the Trojan palace—at the
hands of Hector himself. Similarly, we learn that Oedipus did not really
know the answer to the riddle of the Sphinx, that, furthermore, "la chienne
qui chante" was not really a monster after all, but only a slight young girl
tired of the tribute she exacted and secretly wishing for death.

Not only does the modern dramatist give a fundamentally "personal"
account of events; as we enter their private lives, mythical characters
forswear their very personalities. Cocteau's Orphée no longer loves Eurydice[12]; Medea repents of her sensuality and longs for the purity of

Childhood (Anouilh); Electra forsakes vengence, leaving Orestes to bear alone the burden of a common guilt (Sartre). Such conduct as remains consistent with traditional accounts is explained by unexpected motives. Oedipus really left Corinth—for no one believes in oracles—"pour fuir la cour et satisfaire [sa] soif d'inconnu" (MI, p. 91); Anouilh's Oreste hates Aegisthos, not as the murderer of his father, but because of childhood memories antedating the assassination: a vision of sex as fundamentally impure, not the horror of regicide, motivates this youth who had witnessed as a boy the intimacies of an adulterous couple. Créon, we are told, would secretly have preferred to bury Polynices. Reversing cause and effect as they appear in Sophocles, Anouilh explains the burial edict on the grounds of civil disturbance in Thebes; it is not the king's obstinate pursuit of vengeance which provokes public indignation, rather the rebel's body must be exposed in order to quell incipient revolution. Antigone's motives are also transformed, and the linear action of this particular play could well be described as the systematic destruction of the traditional conflict between the individual and the state in favor of a secret personal drama: the choice between the perfection of a static, untainted image of self, and a humble life of daily compromise.

Revelation thus becomes the favorite pose of the modern mythological dramatist. It is, indeed, only through the mediation of the Secret that his originality can survive the climate of myth. For the author's vision of a mythological subject must remain at least superficially consistent with the common culture of his audience: Orestes must leave the scene pursued by Furies, the Trojan war must take place, Antigone must resolve to die, Medea must have her vengeance. Giraudoux's choice of Elpénor as the subject of his first work is illuminating in this respect: "C'est alors que mourut le matelot Elpénor," reads his epigraph from Homer, "seule occasion que j'aurai de prononcer son nom, car il ne se distingua jamais, ni par sa valeur, ni par sa prudence." But where events are more perfectly known, the supposed secrecy of the "true" account supplies the only plausible explanation for the traditions of our false mythology: since the Trojan poet was silenced by Hector, "le poète grec" could transmit unchallenged his lies to posterity. Had it not been so, Giraudoux could not have written his play. A true account of the Theban political situation had never been given before Anouilh, who relates what Créon terms, in characteristically anachronistic fashion, "les coulisses de ce drame" (A. p. 94). The banal secrets of the intimate decor perish with the actors of the drama: future generations, the modern audience excepted, will not have access to the truth, but only to the mythified versions of the public domain.

Like the anachronistic, the concrete, the intimate and the critical, revelation reflects the profoundly historical consciousness of the modern era. In treating traditional subjects, the modern writer does not seek to play, in Pascal's phrase, a better game of tennis[13]; his intent is to alter the game itself in some new and original way. The author's vision of himself, like his vision of his subject, is basically particularistic, for creativity is a valorization of the act as unique and as such a property of Historical man. The mythographer of the anhistorical era sees himself, conversely, as an imitator, just as he views his subject matter as a timeless and paradigmatic essence. In this sense the classical doctrine of imitation is (or at least purports to be) the heir of a truly mythical mentality; it refuses the concrete, the timely, and the unexpected, recognizing distance as a category of the paradigmatic and transmitting material viewed as immutable. The art of myth—as opposed to the creations of genius—is characteristically and perhaps necessarily an art of embellishment.

The incubus of romantic genius haunts the modern stage, and the modern dramatist is, paradoxically, drawn to the trivial because he values his original intelligence. The most clearly original characters in the modern mythological drama are precisely those episodic and topical figures mentioned earlier as most intimately associated with concrete anachronistic detail: the soldier-guard and "la bonne femme." Legend tells us nothing of the nurse of Antigone's childhood or of the uneventful meeting between an obscure "matrone" and the Sphinx of Thebes (*MI*, pp. 73-82). Pâris' "gabiers" and the several anonymous voices of Giraudoux's *Guerre de Troie*, like the palace guards in *Les Mouches* or the soldiers on the ramparts of Thebes may well be plausible actors in the archetypal drama; they are, however, as artificially modern as the "commissaire" of Cocteau's play *Orphée*. Where precedent for humble characters does exist in ancient literature, the modern dramatist presents a profoundly altered vision. The nurse or "bonne femme" of Anouilh's *Médée* has none of the dignity of her counterpart in Euripides, and Giraudoux's Hécube has more in common with Cocteau's "matrone" than with Homeric prototype. So modern indeed are the tabacco-chewing guards in Anouilh's *Antigone* that authentically classical motifs of a somewhat vulgar cast are perceived as out of place: the dispute over bringing bad news, or the stench which forces these humble characters to gain higher ground (p. 49) are absorbed by the generally anachronistic and original characterization, and it is with some surprise that one rediscovers these motifs in Sophocles.

The traditional body of myth pays little attention to concrete detail: it ignores the secrets of the intimate decor and shuns the banal and the timely in a quest for universals. By the same token, the intrusion of the Historical is, in modern dramatists, a symptom of the presence of Self. The anachronistic and the episodic, like the intimate secrets of central figures, are microcosmic reflections of the author's personal message. Hécube's specifically modern idiom proclaims that a humble and contented life is better than the putative glories of battle, just as a historical and somewhat prosaic Amphitryon is to be preferred to the archetypal perfection of eternal Jove. A different, yet equally original attitude is revealed by the refusal of the banal which typifies Anouilh's heroines: the purity which is their hallmark, dialectically expressed, is grounded in the anachronistic and the concrete. Most of the anachronisms in Sartre's *Mouches* relate to the institution of the Church, viewed as the keeper of guilt; the author underscores in this manner his intense preoccupation with psychological liberty, just as his betrayal of the classical Electra is a commentary on responsibility as a burden which cannot be shared. The particularly modern overtones of the Oedipus theme are sufficiently clear in Cocteau, not only in the intimate scenes of the entire third act of his *Machine infernale*, but also in Jocaste's encounter with a young soldier on the ramparts of Thebes, and in the hero's boyish posture in his meeting with the Sphinx. Significantly, the presence of Self in every instance corresponds to a diminution of mythical grandeur.[14] For the perspectives of History are critical perspectives, and the triumph of historical reality in the several manifestations described above degrade mythical paradigms and often have effects which border on the satirical.

THE TEMPORAL DIALECTIC

Originality, critical revelation, the love of the concrete and the lowly, these are then the ideological postulates of anachronism on the modern stage. Yet if historical attitudes are essential to the apparition of anachronistic motifs, it does not follow that they are sufficient to this end. For all its modernism, Cocteau's film *Orphée* has little that could be termed anachronistic, since practically nothing remains of the trappings of myth.[15] The less fanciful but equally thorough modernism of Anouilh's *Eurydice* is still further removed from the memory of Greece; within the familiar setting of a railroad station and its neighboring "hôtel de province," an entirely new drama takes place.[16] The anachronistic is not to be equated with the modern, for the conditions which preside over its creation are such as to destroy it. Perfect anachronism is tantamount to none.

A distinction must therefore be made between the arbitrary temporal prejudice of the reader of myth and perspectives inherent in the mythical work. For the memory of myth is not necessarily colored by time, and it is quite possible to treat an ostensibly antique subject within a temporal vacuum. This is in fact a fitting description for Gide's earlier mythological plays, whose rarified temporal setting simply excludes all History. Theirs is the time of the philosophical dialog,[17] and Philoctète's account of his solitary exil is equally appropriate to the ideal ontology of *Le Roi Candaule*: "Moi, dans cette île, je me suis fait, comprends, de jour en jour moins Grec, de jour en jour plus homme" (*P*, p. 34). The later *Oedipe* contains many details which have have been termed anachronistic by most commentators[18]: the modernistic character of these items is beyond doubt,[19] although their temporal inappropriateness would be more difficult to establish. The antique is essentially absent from Gide's theater, not only because allusions to the ancient world are rare, but also because those elements presented as History are ironical in tone. It is with a derisive, not a historical intention, that Créon refers to Antigone, upon learning of her decision to take religious orders, as a Vestal (*O*, p. 66). If *Oedipus* survives in *Oedipe*, it is only as material for comment, not as myth. Any temporal frame of reference the play may have derives from our knowledge of Sophocles, not from the intent of the author[20]: "Me voici tout présent," affirms Oedipe as the play begins, "complet en cet instant de la durée éternelle." (*O*, p. 57)

Where temporal considerations are present in the theater of myth, anachronism is defined, if a word may here be coined, by chronism. This is the use of concrete historical detail for its value as a sign of temporality on a plane removed from that of the performance. The spectator's perception of antiquity is thus as vital to anachronism as his awareness of contemporary history. The direct juxtaposition of chronism with present History creates some striking cases of temporal disequilibrium in the myths of the modern stage. The text of *Antigone* clearly indicates that the play is to be performed in modern dress, yet Antigone refers to her uncle's crown (p. 84) and herself wears sandals which seem almost inappropriately Greek (p. 15). Recalling that his edict has been proclaimed "aux carrefours" (p. 71), Créon alludes to information techniques appropriate to classical times, yet in the self-same phrase supposes the existence of media more logically situated in the post-Gutenberg era ("tu as lu l'affiche sur tous les murs de la ville," p. 71). The conjugation of modern measures with ancient weapons in Giraudoux has been mentioned above; the same sort of temporal paradox can be found in the most minute details of his *Guerre de Troie*, as a reference, made in mixed company, to a "révolte de gynécée" (p. 48). Helen too is carried to Troy in an appropriately Greek—or Trojan—"trirème", yet this one-masted ship has a "mât de misaine" (p. 75) like the ocean-going ships of more recent eras. There is, again, much that is modern in Anouilh's account of Jason's wedding, but sacrifices and athletic games are part of the ceremony, as is the traditional "chant d'hyménée" (pp. 355, 358).

Such immediate juxtaposition of past and present is not the rule in the modern mythological theater, but none of the categories of anachronism mentioned above is entirely lacking in its chronistic analogues. What is perhaps the only specifically classical motif from the gustatory sphere—the Greek taste for "vin à la résine"—is found in Giraudoux (*GDT*, p. 96), whose plays are particularly rich in chronistic as well as anachronistic detail. Ancient weaponry is, on the other hand, the chronistic category most often represented. Anouilh's Hémon is armed with a sword (p. 128); Demokos is slain by Hector's spear (*GDT*, p. 181). Where warfare is present as an element of decor, it is siege warfare: Ilion is a focal point of the modern image of ancient conflict, and it would be no great exaggeration to say that for the modern mind Greece is the high wall of the fortified city. Witness the "terrasse d'un rempart dominée par une terrasse et dominant d'autres remparts" of the *Guerre de Troie* (p. 7), the "chemin de ronde" of Cocteau's *Machine infernale* (p. 15), the "créneaux" of Sartre's *Mouches* (p. 15), or Cocteau's decor ("murs de pierres grises," p. 101) for the earlier adaptation of Sophocles' *Oedipus Rex*.

In the area of domestic chronism, although the ubiquitous windows and doors suggest a basically modern interior, reference is made to "la plinthe du palais" in Giraudoux (*GDT*, p. 30), and the Sphinx at home on her pedestal seems to owe as much to a well-known artefact as to Cocteau's fancy. Comfort is usually a category securely within the modern domain, but if Giraudoux's Helen prefers soap to pumice stone (*GDT*, p. 70), olive oil is mentioned upon occasion as part of the "ancient" toilette (*M*, p. 358).

Measures do not necessarily follow the metric system: a vague but sufficiently Greek "douzième borne" is found in the *Machine infernale* (p. 74), and one of Pâris' "gabiers" estimates distances in paces (*GDT*, p. 159). Troy's gates of War, whose hinges are bathed in olive oil, can be contrasted temporally with the anachronistic image of a "coffre-fort", used to describe the gates themselves (p. 118). And if Anouilh's characters play at cards, Cocteau's soldiers have not forgotten dicing (*MI*, p. 19). Antiquity awaits in all its facets the intrusion of the modern: two eras share the stage. Temporal homogeneity of either ancient or modern civilization is thus avoided through the concrete details of History confounded.

On a plane removed from the concrete, but not from the temporal, many traditional attributes of the classical character survive. Orphée may live in a modern apartment, but he is still priest of the sun in Cocteau's stage version of the myth. Sartre's Jupiter throws the thunderbolt, and, one suspects, rolls up his sleeves to do so (*LM*, p. 18). Giraudoux alludes to "la ruse d'Ulysse" (*GDT*, p. 177), Helen is still (or perhaps already) aware of a proverbial Greek cleverness (p. 70) and the somewhat effete sensuality which the Greeks ascribed to Eastern peoples seems equally well-known ("l'idée qu'il y avait des Troyens," p. 156). Nor is linguistic chronism entirely absent from the modern mythical drama. Examples are for the most part allusive, e.g., "la Parque" as a figure for death in Cocteau's play *Orphée* (p. 51), but occasionally an entire sentence in the Greek French style can be found. Giraudoux's Ulysse is appropriately eloquent: "Au-dessus de votre couple, les étoiles ont paru et disparu trois fois" (*GDT*, p. 156).

Chronism then, like anachronism, can consist in the use of motifs whose temporality is wholly conventional: it need not be objectively authentic as long as it seems to be. For who would dare to challenge the authenticity of Giraudoux's "colza"? (*GDT*, p. 173) The shades of the unburied dead, who "errent éternellement sans repos" (*A*, p. 70), belong to epic tradition, not to Sophocles, yet no one would judge the presence of the motif inappropriate in *Antigone*. A similar and more pointed example is Tirésias' blindness in Cocteau: myth associates the seer's second sight with physical blindness[21], yet Jocaste's allusion to devination by birds ("entrailles de poulets") seems to imply that his vision is still intact. Cocteau avoids this difficulty by making Tirésias only partially blind ("je suis presque aveugle," p. 35), and since myth does teach that the prophet was sensitive to the speech of the birds, ancient tradition, imperfectly remembered, satisfies the modern need for historical color.

Elements of such a neoclassical *vraisemblance* are systematically offset by a self-conscious awareness of myth as literature on the part of the dramatist and his characters. Just as anachronistic and incoherent reality is created through the interference of past and present, so do the persons of the drama become temporally schismatic figures because they perceive their traditional roles from the vantage point of the present. This consciousness of role is indeed the most important driving force in Anouilh's dramaturgy.[22] His characters "are there" to assume a preordained and arbitrary being. This is also true, in a sense, of the protagonists in Cocteau's *Machine infernale*, although the awareness of self in the main characters is dream-like and intermittent. Yet if the term is a paradox, subconscious awareness is precisely the author's theme, and Tirésias, who as a clairvoyant spectator can comment on the drama objectively, knows full well his place in history: "...le cercle se ferme: nous devons nous taire et rester là... laissez la fable tranquille" (p. 180).

In Giraudoux, where the traditional appears in yet another vein, consciousness of role is set in an ironical mode. The poet Demokos does not speak seriously of the divine inspiration of his "transes" ("Je délire, j'écume, et j'improvise," *GDT*, p. 81), and Pâris comments lightly on the disadvantages of being cast in the role of "fils séducteur" (p. 57). While myth teaches that Cassandra's prophecies were necessarily ignored by a sceptical audience, Giraudoux's Cassandre refers flippantly to her "spécialité de parler à l'invisible" (*GDT*, p. 81), and Hector makes light of her prophetic vision ("Ce sont toujours les devineresses qui questionnent," p. 69). This last remark is reminiscent of Jocaste's "il fallait deviner" (*MI*, p. 51), addressed precisely to the "devin" Tirésias, whose knowledge of the present compares so unfavorably with that of the young Theban soldier.

But whether serious or ironical, the roles of the theatrical present are constantly perceived and justified in terms of the historical future of the audience. The "habitudes des cerveaux et des siècles" will be formed by events at Troy (*GDT*, p. 132); the names of Jason and Médée will be "liés ensemble pour les siècles" (*M*, p. 372); Tirésias knows that Oedipe and Jocaste will belong "au peuple, aux poètes, aux cœurs purs" (*MI*, p. 190). The ontology of the mythical theater is thus a subjective ontology. What might be termed, existentially, the category of the "être-là-pour" implies an omniscience not unlike that of Augustine's God: it is only knowledge, not foreknowledge, since the perceiving consciousness is uncircumscribed by time. When asked by the Sphinx to account for the presence of an Egyptian god in ancient Greece, Anubis makes an observation which applies to the mythological drama taken as a whole: "l'Egypte, la Grèce, la mort, le passé, l'avenir, n'ont pas de sens chez nous." (*MI*, p. 72)

The very intelligibility of much that is anachronistic depends upon the omniscience of the anachronistic consciousness. Citations, for example, derive their value as citations from the authority of a literary past. It follows that quotations from non-Greek sources must function through the mediation of a common future. At least three temporal planes are involved in Pâris' witticism: "Un seul être vous manque, et tout est repeuplé." (*GDT*, p. 32) Pâris the son of Priam must become the creation of Giraudoux if he is to rewrite Lamartine for the amusement of the Trojan court. Only a consciousness uncircumscribed by time can give meaning to anachronisms drawn from literature, which appear, under the form of Biblical citations in the main, in Cocteau and Anouilh as well. A self-contained paradox of the same sort is the "mot historique" set in classical context, e.g., "La politesse des rois, c'est l'exactitude." (*MI*, p. 31) The same logic holds true for the more concrete forms of history, as for example the allusion made as Hélène descends towards the Greek ships: her pathway is "long comme le parcours officiel des rois en visite quand l'attentat menace" (*GDT*, p. 177).[23]

Comments made on purely objective anachronisms also reveal, on the part of the players, a contemporary perception of the past. Giraudoux's Hélène draws attention to her reference to soap, and substitutes an appropriate chronism ("ou de la pierre ponce, si vous aimez mieux," *GDT*, p. 70). The rhyming poetry written by Demokos does not escape Hector's criticism on more than one ground: "Tu as fini de terminer tes vers avec ces coups de marteau qui nous enfoncent le crâne." (p. 58)[24] Cocteau's soldiers comment on their use of the expression "petite vache," glossing the particular meaning of the expression for the modern military (p. 30, cf. 17). In *Amphitryon 38*, Alcmène wears "une tunique de linge inconnu, qu'on appelle la soie, soulignée d'un rouge nouveau, appelé la garance" (p. 112). These are the quintessential anachronisms: they appear as temporal paradoxes, not by exterior criteria, but by virtue of an interior incoherence.

This flagrant dialectic of the old and the new is a flight into fancy not atypical of the cumulative effects of anachronism within the context of a given play. For the modern theater of myth presents historical reality only in the self-destructive mode created through the interference of the ancient with the modern. In such a setting of temporal fantasy, the concrete can only be considered historical in the sense that it is a valorization of the Event. Antique authenticity does not necessarily heighten our sense of historical accuracy, any more than the modern need create in all cases the greater immediacy of a realistic setting. Events may destroy others of their kind. Indeed, History exists on the modern stage for that very purpose: it abolishes Time and the unique and calls forth, through its dialectic of the old and the new, a new world of exemplary forms.

THE NEW PARADIGM

Despite the incursion of a post-Hegelian historicism into the world of myth, the paradigmatic remains its essence. A mythological title alone will serve as a minimal paradigm, and Cocteau's film *Orphée* must immediately be understood as a statement on the Poet. It matters little that the content of classical myth has been replaced by a modern message, that it is expressed through a new series of events and is set in a thoroughly modern decor. Nomenclature is in itself sufficient to the creation of myth, and Anouilh's *Eurydice* similarly offers a new mythology of love and dreams. Just as the messages of ancient myth can, as universals, claim some validity for modern man, so do the versions of Cocteau and Anouilh reflect backwards through time on Greece: they are new myths in modern dress, yet as myth they speak to all mankind.

A mythological setting signifies at once an indifference to temporal difference and a commitment to preaching. Within the French tradition ancient subject matter has retained the exemplary cast of its primitive ontology, and the choice of mythological personae is the external sign of a didactic orientation. This is doubtless the lowest common denominator in the modern taste for myth, and the addition of didactism into an equation of time and theatrical fantasy will account for the most striking variations in anachronistic technique among the authors studied here.

Sartre seems to have been drawn to the theater because of its aptness as a means of propaganda; indeed his brush with classical subject matter in *Les Mouches* has been attributed by some to the presence of the censor.[25] Consequently, the author's anachronism merely underscores the message that "ancient" events apply to modern life, and the persistent association of modern elements with the themes of religion, sin, and guilt separates chronistic and modern elements into neatly defined temporal planes. The play thus appears as a basically pseudo-classical work, and its anachronisms heavy-handed, if not gratuitous.

Gide's didactic vocation is even more obvious, but he seems to have been far less preoccupied with the theater as a demonstrative art form. The ideal performance of *Oedipe*, if we are to believe the author, was in fact one in which "l'illusion théâtrale était nulle."[26] Since all concrete forms are rare in Gide's theater, anachronisms—other than those of the ironical sort—are for all intents and purposes absent from his plays.[27] Irony and self-analysis supply a more direct and intelligent abstraction: that of the frank didactic intention.

The didactic ends of Cocteau, Giraudoux, and Anouilh are far less obvious. These dramatists are, however, intensely preoccupied with theatricality and show a pronounced taste for dramatic fancy.[28] It is thus in their work that the anachronistic, as a junction of independent temporal planes, finds it purest expression as an esthetic form. All three consider myth the native environment of purity, and they have found in anachronism a common tactic for the accommodation of History in a search for type. One of the epigraphs of the *Machine infernale* alludes to "l'impeccable naïveté" of myth; another refers to the usefulness of systems where one can "prêcher à son aise." Both sentiments are echoed in the admonitions addressed by Tirésias to Créon in the closing scene of the play: the new king must not interfere with myth, as Oedipe, Jocaste, and their children now belong "aux cœurs purs" (p. 180), i.e., "aux poètes." The chorus of *Antigone* expresses a mythological credo whose terms recall those found in Cocteau: "propre... reposant... sûr... on est tous innocents... pour les rois" (pp. 56-58). The same themes are developed in strikingly similar fashion in the gardener's lament of Giraudoux's *Electre*: "On réussit chez les rois les expériences qui ne réussissent jamais chez les humbles, la haine pure, la colère pure. C'est toujours de la pureté. C'est cela que c'est, la Tragédie, avec ses incestes, ses parricides; de la pureté, c'est-à-dire en somme de l'innocence." (p. 117)

There is thus a common recognition, among those dramatists who can most clearly be considered masters of anachronistic technique, that the pure and exemplary figure is not a character drawn from life. It is rather in the frankly illusory that truth is to be found, and it can be said of their plays that the exemplary owes its didactic value to the imaginary mode of its existence. Recognizing the unique nature of the Event, classical doctrine, as epitomized in Boileau, held that "le vrai peut quelquefois n'être pas vraisemblable." (*AP*, III, 48) But modern mythical personae, unlike the "caractères" of French neoclassicism, do not attain universality by shedding their concrete attributes. The modern theater, holding that "l'invraisemblable peut être le vrai," solicits historical reality in a paradoxical creation of the pure and archetypal.

For while none of the authors discussed in this paper could embrace realism, all recognize the legitimacy of the historically real. As antithetical realities conflict in Time, the historical destroys History, and theatricality, in the artificial world of the stage, becomes a major force for abstraction in the modern search for type. Artifice is the new paradigm in the myth of the modern stage. Anachronism, in the strict sense of the term, is one of the major aspects of this theatricality. In its broadest sense, as the essentially timeless atmosphere of a paradigmatic stage, it is that theatricality itself.

University of Maryland

Notes

[1] Tr. Willard R. Trask, London (Routledge & Paul), 1955, p. 141.

[2] An eminent professor of History reminds us that the sense of historical perspective is a fairly recent development, and that the anhistorical attitudes of the past were "not completely shaken off until the triumph of historicism in the nineteenth century. No popular representation today of imperial Rome or of Old Testament Judea such as Hollywood has from time to time given us would be attempted without all the apparatus that archeology and history, fake or real, could supply. But down through the eighteenth century popular audiences were not bothered by the fact that Greeks of the Age of Pericles appeared in the costumes of Versailles." Myron P. Gilmore, *The World of Humanism*, New York (Harper and Brothers), 1952, p. 201.

[3] This conflict is tacitly assumed by Professor Peyre in "History and Literature in France" (*Historical and Critical Essays*, University of Nebraska Press, 1968) when he notes: "Obviously, every situation is a new one and there is no trace of an eternal recurrence in human affairs. The past can hardly be expected to provide a solution to a problem which is set in new terms." (p. 6)

[4] Cf. Gilmore's remark that "the attainment of a sense of distance in time and space which is one kind of reality has been accomplished at the sacrifice of another kind of reality." (*Humanism*, p. 201)

[5] Wherever possible, reference is to current editions. This has resulted is some duplication of volumes, but it was felt that greater convenience would result from citing the most readily available edition. In the order of their citation, the following signs or designations are used: "the play *Orphée*": Jean Cocteau, *Orphée*, in *Œuvres complètes*, t. V, Genève (Marguerat), 1948; *A*: Jean Anouilh, *Antigone*, Paris (La Table Ronde), 1967; *MI*: Jean Cocteau, *La Machine infernale*, Paris (Livre de Poche), 1964; *GDT*: Jean Giraudoux, *La Guerre de Troie n'aura pas lieu*, Paris (Livre de Poche Université), 1964; *A38*: Jean Giraudoux, *Amphitryon 38*, Paris (Grasset), 1939; *LM*: Jean-Paul Sartre, *Les Mouches*, in *Théâtre*, Paris (Gallimard), 1947; *E*: Jean Giraudoux, *Electre*, Paris (Grasset), 1959; *M*: Jean Anouilh, *Médée*, in *Nouvelles Pièces noires*, Paris (La Table Ronde), 1957; Oreste, in Robert de Luppé, *Jean Anouilh, suivi des fragments de la pièce de Jean Anouilh, Oreste*, Paris (Classiques du XXe Siècle), 1961; Jean Giraudoux, *Elpénor*, Paris (Grasset), 1950; "the film *Orphée*": Jean Cocteau, *Orphée*, Paris (La Parade), 1950; Jean Anouilh, *Eurydice*, in *Pièces noires*, Paris (Calman-Lévy), 1949; André Gide, *Le Roi Candaule*, *P*: *Philoctète*, in *Œuvres complètes*, t. 3, Paris (*NRF*), 1933; *O*: André Gide, *Œdipe*, William S. Bell, ed., New York (Dell), 1968; "Sophocles' *Oedipus*: Jean Cocteau, in *Œuvres complètes*, t. 5 (v. supra).

[6] Where French names are used, the modern characters are intended; English names designate the classical figures, either as types or as characters in Greek literature.

[7] The French-speaking Greek is a paradox of the modern stage. Soldiers in all ages have undoubtably had their own particular idiom, and perhaps even precise equivalents for phrases like Cocteau's "s'inscrire au Sphinx." If historical Greek soldiers or nurses had spoken French, they very probably would have employed the "vulgar", i.e., everyday idiom of the modern stage. But the contemporary world enjoys a monopoly on linguistic cliché, and no matter how appropriate such language may seem upon reflecting, the theater leaves little time, precisely, for reflection, and operates within the confines of clearly defined conventions. Colloquialism may appear to be a form of historical authenticity, but its effects are invariably anachronistic in the classical context.

[8] Cf. Hugh Dickinson, *Myth on the Modern Stage*, University of Illinois Press, 1969, p. 264: "Show Antigone as having lived intensely... But be careful: don't present these things as good in themselves. After all, they are part of corrupting life..." (*Subsequently cited as* "Dickinson").

[9] The passage requires perhaps 90 seconds of stage time.

[10] The point is, of course, that both brothers were rascals.

[11] Dickinson's concluding statement on the use of myth in modern dramatists is that "with few exceptions, they offer us a diminished image of man" (p. 340).

[12] See Dickinson, pp. 81-82, for a discussion of Cocteau's debt to Offenbach.

[13] "Qu'on ne dise pas que je n'ai rien dit de nouveau: la disposition des matières est nouvelle; quand on joue à la paume, c'est une même balle dont jouent l'un et l'autre, mais l'un la place mieux." (*Pensées, texte de l'édition Brunschwig*, Paris, Garnier, 1958, p. 79)

[14] Cf. Bell's remark that "La Rencontre avec le Sphinx" has often been called Cocteau's only original contribution to the myth (bibliographical data in note 5), p. 32; this is also the scene in which the hero appears in the least heroic posture.

[15] Such vestiges of the traditional as remained in the stage version of the theme were systematically purged in the adaptation for the screen. Antique detail, such as references to laurel crowns or the region of Thrace, simply does not occur in the later work; the dominant classical motif of the play—Orphée's horse, with its suggestion of the Pegasus theme— is of course replaced by the Rolls Royce automobile equiped with short wave radio.

[16] Orphée is cast as a poor musician, but his music really is irrelevant to his role. There is, in addition, no significant relationship between the theme of poetry or music and the death of the lovers. John Harvey would seem to find this relationship, however, in the theme of dreaming. But the poet as dreamer is a post-romantic conception, and has little to do with the Orpheus of classical myth. (*Anouilh, A Study in Theatrics*, New Haven and London, Yale University Press, 1964, p. 85; *subsequently cited as* "Harvey".)

[17] *Philoctète* "examines the ethics, rather than the psychology, involved in the myth..." (Dickinson, p. 37); cf. p. 38, where the work is referred to as "a conversation piece on the question: What is virtue?"

[18] e.g., Dickinson, p. 60; Bell, p. 37. Bell also remarks in this excellent introduction to the two modern French Oedipus plays that the result of anachronism in Gide is "less an updating than it is the removal of the myth from historical and legendary time so as to place it in universal time." This is, in my opinion, a true statement, but it is a statement which suggests that it is fallacious to call such motifs anachronisms.

[19] One encounters details that are concretely modern (e.g., the automobile); religious problems are formulated in consistently modern terms ("bien-pensants", convents, etc.); there are also many proverbial or Biblical phrases which seem inappropriate to ancient context.

[20] Cf. Dickinson, p. 60: "*Oedipus* depends immensely on one's familiarity with the original, as it relies on one's knowledge of the myth; and it is difficult to imagine what its effect would be without them."

[21] Ovid, *Metamorphoses*, III, 316 ff.

[22] This is the principal thesis of Harvey's study.

[23] Alexander of Yougoslavia was assassinated in Marseilles in 1934.

[24] Cf. *Faust* II, III. Akt:

Vielfache Wunder seh' ich, hör' ich an.
Erstaunen trifft mich, fragen möcht' ich viel.
Doch wünscht' ich Unterricht, warum die Rede
des Manns mir seltsam klang, seltsam und freundlich.
Ein Ton scheint sich dem andern zu bequemen,
und hat ein Wort zum Ohre sich gesellt,
ein andres kommt, dem ersten liebzukosen.

(9365-71)

[25] For Sartre's didactic ends, see Dickinson, pp. 220-21; Philip Thody is cited on p. 222: "It is highly probable that... he used these myths principally because of the need to get past the censor."

[26] Hartung's production in Darmstadt. Gide also notes in his *Journal* for 5 février 1930, from which the citation is taken, that his "volonté de ne point chercher à [obtenir cette illusion] devenait du coup évidente." Cited in Helen Watson-Williams, *André Gide and the Greek Myth*, Oxford (The Clarendon Press), 1967, p. 120.

[27] "...time, or any kind of distance, allows an image to reach us only after it has been stripped of everything episodic, bizarre, and transitory, leaving only its portion of profound truth." From Gide's lecture on the "Evolution of the Theater," cited in Dickinson, p. 46.

[28] Giraudoux is said to have taken a "night course" on Cocteau (Dickinson, pp. 184, 189, 201); for Anouilh's admiration of Giraudoux, see Harvey, p. 6. There is a definite thread of influence between the three authors, or at the last, a line of admiration and respect.

In the early evening of May 28, 1959, on a spot known as the Pnyx, close beneath the towering cliff of the Acropolis, André Malraux rose to face an enormous crowd. The silent multitude that was spread far out over the hillside included not only Greeks, but representatives from a great many other nations as well, some as far distant as the United States and Japan. Philosopher, novelist, art historian, and Minister of Culture in the de Gaulle government, he had been invited to deliver an address on the occasion of the first "son et lumière" program at the Acropolis. As he stood beneath the timeless stars of the Greek sky on the very rock from which the great national leaders and orators of antiquity—Aristides, Themistocles, Pericles—had spoken to the citizens of Athens, Malraux was acutely conscious of what his presence in that historic place symbolized. It is not surprising that he took the occasion to summarize his view of the role that Greece and the Greek ideal had played in the life of Western civilization.[1]

It was most appropriate that Malraux should have been called upon for this task, because he is a truly remarkable representative of the long line of French thinkers and writers who have looked back to Greece for moral guidance and artistic inspiration. Indeed, as Professor Peyre suggests in his article, "What Greece Means to Modern France," many Frenchmen "have celebrated the uniqueness of the Greek miracle" since the 18th century,[2] but Malraux is particularly well qualified to do so by virtue of his perceptive intelligence, his temperament, his broad-ranging knowledge, and his eloquence. Yet, in an even deeper sense, one may say that Malraux has an exceptional insight into (and affinity for) the spirit of ancient Greece because his metaphysical view of the relationship between man and the universe is basically Greek. As the following study points out, like the great artists and thinkers of the Golden Age of Pericles, Malraux is acutely aware of the limits of the human condition and of its essential tragedy, but his determination to transform these elements into victories—in his life as well as in his art—makes him the very personification of the Greek humanist ideal, translated into 20th century terms. It is particularly fitting that this collection of essays on Hellenist influences in French literature should close with an examination of what he considers to be the major elements which the Greeks have left as their legacy to all of us in the West.

Notes

[1] Most of the Paris newspapers carried accounts of the events in their issues of the following day, May 29, 1959. See in particular the story from Michel Clare, the special correspondent for *L'Equipe*, on that date, p. 7. Mimeographed copies of the full text of the speech were subsequently distributed by the French Cultural Affairs Office, under the title "Discours prononcé à Athènes le 28 mai 1959...".

[2] This article, reprinted from *Yale French Studies*, no. 6 (December, 1950), pp. 53-62, is included in Peyre's recent collection, *Historical and Critical Essays* (University of Nebraska, 1968), pp. 100-112. Cf. p. 104.

MALRAUX AND THE GREEK IDEAL

By Walter G. Langlois

André Malraux has long been known as a man of unusual perception and broad insights, which he often formulates in remarkably incisive aphorisms. He began his brief but very eloquent 1959 speech in Athens with the affirmation that Greece in the Age of Pericles was unique among all the nations of antiquity because it was the first civilization in which "le mot intelligence a voulu dire interrogation."[1] The rest of the ancient world, still "ivre d'éternité" as he put it, could not comprehend this new culture because life without a Sacred Book as a guide seemed inconceivable. Yet it was precisely this freedom from the Sacred and the new spirit which accompanied it that had permitted Greece in less than fifty years to achieve three victories that were awesomely important for the future history of mankind, particularly in the West (which became the most direct heir of that classical civilization). As he formulated them, these "conquêtes" were "celle du cosmos par la pensée, celle du destin par la tragédie, celle du divin par l'art et par l'homme." This succinct statement serves as an excellent guide to the numerous comments about the nature of the Greek achievement that Malraux has made throughout his life, but most particularly in the three books with which we shall be primarily concerned here: *La Tentation de l'Occident, Les Noyers de l'Altenburg*, and *Les Voix du silence*.[2]

I

As a youth, Malraux was evidently first attracted to ancient Greece because in that civilization he found answers to certain of the problems that were pressing him and others of his generation so urgently. During the early 1920's, a whole group of young Frenchmen exhibited the symptoms of what Marcel Arland has called a "nouveau mal du siècle."[3] Their adolescence and early youth had been marked by the horrors of the First World War, and their utter disillusionment with the values inherited from their elders brought them to manhood with a strong desire to seek new and better answers for their lives. Not unlike many of today's young people faced with the war in Vietnam, these Frenchmen were determined either to sweep away or to profoundly modify their cultural heritage because they felt it was meaningless—if not actually injurious—to them.

Highly sensitive and intelligent, Malraux was aware of the malaise of his generation to the point of anguish. His close friend Arland summed up his state of mind at the time: "Si l'on peut parler d'angoisse, c'est bien à propos de cet homme qui, à 23 ans, a plus vécu, plus pensé, plus souffert que la plupart de nos vieillards... Son admirable intelligence avive encore ce tourment; elle l'a jeté tour à tour vers toutes les possibilités qui s'offraient à lui; il les envisage, il s'y livre maintes fois; mais il garde jusqu'au bout sa lucidité, qui l'alimente d'amertume, son frémissement qui fait de lui un artiste, et son malaise, qui le pousse sans cesse plus avant." [4]

A short article Malraux wrote in 1923, just before he left for Indochina, helps to illuminate the direction which his search for new basic values was beginning to take. His preface to a re-edition of two Maurras texts, *Mademoiselle Monk*, *suivi de Invocation à Minerve*, reveals that he—like Maurras—found certain values in the classical tradition which could be of great use in the contemporary world. He is favorably impressed, for example, by the fact that Greek philosophers were "accoutumés de mettre en harmonie leur vie et leur philosophie." [5] Certain moderns have tended to scorn Maurras, but Malraux admires him because "son système est formé de théories dont la force que représente leur application fait une partie de la valeur." Evidently, for Malraux—as for many others of his generation—Maurras was "une des plus grandes forces intellectuelles d'aujourd'hui" and a worthy successor to the Greek thinkers of old, precisely because his philosophy was more than the abstract, rationalist structure of an ivory-tower thinker. It represented an inner commitment to values that had real meaning for life as it was experienced by the young generation in Europe.

Malraux felt that in the West it was particularly difficult to bridge the gap between a system and a life, to make a philosophy into a living commitment, as it were, because two separate orders of reality were involved. As he noted in his Maurras essay, "la raison est peu puissante contre la sensibilité" (p. 8) since each belongs to one of the two "reals"—intellectual and emotional—between which Western man has been forced to divide his existence. To be sure, reason may act to modify an emotion, but only by using another emotion to do so, and any philosophical system which seeks to be valid and operative in the real lives of men must be rooted in something that is felt or experienced, rather than simply conceived of, intellectually. Malraux is here suggesting an idea that later became a primary element in his whole world view, namely that to be really meaningful a philosophy must be aesthetic, rather than merely rational or activist. As he points out, Maurras' aesthetic base was his admiration for the creations of "le génie français," and he loved Rome and Greece precisely because it was their legacy that had determined the character of that "génie". As we shall see, Malraux's admiration for Greece had a similar origin, but went much further.

The 1923 Maurras essay clearly indicates that even before his journey to Indochina, Malraux correctly understood the metaphysical impasse in which his generation found itself. Disoriented, discouraged, anarchistic, with an acute awareness of the enormous gap that separated what they *felt* from what they *knew*—their emotional from their intellectual existence— the young people of the early post-war years did not know how to redeem their lives so that they would be worth living, nor how to reorganize their world so that it would be meaningful. Malraux was one of the few who realized that before satisfactory answers could be found it was first necessary to understand the profound and distinctive character of the cultural tradition that had formed Western man and brought him to the point where he was. Because he felt that understanding arose primarily from the juxtaposition of contrasts,[6] he began to formulate an inter-cultural dialogue between the West and the non-West which would illuminate the fundamental assumptions that gave these cultures their distinctiveness. The book—in the form of an exchange of letters between a Frenchman and a Chinese, with comments by an Indian friend—was apparently planned as early as 1921; it was to be based on Malraux's extensive reading and his knowledge of art, as well as on his personal ideas about the different value systems upon which the three major cultures of the world were based. His two-year sojourn in the Orient in 1924 and 1925 brought him much meaningful experience and made him more aware than ever of the distinctive character of Western culture, particularly as it had been derived from the classical world.[7] He worked on revising his text (the Indian commentator was finally dropped) during the boat-trip back to France early in 1926, and it was published that summer under the title *Tentation de l'Occident*.[8]

As has been suggested, this book is young Malraux's effort to reach some conclusions about the essential characteristics of the culture of which he was a part, and to trace the historical evolution by which it had become what it was. His perceptive and occasionally lyric inquiry in dialogue form may not always have the clarity and coherence of a philosopher's analysis, but in a provocative way it illuminates many of the concerns that have been with him throughout his life. It is particularly relevant to the discussion here because several important letters deal with his views on the role that the Greco-Roman tradition—particularly the intellectual achievement that he called "la conquête du cosmos par la pensée"—has played in shaping the European cultural heritage.

The letters that comprise the text of the volume have been selected from an exchange between A. D., a young Frenchman visiting Asia, and Ling, a Chinese youth who is travelling in Europe. This literary device permits Malraux to bring out the differences between the two civilizations in a particularly concrete and striking manner. Each of these young men feels himself very much of an alien in the world of the other because that world was the result of a cultural tradition based on radically different principles. In Europe, Ling for the first time becomes acutely conscious of the ways in which he is a Chinese and not a Westerner through the contrast he senses between himself and the reality into which he has ventured, just as A.D. comes to better know himself and the character of the European civilization that had formed him through his travels in the East.

In his very first letter, Ling makes it clear that he has come to the West with "une curiosité hostile," not in quest of the "beaux fantômes" of

Europe's past, or indeed of any other of its "formes", but in search of the secret of Europe's *thought* (T, p. 27). For Asians believed that it was this thought which had enabled the West to make so many achievements and which presumably held the secret of its strength. Even before he had actually arrived, Ling's reading and study had given him the image of a vast continent "dévoré par la géométrie" where nature, man, and even the process of thinking itself bore the marks of the willed imposition of a reasoned order. To Ling, French-style European gardens—so unlike Chinese landscapes—"démontraient... des théorèmes" and symbolized the manner in which Westerners constantly corrected and humanized the natural order of nature, dominating and restructuring it according to human reason. It was inevitable that in such a civilization " la soumission à la volonté de l'homme dominait les formes" (T, p. 28).

During the earliest period of his sojourn, Ling is particularly sensitive to the exterior signs of Western culture which support this preconceived idea of Europe's energetic activism and overpowering rationalism. As he put it, what Europeans called "culture" impressed him as being little more than "une barbarie attentivement ordonnée, où l'idée de la civilisation et celle de l'ordre sont chaque jour confondues" (T, p. 34). Geometers in all things, Europeans even sought to organize time, to give it a reason or purpose, while Asians preferred to seek to attune themselves with it: "Le temps est ce que vous le faites, et nous sommes ce qu'il nous fait," he notes succinctly (T, p. 50). To an outsider, such a taming of the universe (to the ultimate use of Man) by human understanding was made possible by the special character of the terms in which Europeans comprehended or viewed reality.

Moreover, as Ling begins to know Westerners a little better he comes to realize that to a certain degree these same terms are operative even on the most intimate psychological level. Among other things, he is struck by Europeans' efforts to arrive at a profound understanding of their emotional and psychological life via reason. Their overpowering interest in learning the "truth" about themselves, their desire for sincerity seem to Ling to be attempts to integrate the human personality into the same geometric and reasonable system by which the exterior material world is dominated. He feels that the "demon" of ordered rationality has taken possession of the Western mind and so deformed it that Europeans can no longer perceive life except in fragments. To "comprehend" their existence, they must deal with it in an orderly manner, breaking it down into parts that human reason can dominate, thus destroying that living ensemble which—to an Oriental—is the very essence of creation.

As the Frenchman A. D. read his friend's first three letters, he evidently concluded that Ling was not fully understanding much of what he was observing in the West, and he suggested that a visit to Rome and Athens might provide a helpful historical background. Ling follows this advice, and his fourth and fifth letters are accounts of his reactions to the two cities that are the sources of the basic elements that had formed the culture of Europe and the "sensibilité" of Europeans. Ling's initial response to Rome was somewhat favorable because the Chinese cultural "grill" through which he perceived the world made him particularly susceptible to "le charme de ce beau jardin d'antiquaire à l'abandon" (T, p. 53). Thus, for him the immediate appeal of the ancient city was primarily that of its disorder—a confusion of past and present, of ruin and non-ruin, of Christian, Roman and modern. Yet even though he gradually became aware that these remains offered "quelques-uns des plus puissants sujets de méditation que recèle l'Europe," he notes that he had not been able to find in them that "sentiment qui, pour nous [Chinois], fait tout le prix des lieux autrefois élus" (T, p. 51). Moreover, in spite of the superficial pittoresque attraction of this "paysage où des souvenirs classiques tentent en vain d'ordonner un vide infini" (T, p. 54), he was much more interested in looking deeper, to try and determine what ancient Rome had really represented, to see if he could discover in her any distinctive values that had been passed on to subsequent European civilization.

To a large extent, these values were expressed in Christian terms, but Ling felt that most of the non-materialist tendencies of the original Christian message had been altered by the forceful and realist character of Rome itself. For him, the ancient Imperial capital with its many "symboles de pierre de la Volonté" (T, p. 56) mirrored the basic character of the Roman Empire, the "victoire de hauts esprits sur leurs rêves." Although the structures of the Church had ostensibly been elaborated to preserve Christ's message, in reality they had also kept alive the Imperial exaltation of organized, material power. The Roman Church replaced devotion to the Empire or the semi-divine person of the Emperor with an ideal of service to its own organizational structure, dominated by a scholastic God, and in the capital city of Christendom many Europeans heard little more than echos of the old Roman "appel de l'Empire" (T, p. 57).

To an Asian, such servitude to what was little more than an "allégorie ordonnée" of Force, imposed by an ordering human reason, was unworthy of man. As a Chinese, Ling protests that "si je m'abaissais jusqu'à l'ordre, je voudrais qu'il fût fait pour moi, et non pas moi pour lui" (T, p. 58). He further notes acutely that the traditional Western and Christian exaltation of "cette amère vertu de la force" had often caused Europeans to confound the Roman soul with "l'éclat de sa puissance" as an Empire. Asia may need Rome's forceful ordering strength in order to organize her universe and achieve progress in the modern world, but before the finest symbols of such power, Ling cannot help but feel disgust. As he closes his letter, he indicates that he intends to probe further into the secrets of the Western cultural past by making a trip to Greece.

Ling's fifth letter, one of the most provocative sections in the *Tentation*, deals with his visit to Athens, and it serves to clarify many of young Malraux's ideas about the character of the Greek legacy to the West. Ling had gone to Greece because he hoped that there he would find the essence of the classical spirit, a kind of "nouvelle pureté persane" (T, p. 64), not unlike the ideal that characterized the golden moments of Chinese civilization. Yet, at the time, Athens had seemed to him to be little more than a curious "symbole d'un peuple lauré, dressé sur les murs d'une forteresse," and this had left him filled with uncertainty. It was not until his return to contemporary Europe with all its resonances of the classical tradition that he really began to understand the primary meaning of what he had seen in Greece. All his impressions seem to converge on a certain Greek landscape ("ces colonnes brisées et ... ce dur horizon") and on a piece of sculpture— "le meilleur symbole que je connaisse aujourd'hui de l'Occident"—which he had seen in the small Acropolis Museum (T, p. 64). This "tête de jeune homme aux yeux ouverts" personified the triumph of the fundamental Greek attitude, so foreign to all the Orient but so characteristic of Western civilization: "Mesurer toute chose à la durée et à l'intensité d'*une* vie humaine" (T, p. 66).

This act of faith in the all-encompassing value of the individual human life, this reducing of the universe to a human scale was incomprehensible to an Asian because it made the force of each personal existence so over-powering that "tout s'ordonne par rapport à lui." As Ling saw it, even the Greek gods mirrored this attitude because what distinguished them was not so much that they were human, but rather that they were "personnels", i.e., individualized (T, p. 67). To be sure, many of the traditions of Asian religious and philosophical systems gave importance to Man and to his potential, but it was always in a larger context that prevented him in his pride from taking himself as the measure of the universe. As Ling put it, "nous concevions le monde dans son ensemble, et étions sensibles aux forces qui le composent autant qu'aux mouvements humains" (T, p. 67), and this awareness of being important only as a part of some larger whole inevitably led Asians to a "notion toute abstraite de l'homme." The Greeks' emphasis on the life-span of a single, separate, specific being who is born, grows old, and dies led them to a quite different fundamental awareness of the Self. For the Eastern idea of a human "genre," they "substituèrent la conscience d'être un être vivant, total, distinct" on an earth whose only unconquerable elements were the sea, and Man himself (T, p. 68).

Against this newly-understood background of the Greek tradition, Ling becomes even more aware that Rome's primary importance in Western cultural history was as the transmitter—and transformer—of the Greek and Christian messages. But in a sense, the change from Athena to Minerva was not so much a change in basic attitude as it was a change in degree. Both the Greeks and the Romans believed in the strength of the will and in the power of the mind of Man—through its own efforts—to find an order in the world, but in Greece that order never became an end in itself; man's intellectual inquiry was never frozen into the legalistic categories mirrored in Roman law and administration, and the universe did not become a hieratic machine. In Rome, the Greek ideal of the alert, questioning, individual mind seeking order in existence became an ideal of servitude in an ordered world in which the Emperor had become a semi-human God. In essence, Rome sought less to *understand* the world than to conquer, organize, and rule it.

Christianity, following the Roman pattern, made a virtue out of the sacrifice which an individual made of himself to a similar higher order, emphasizing—as Ling put it—that "celui qui se sacrifie participe à la grandeur de la cause à laquelle il s'est sacrifié" (T, p. 59). In this sense, the ancient city was "le lieu unique où la plus vaste pitié se réduit lentement à la force. Que l'individu s'exalte ou s'observe, les sept collines lui enseigneront à s'incliner" (T, p. 69). In a real way, this was of course in direct opposition to the ideal of the earlier Greeks, for they were precisely the ones who had liberated themselves from service to any order higher than Man himself. The Western Christian emerged as the child of both the exalted and forceful individualism of Rome and the probing, questioning individualism of the Greeks. Whether his faith was primarily "la voix avide" of the Attic philosopher seeking understanding, or "la voix hautaine" of the Roman citizen and conqueror, he would find his place in Holy Mother Church, where one voice "chantait la gloire de Dieu, [et] l'autre l'interrogeait sourdement" (T, p. 70).

When Ling returns to Europe from his Mediterranean trip, he has a broader view of Christianity, the central pillar of Western culture, as being to a large extent an amalgamation of Imperial Rome's ideals of glory and power, and Greece's efforts toward knowledge and individual experience. (Interestingly, he makes no reference to Christianity's Judaic elements.) This particular cultural heritage had marked Westerners in a unique way, one that was especially evident when viewed from the vantage point of a non-Western tradition. Ling sums up the fundamental intellectual distinctiveness of European civilization as inherited from Greece—and transmitted by Rome and Christianity—in a very revealing passage:

Entre l'esprit oriental et l'esprit occidental s'appliquant à penser, je crois saisir d'abord une différence de direction, je dirais presque de démarche. Celui-[ci] veut dresser un plan de l'univers, en donner une image intelligible, c'est-à-dire établir entre des choses ignorées et des choses connues une suite de rapports susceptibles de faire connaître celles qui étaient jusque-là obscures. Il veut se soumettre le monde, et trouve dans son action une fierté d'autant plus grande qu'il croit la posséder davantage. Son univers est un mythe cohérent. L'esprit oriental, au contraire, n'accorde aucune valeur à l'homme en lui-même; il s'ingénie à trouver dans les mouvements du monde les pensées qui lui permettront de rompre les attaches humaines. L'une veut apporter le monde à l'homme, l'autre propose l'homme en offrande au monde....

En face d'un monde dispersé, quel est le premier besoin de l'esprit? Le saisir. Nous [Orientaux] ne pouvons le faire sur ses images, puisque nous sommes sensibles d'abord à ce qu'elles ont de transitoire; nous voulons le faire sur ses rythmes. Connaître le monde n'est pas en faire un système, non plus que connaître l'amour n'est l'analyser. C'est en prendre une conscience intense. Notre pensée (lorsqu'elle n'est pas au service de combats dogmatiques) n'est pas, comme la vôtre, le résultat d'une connaissance, mais l'armature, la préparation de cette connaissance. Vous analysez ce que vous avez éprouvé; nous pensons afin d'éprouver (T, pp. 154-159).

Ling concluded that a Greek pilgrimage was particularly appropriate for "de belles âmes lucides et avides de se bien connaître" from the West, for it was from Greece that they had inherited their characteristic desire for meaningful knowledge of both the universe and the Self. The self-awareness of the Greeks and their growing belief in the power of the human mind to make sense out of the universe had led them to a new confidence in Man. In young Malraux's view, this effort to wrest understanding from existence, to reduce the universe to an intelligible human dimension, "la conquête du cosmos par la pensée," as he put it in his Athens speech, was mankind's first intellectual interrogation of the Divine *as an equal*. For him, the face of the youth in the Acropolis Museum clearly reflected this courageous presumption.

II

Although the intellectual heritage from Greece and Rome was a major source of Europe's strength, it was also the origin of great weakness. As Ling pointed out to his friend, A. D., the free human intelligence awakened by the Greeks was a very powerful and creative force, but it was a double-edged sword; for along with a knowledge of what man *could* do, it also brought him a fuller awareness of the limits of his condition. In the profane world where he himself had to be the measure and guarantee of all things, thinking man came to realize the awfulness of his situation. From this point of view, the Greek head from the Acropolis Museum was also very significant. Ling readily admitted that it was one of the most revealing and evocative forms that the Greek genius had ever produced. Yet, as a Chinese, he felt that the sculpture could not be otherwise than defective because its purity and harmony were exclusively human. To a non-Westerner, the open-eyed youth was a symbolic Oedipus, and the Sphinx he had encountered represented those enigmas in human life and experience "que tenta de réduire la Grèce" within its framework of rational inquiry (T, p. 66). Oedipus may have triumphed at Thebes, suggesting Man's ability to solve the riddle of his existence with his intellect, to find a meaning in life outside of a divine frame of reference. But, notes Ling, this victory of the understanding over the mysteries in the universe was not a lasting one: the Sphinx was reborn "chaque fois que les hommes demandent à la vie plus que ne peut leur donner la pensée" (T, p. 66). In this sense, the Greek voice was one "alternativement d'exaltation et de désespoir" and after the death of the Sphinx, Oedipus attacked himself and went mad.

Faced with his mortality, his solitude, his ultimate inability to cope rationally with certain elements in his experience, profane Western man—the intellectual descendant of the classical Greeks—had gradually been forced to a similar realization of his fundamental Absurdity in a world to which he had tried to bring order with his intelligence and his courage. Shortly after his arrival in Europe, Ling had become aware that "*au centre de l'homme européen, dominant les grands mouvements de sa vie, est une absurdité essentielle,*"[9] but it is not until near the end of their exchange that A. D. himself formulates in greater detail the intellectual dichotomy which Western man has inherited from his classical ancestors: "Il est au cœur du monde occidental un conflit sans espoir, sous quelque forme que nous le découvrions: celui de l'homme et de ce qu'il a créé. Conflit du penseur et de sa pensée, de l'Européen et de sa civilisation ou de sa réalité, conflit de notre conscience indifférenciée et de son expression dans le monde commun, par les moyens de ce monde" (T, p. 210).

Yet, to be in a struggle without hope is not necessarily to be in despair. The Greeks have led the West into this dilemma—which also existed for them, albeit in a less acute form—but they have also shown a way in which it may be resolved or transcended. This second victory—the "conquête du destin par la tragédie," as Malraux put it in the somewhat elliptical language of his Athens speech—was no less important a Greek contribution to the Western cultural heritage.

As we have seen from certain passages in the *Tentation*, young Malraux felt that the Greek intellectual effort to find a non-sacred meaning in the world was essentially the triumph of a human interrogation. The men of the Golden Age—like their European descendants—did not consider their lives to be completely determined by mysterious and incomprehensible forces before which they could only grovel abjectly. As Malraux pointed out, the refusal to accept any Sacred explanation for the universe and the subsequent efforts by Greek thinkers to find coherence in creation were extremely significant for the history of mankind, for such a denial that any non-human Absolute should be the measure of the human put Man, rather than a god, at the center of the world. This metaphysical revolution on the Attic peninsula meant that "pour la première fois, le vrai caractère de l'Asie: l'ordre établi par rapport à l'Absolu, disparut de la Méditerranée du Nord."[10]

The Greeks' rejection of any non-human order—in the name of one based on the possibilities of Man—was precisely what made their culture so distinctive. Yet, as Ling pointed out, the efforts by the Greek philosophers to humanize the universe with their intelligence were never entirely successful. There always remained certain things in a man's life—such as the gap the individual felt between himself and the Cosmos, his helplessness before aging and death, his awareness of the power and unreasonableness of passion—that inevitably brought him back to a recognition of the dimensions of his condition, the inevitability of his Destiny.

Critics have often pointed out that Malraux is almost obsessed with what he calls "le Destin," and the word appears frequently in his work. He has perhaps most succinctly summed up its meaning for him in the well-known passage where he writes: "Le destin ... est fait de tout ce qui impose à l'homme la conscience de sa condition" (V, p. 628). Destiny forces man to take cognizance of his limits, and his feeling of absurdity is due to the realization that he is master neither of time, nor of anguish, nor of evil. Stated in these terms, this is not a particularly optimistic view of the human situation, but it was the intellectual conclusion that the Greek thinkers reached. Yet, even though they were forced to recognize that they could not overcome Destiny by thought, they refused to accept this as a defeat and to cower anew before some superhuman Sacred. Out of this refusal grew a new victory, for they gradually discovered that they could reduce the Unknowable to human dimensions not through an intellectual order, but rather through a tragic one.

This is the kind of attitude that underlies the life and writings of men like Pascal, Camus, and Malraux himself. These men understand that the anguish or absurdity of the human condition cannot be dispelled by the intellect, but that it can be reduced or made fecund by a human attitude, especially as that attitude is translated into a life or mirrored in a literary creation. Thus it is that Malraux, the Prix Goncourt of the 1930's—pushing further the intellectual inquiry he had begun with the *Tentation*—follows closely in the footsteps of the tragic playwrights of antiquity whom he so greatly admired, and in a very real sense, he makes the Greek "conquête du destin par la tragédie" also his own, through his novels.

III

As we have seen, for Malraux the fundamental element of the Greek spirit was its relentless assault on everything that transcended man. The intellectual conquest by Greek thinkers had been continued and extended by the tragic victory of Greek poets, and their achievements on rational and emotional levels had been remarkable. However, in the final analysis Malraux felt that the Greeks' attempt to reduce the inhuman in their lives by reason or tragedy was not as significant as what he called their "conquête du divin par l'art et par l'homme." This victory was more important because it was primarily aesthetic, that is an amalgamation of both intellectual and emotional elements. Like his other views on the nature of the Greek legacy, Malraux's ideas about the Greek artistic achievement are part of a very personal ensemble. Although some specialists may take exception to certain specific details of his position, in its general lines his conception of the evolution and meaning of Greek art is both justifiable and provocative.

As a focal point for an important dialogue in his last novel, the 1943 *Noyers de l'Altenburg*, Malraux makes striking use of the beautiful sculptured head from the Acropolis Museum that had figured in his very first serious work, the 1926 *Tentation de l'Occident*. Vincent Berger, a principal figure in the story, comes back to Europe from a long stay in the Middle East and arrives at the ancient monastary of Altenburg—now a meeting place for intellectuals—shortly after his father has committed suicide. In the library of this "cloître de la pensée," his uncle, Walter, asks him if he can give any reasonable explanation for the father's self-inflicted death. Having just returned from lands where Islamic fatalism makes suicide virtually unknown, Vincent is particularly sensitive to the contrastingly aggressive and "volontaire" character of Europe. On landing in Marseilles a week earlier, he had already been forcefully struck by the "angoissante liberté" that was so fundamental to Western civilization, and now he suggests that perhaps old Berger had *chosen* his death in no less meaningful a way than he had chosen his life, as a function of his freedom. In death, as in life, he had preferred not to submit to his destiny, but to create it. For Vincent, such an action revealed the profound difference between "la mystérieuse liberté humaine" (N, p. 68) that characterized life in the West, and the crushed, insect-like existence of men in those other parts of the world where some element of an inhuman Sacred still ruled.

Vincent further points out to his uncle that after all, man—particularly Western man—was not reducible to an explanation, and that sometimes there were incidents in the human adventure which were beyond reason. After reflection, Walter admits that through art he has occasionally known such transcendentally unreasonable moments—as when the mad Nietzsche unexpectedly sang a sublime song in the utter darkness of a railway car during the passage through the Saint-Gothard tunnel. Walter recalls that at that instant, he had experienced the revelation that "le chant était aussi fort qu'elle [la vie]. Je venais de découvrir quelque chose. Quelque chose d'important. Dans la prison dont parle Pascal, les hommes sont parvenus à tirer d'eux-mêmes une réponse qui envahit, si j'ose dire, d'immortalité, ceux qui en sont dignes" (N, p. 71).

Continuing along these lines, Walter affirms that for him the "vertigo" that overwhelms man before the incomprehensible mysteries of death, the infinity of the universe, the march of history—in short, before everything that transcends the human condition—can be calmed or dissipated only by certain works of art. Pointing to a photograph of the sculptured head of a youth from the Acropolis Museum, he says that he particularly valued it because it was "la première sculpture qui représente un visage humain, simplement un visage humain; libéré des monstres... de la mort... des Dieux" (N, p. 72). In his view, it was by such creations that Man could equal God ("Ce jour-là, l'homme aussi a tiré l'homme de l'argile" [ibid.]), for from his mortal condition he had succeeded in drawing something that was immortal. For Walter, art had evidently taken the place of a de-throned Sacred Absolute, and he valued the head above all as an affirmation of transcendence. In an epigram reminiscent of Pascal—but which goes further—he sums up his position: "Le plus grand mystère n'est pas que nous soyons jetés au hasard entre la profusion de la matière et celle des astres; c'est que, dans cette prison, nous tirions de nous-mêmes des images assez puissantes pour nier notre néant."[17]

To a certain extent, this position was also Malraux's. However Vincent's subsequent meditation suggests Malraux's fear that Walter's excessively aesthetic attitude might lead to an exaggerated "mandarin" or essentialist view of art. To Malraux—as to Vincent—Man's existence meant more than just the possibility of giving birth to a certain number of transcendent artistic creations like the Greek head. For although the head—as art— could be a general consolation for the human condition, it was quite ineffective in face of a strong personal emotion. An artistic masterpiece might recompense mankind for the existence of Death, for example, but it could not offer solace that would blot out the intimate suffering an individual felt at the disappearance of a loved one. For this, an *attitude* was required, similar to the one old Berger had shown. He had not conquered his condition and vanquished his Destiny, as it were, by a single "immortal" or transcendent work of art; rather he had overcome his human condition by living a life of choice, in full awareness of the limits of that condition. In a sense, his whole existence had been a defiance of mortality similar to the one reflected in the youthful face of the Greek statue from the Acropolis Museum. To Vincent—as to Malraux—the possibility of this human attitude seemed a more Sacred greatness than any object that issued forth from the creative potential of the artist—to which, in any case, it was linked. Malraux himself once wrote that to transform "un destin subi en destin dominé"[18] was one of the highest callings of mankind, suggesting that for him a work of art was only one manifestation of what in some men was a life-long attitude, and in some cultures—such as in Greece during the Golden Age—the attitude of a whole people.

In subsequent discussions at Altenburg, it becomes clear that Walter's position remains essentially that of an aesthete whose primary affirmation is of the transcendence of man the artist. To be sure, he is sufficiently shaken by the suicide of his brother to change the topic of the colloquium from "les éléments éternels de l'art" to "Permanence et métamorphose de l'homme" (N, p. 77—"l'éternité va mal," commented one of the visitors), but his ultimate faith is in the artist and in the works he creates. During the colloquium, certain points relating to this general problem are developed and refined, and at one point the discussion turns to an examination of the Western views of man, particularly as those views are related to Europe's intellectual heritage from Greece.

Echoing ideas that Malraux had first formulated in the *Tentation de l'Occident* some years earlier, Vincent Berger says that for him a primary characteristic of the Greeks—as of modern Western man—was their awareness of everything that lay beyond the control of the human will, such as birth, aging, death, passion, and the individual's separation from the life of the Cosmos. The classical Greek felt the presence of Fate in areas like these, precisely because they imposed upon him a recognition of "l'indépendance du monde à son égard" (N, p. 90). He knew that the world was not on his scale, yet he still wanted it to be. So he "reconstructed" it in a human dimension and according to a human ordre. In Greek art, this effort was particularly evident. Vincent asks pointedly: "Qu'est-ce que l'acanthe grecque? Un artichaut stylisé. Stylisé [i.e. "ordered"], c'est-à-dire humanisé; tel que l'homme l'eût fait s'il eût été Dieu" (N, p. 90). Much Western art—so heavily influenced by the Greek ideal—may be considered to be a similar "rectification du monde, un moyen d'échapper à la condition d'homme" (ibid.). After emphasizing that to be aware of and represent a fatality like Destiny in a work of art is not to submit to it, but rather virtually to possess it (as in Greek tragedy), Vincent concludes his discussion by observing that the fundamental value of Western art—one that clearly linked it to Greece—was its attempt to carry out the same kind of "humanisation du monde" that was so clearly evident in the head of the Greek youth from the Acropolis Museum. In a striking way, this sculpture of a human countenance represented—perhaps for the first time in history—an effort to question and know the world, then to rectify and humanize it. For it was thus that the Sacred—including Destiny—could be dominated by Man, the artist.

Malraux amplifies and illuminates this theme in his next work, the treatise on the history and aesthetics of art entitled *Les Voix du silence*. In several important passages of this book, he sums up the fundamental points regarding the Greek achievement that he had already made—usually in less specifically artistic terms—in the *Tentation de l'Occident* and in the *Noyers de l'Altenburg*. He particularly emphasizes his basic conviction that "pour maint d'entre nous, la découverte fondamentale de la Grèce, c'est la mise en question de l'univers" (V, p. 72). As he sees it, it was this inquiring attitude, this desire of man to know for himself and by himself, this "opiniâtre *question* qui fut la voix même de la Grèce," that succeeded in less than 50 years in destroying the essentially uncreative, inhuman and static "litanie thibétaine" that characterized man's responses to the universe in most of the rest of the ancient world. Echoing certain statements that he had made earlier in his novels, Malraux reaffirms his belief that this revolution had also brought about the

fin de l'unique au bénéfice de la multiplicité du monde, fin de la valeur suprême de la contemplation, et des états psychiques où l'homme croit atteindre l'absolu en ne s'accordant à des rythmes cosmiques que pour se perdre dans leur unité. L'art grec est le premier qui nous semble profane. Les passions fondamentales y prirent leur saveur humaine; l'exaltation commença de s'appeler joie. Car même les profondeurs devinrent celles de l'homme; la danse sacrée dans laquelle apparaît la figure hellénique, c'est celle de l'homme enfin délivré de son destin... Au destin de l'homme, l'homme commence et le destin finit (V, p. 73).

During the Golden Age, Greece had gradually reduced "à la dimension humaine les formes de la vie" (V, p. 74), and thus the whole Greek world, "conquis sur sa servitude," had arisen from its prostration before the Divine to become the universe "qu'eût créé un dieu qui n'eût pas cessé d'être un homme" (V, p. 74). The classic acanthus, the form man would have given the artichoke leaf if he had been god, symbolizes this achievement because it was so obviously one of the "formes choisies par l'homme, réduit à l'homme" (V, p. 74).

The fundamental interrogation of this humanist culture caused a profound artistic revolution. The most important element in what Malraux refers to as the "métamorphoses d'Apollon" was "une obsédante poursuite de l'homme" (V, p. 83). The awakening of man to his humanity is graphically reflected in the evolution of the sculpture of the Golden Age. Greek artists continued to sculpt figures of gods, but they "arrachèrent des dieux à la terreur, au domaine du non-humain." As Malraux points out, the 6th century "Tête d'Ephèbe" from the Acropolis Museum—the sculpture to which he had referred earlier in both the *Tentation* and the *Noyers* but which he here specifically identifies for the first time— impresses us so deeply precisely because it is one of the first utterly human faces in the history of art.[19] Probably its most remarkable human quality— along with the open-eyed, fearless gaze of inquiry that had struck Ling in the *Tentation*—was the hint of a smile.[20] This smile was very important, as Malraux saw it, because "chaque fois qu'il reparaît, quelque chose de la

Grèce est près d'éclore... et chaque fois qu'il devient roi, l'homme accordé au monde (plutôt qu'au sacré) a reconquis la royauté fragile du royaume obsédant et limité qu'il conquit pour la première fois sur l'Acropole" (V, p. 78). Such a warm human reaction characterizes man as he enjoys living, the joyful movements of dancers, "soumises non au rite mais à l'instinct," and the voluptuous human pleasure represented by the female nude.

To the other sacred civilizations of the ancient world human happiness, the desire to understand the world in human terms, or indeed man himself had never been of major importance; thus they were seldom represented in art. To be sure, the non-Greek Oriental artist recomposed the world, but it was not according to *human* values. His basic beliefs were all sacred, and the most constant of them was an inhuman Eternal. It was only in Greece that "l'homme grandit ses valeurs jusqu'à l'idée qu'il se fait de l'univers" (V, p. 75). Thus, in a sense, the sculpture from the Acropolis Museum represented not only the victory of the artist over his material and over archaic sacred tradition; in its expression it also bore witness to the even great spiritual victory of "la mise en question *par* l'homme de tout ce qui lui échappe." To be sure, this conquest was subsequently transformed by Rome and Christianity into a "mise en question *de* l'homme par tout ce qui lui échappe, par ce qui le dépasse, le transcende ou l'anéantit."[21] Yet, as Malraux saw it, something resembling the Greek attitude subsequently came alive again at various times in the history of the West whenever men sought to continue that early "conquête du divin par l'art et par l'homme."

In the closing lines of his Athens speech, Malraux noted pointedly that "une Grèce secrète repose au cœur de tous les hommes d'Occident,"[22] and although—as we have seen from the essays in the present volume—the configurations of that Greece may have differed somewhat from century to century and from author to author, it is clear that this is essentially true. For the same humanist interrogation that gave meaning to the life and world of a Greek of the Golden Age has also given meaning to ours, particularly since the end of the 18th century. Thus, in a very real way, the sculptured head from the Acropolis Museum is a portrait not only of an Attic youth of the 6th century B. C., but of modern Western man as well.

The University of Kentucky

Notes

[1] Malraux's speech was reproduced—whole or in part—in a number of French newspapers at the time. However, we shall quote from the official mimeographed text released by the Minister of Culture, entitled "Discours prononcé à Athènes le 28 mai 1959 par Monsieur André Malraux, Ministre d'Etat du Gouvernement de la République Française." The quotations in this paragraph are all from the second page of this document.

[2] *La Tentation de l'Occident*, first published by Grasset in 1926, has recently been reprinted, and it is from this 1951 edition (abbreviated T in the text) that we shall quote. *Les Noyers de l'Altenburg* originally appeared under the title *La Lutte avec l'ange—Les Noyers de l'Altenburg* in 1943 (Editions du Haut-Pays), but was reissued in an edition of 5,000 copies by Skira (Geneva) in 1945. It is from this printing (abbreviated N) that quotations will be made. *Les Voix du silence* is a much reworked version of the earlier 3-volume text that Skira published under the collective title, *La Psychologie de l'art*. We will quote from the one-volume Gallimard edition of 1951, abbreviated V.

[3] Cf. Marcel Arland's article, "Sur un nouveau ' mal du siècle'," that appeared in the February, 1924, issue of the *Nouvelle Revue Française*. The text has been published in English in Justin O'Brien's *From the N.R.F.* (New York, 1958), pp. 28-38.

[4] This quotation is taken from the moving statement Arland wrote in support of his friend Malraux when the latter was accused of the theft of some statues from a jungle ruin in Indochina. It was published as a kind of preface to excerpts from Malraux's fanciful "Ecrit pour une idole à trompe," in the October-November, 1924, issue of Arland's little review, *accords* (p. 55).

[5] These texts were published by Stock in a volume that was part of a series called "Les Contemporains. Œuvres et portraits du XXe siècle." Malraux's introduction is found on pp. 7-9, and the quotations in this paragraph are taken, respectively, from pages 7 and 9.

[6] Young Malraux made a particularly striking statement of this belief in his 1922 essay, "La Peinture de Galanis," when he wrote: "Nous ne pouvons sentir que par comparaison. Quiconque connaît Andromaque ou Phèdre sentira mieux ce qu'est le génie français en lisant *Le Songe d'une Nuit d'Eté* qu'en lisant toutes les autres tragédies de Racine. Le génie grec sera mieux compris par l'opposition d'une statue grecque à une statue égyptienne ou asiatique, que par la connaissance de cent statues grecques." Quoted from the reprinting of this text in *Malraux Miscellany*, vol. I, no. 2 (Autumn, 1969), p. 8. In the *Tentation de l'Occident*, he reaffirms this position, for in one of his letters Ling writes to A.D.: "Comment me trouverai-je, sinon en vous regardant?" (p. 77).

[7] In a letter to his publisher, dated Saigon, October 4, 1925 (in the collection of the author of this essay), Malraux characterized the book as "lettres échangées entre un jeune Occidental et un jeune Chinois, et annotées par un de leurs amis indiens."

[8] The *achevé d'imprimer* is dated July 2, 1926. The text contains a large number of typographical errors, and it is possible that Malraux was away from Paris when the proofs were ready to be corrected. Three of the letters in the volume had already appeared in slightly different form in the April, 1926, issue of the *Nouvelle Revue Française*, under the title "Lettres d'un Chinois" (pp. 409-420). It is interesting to note that one of them is precisely the letter which presents the Chinese youth's reactions to his visit to Greece (pp. 412-415).

[9] This crucial passage, underlined by Malraux, is on page 78.

[10] Cf. Malraux's "D'Une Jeunesse européenne," in *Ecrits* (Grasset, 1927), p. 138, note 1.

[11] Cf. V, p. 628, and the preface Malraux wrote to Manès Sperber's novel, *Qu'Une Larme dans l'océan* (Paris, 1952), pp. xix-xxi.

[12] Cf. Malraux's preface to the translation of William Faulkner's novel, *Sanctuaire* (Paris, 1933), p. iv. A number of critics have dealt with this aspect of Malraux's work, but for the most extended and provocative discussion see Charles Blend's superb book, *André Malraux, Tragic Humanist* (Ohio State, 1963), particularly the chapter on "Humanism and Tragic Poetry" (pp. 49-74). Professor Blend treats the problem from a slightly different viewpoint, but our conclusions are in complete agreement.

[13] He had already made this position clear in his youthful essay, "D'Une Jeunesse européenne" (1927), particularly on pages 138-139.

[14] Sperber, p. xx.

[15] Sperber, p. xxi.

[16] Sperber, p. xx.

[17] *Noyers*, p. 72. Interestingly, Malraux includes this passage in his recently-published *Antimémoires* (Paris, 1967), p. 40, but there he adds the following: "Et pas seulement des images... Des... enfin, vous voyez."

[18] This, of course, is one of the basic messages of his novels.

[19] Cf. *Voix*, p. 75. A large size photograph of this head—and of the equally significant Koré d'Euthydikos—are to be found on pages 76-77 of this volume.

[20] This smile is even more evident in a figure like the Kouros of Kaliva, pictured on page 78 of the *Voix*.

[21] *Voix*, p. 178, my italics.

[22] "Discours," p. 2.

EPILOGUE

In a recent provocative article entitled "The Crisis of Modern Man..."[1] Professor Henri Peyre has emphasized that few world literatures of the last three or four centuries have been more "metaphysical" in nature than that of France because a majority of the greatest French writers have been essentially moralists, "bent upon improving man's fate or sharpening his awareness of it." If various authors from Voltaire and Rousseau to Péguy and Giono have turned to Greece, it was because they believed that that humanist culture from which Western civilization had evolved contained elements which would aid them in understanding—and in putting into literary form—some of the major problems that face men in life. Today's world is in a greater state of crisis than at any time in the past, and contemporary writers are acutely aware of this fact. Technology, a number of common concerns, and the decline of certain separatist Absolutes may have brought men closer together in some ways, but ironically it is precisely these elements that have also pushed us to the brink of a cataclysm that may shortly bring total destruction to the entire planet. Not surprisingly, as Peyre points out, authors like Malraux, Camus and Sartre are seeking solutions, so that we may possibly avoid the catastrophe before us: "Their novels, their maxims, their essays aim at nothing less than the redefining of man in his relations to the past, to other men, to the divine or its substitutes, to the future." In his view, these writers "have undertaken, in their soteriological literature, to point the way to man's salvation." In this effort, the legacy the Greeks have left to the West can be of enormous value.

As we have seen, in his Athens speech, Malraux had forcefully pointed out that Greece in the Age of Pericles was unique in the ancient world because by throwing off the yoke of the Divine she had "créé un type d'homme qui n'avait jamais existé."[2] In other contemporary civilizations, dogmatic indoctrination, blind faith, and ritualism formed men who were subservient to the higher authority of some sacred Absolute, but Greece— having no Holy Writ to provide answers to the why and whither of human life and to give form and direction to her civilization—had to look to culture, the "ensemble des créations de l'art et de l'esprit," for this guidance (D, p. 2). The first civilization in history to make such non-sacred elements "un moyen majeur de formation de l'homme," she had created mankind's first *humanist* civilization, a "civilization d'interrogation" of the Divine, at whose base lay a belief in the possibilities of the *human* spirit, rather than any Absolute.

Greek culture was vivified by the fundamental questions that profane man put to everything in the universe that transcended him, but this attitude would almost certainly not have produced such extraordinary results if it had not been coupled with another quality of the men of the Golden Age, namely courage. For Malraux, the Acropolis was "le seul lieu du monde hanté à la fois par l'esprit et par le courage" (D, p. 1), because only in Greece had early man combined a lucid awareness of his condition with the courage to face the consequences of his awful predicament, without subterfuge. Indeed, the very statue of the goddess which the temple had been constructed to house—an "Athéna pensive appuyée sur sa lance"—suggested the classical Greek's desire both to use his human faculties to understand himself and his world, and his courage and determination to act in the light of that understanding, however great the odds—physical or metaphysical—might be. In a like manner, many men in the modern world (where God is apparently dead or dying) have refused to take refuge behind the shield of the Sacred and fatalistically accept whatever Fate decrees. In Malraux's view, it was essentially this attitude that would enable contemporary man to continue and extend the three remarkable "conquêtes" that constituted the bulk of the Greek legacy to the West and would perhaps even enable mankind to lay the foundations of a new, world-wide civilization of tomorrow.

Greek humanism had not only revolutionized philosophy, literature, and art, but it also gave the Greeks an entirely new view of history and of man's role in historical time. As Malraux points out, when Pericles before the Acropolis had cried: "Si toutes choses sont vouées au déclin, dites du moins de nous, siècles futurs, que nous avons construit la cité la plus célèbre et la plus heureuse" (D, p. 1), he had spoken to the future. His words would have been unintelligible to the other civilizations of the ancient world because the whole Orient was still blindly wandering on some Sacred Way. The Greeks conceived of a development of the human adventure in time that was unlike anything that had been envisaged before. This view—strengthened by elements from the Judaic tradition—had been passed on to most of the cultures of the West, but it was not until very modern times that it had begun to become meaningful for non-Westerners as well. As Malraux sees it, the revolutions, political upheavals and other dislocations that have characterized so many of the "under-developed" nations of the world for the last generation clearly indicate the extent to which men everywhere have now come to accept the Greek belief that they can indeed change the course of history and shape their own destinies.

The idea of men being able to act in and on history required that they be given mechanisms which would enable them to do so, and in his Athens speech Malraux recalls that the contemporary West has derived many of its uniquely democratic political ideas and institutions from the Greeks. In modern times, this ideal has spread throughout the world and so caught the imaginations of men everywhere that—ironically—even the most oppressive regimes in Africa and Asia pay lip service to it. But Malraux is careful to emphasize that to be meaningful the political ideal of classical Greece must not be separated from her aims in the other areas of human life, for everything is inter-related. Acting as the mouthpiece for an imaginary orator of ancient times, Malraux sums up the progression by which the basic elements of Greece's remarkable ideals of personal and political freedom had been elaborated: "J'ai cherché la vérité, et j'ai trouvé la justice et la liberté. J'ai inventé l'indépendance de l'art et de l'esprit. J'ai dressé pour la première fois, en face de ses dieux, l'homme prosterné partout depuis quatre millénaires. Et du même coup, je l'ai dressé en face du despote" (D, p. 2).

Here Malraux is also calling attention to the very important (but often forgotten) fact that the giants of Greek literature were not ivory tower aesthetes. They were active *citizens*, precisely because the Greek cultural formation inculcated an ideal of collective political responsibility along with other values. Sophocles was every bit as much a "servant de la cité" as he was a philosopher and playwright. As Malraux sees it, one of the greatest human problems in the 20th century is to "concilier la justice sociale et la liberté." Classical Greek culture offers a valuable modern lesson, precisely because it succeeded in forming not only artists and thinkers but citizens as well—men who were acutely aware of their duties and responsibilities as part of a larger human whole. Viewed in this light, the life-long political commitment of Malraux himself—which began in Indochina in 1924 and culminated in his participation in various de Gaulle governments in the post-war years—is a continuation of a similar humanistic effort; like the Greeks, he is above all seeking to encourage those values which will give man most dignity—and make him most fecund.

As Malraux stood at the foot of the floodlighted Acropolis before the dignitaries from many nations of the globe, he took pains to point out that the "symbole illustre de l'Occident" shining above him would in a sense henceforth be illuminated *by* the whole world because it had a message *for* the whole world. In his view, the classical Greek "civilisation de l'esprit" was not only a major source of the West's unique cultural heritage, but also it was the best possible base on which secular, humanist man in the 20th century could construct "la première civilisation mondiale." In an age that was witnessing the death of the Sacred on every side, men of every nation of the earth found themselves at the same point of interrogation where Greece had stood at the dawn of the Golden Age. Unfortunately, the new world culture that was being born had not yet found its human model, "le type d'homme exemplaire, fût-il éphémère ou idéal, sans lequel aucune civilisation ne prend tout à fait forme" (D, p. 2). To be sure, contemporary events are dominated by several super-nations, but those "colosses tâtonnants"—almost entirely preoccupied with political and economic struggles between themselves—have a very limited and materialist view of what the human adventure is all about. They "semblent à peine soupçonner que l'objet principal d'une grande civilisation n'est pas seulement la puissance, mais aussi une conscience claire de ce qu'elle attend de l'homme, l'âme invincible par laquelle Athènes—pourtant soumise—obsédait Alexandre dans les déserts d'Asie" (D, p. 2).

Thus it remains for thinking men everywhere, especially those in the "vieilles nations de l'esprit" who are the true inheritors of the Greek tradition, to set about the formulation of such an ideal. Malraux is firmly convinced that in our modern, increasingly secular world of many races and backgrounds, only an ideal rooted in the Greek humanist belief in the potential of the enlightened human spirit can give us any hope for the future. He seems basically optimistic as he exhorts young people of the West to turn again to Greece for guidance in their struggle to protect human dignity and freedom. "Au seuil de l'ère atomique, une fois de plus, l'homme a besoin d'être formé par l'esprit. Et toute la jeunesse occidentale a besoin de se souvenir que lorsqu'il le fut pour la première fois, l'homme mit au service de l'esprit les lances qui arrêtèrent Xerxès" (D, p. 2). Culture and courage should be the watchwords of today's youth, as they had been in the days of Greece's glory.

Thus in Malraux's view the Greek ideal and the enormous potential of human freedom in its broadest sense are inextricably entwined. Indeed, as he put it, "en face de l'esclavage pétrifié des figures de l'Asie, le mouvement des statues grecques est le symbole même de la liberté." In Greece for the first time, "la liberté de l'homme voulut s'égaler au destin," and such human autonomy before the Sacred was the characteristic "forme de la victoire grecque" in all things.[3] Greece, then, is for him primarily an *attitude*, a spirit which summons us to the highest achievements of which we—as men—are capable. Nothing less is required of us if we are to continue to survive on our shrinking planet. Thus the head from the Acropolis Museum will no longer be simply a portrait of a Greek of the Golden Age, or indeed of a youth of Europe; it will be the face of Everyman, everywhere in the world. As Malraux put it, the basic spirit of our Hellenist heritage urges us not to "nous réfugier dans notre passé," but rather to "inventer l'avenir qu'il exige de nous" (D, p. 2).

That future can only be world-wide.
Will we be capable of this high task?

Notes

[1] Cf. Peyre's *Historical and Critical Essays* (University of Nebraska Press, 1968), pp. 265-282.

[2] "Discours prononcé à Athènes...," p. 1.

[3] *Les Voix du silence* (Paris, 1951), pp. 74, 147, 150.

The editor of this collection wishes to express his deep gratitude to the Kentucky Research Foundation (Vice President Lewis W. Cochran, Chairman) for its generous financial support in the preparation of the volume.

ACHEVÉ D'IMPRIMER
SUR LES PRESSES DE
L'IMPRIMERIE STUDER S.A.
À GENÈVE
EN JUILLET 1971